Munkey Diaries
1957–1982

JANE BIRKIN

W&N

WEIDENFELD & NICOLSON

First published in France in 2018 by Fayard
First published in Great Britain in 2020 by Weidenfeld & Nicolson
This paperback edition published in 2021 by Weidenfeld & Nicolson
an imprint of The Orion Publishing Group Ltd
Carmelite House, 50 Victoria Embankment
London EC4Y 0DZ

An Hachette UK Company

The authorised representative in the EEA is Hachette Ireland,
8 Castlecourt Centre, Dublin 15, D15 XTP3, Ireland (email: info@hbgi.ie)

20 19 18 17 16

A CIP catalogue record for this book is
available from the British Library.

ISBN (Mass Market Paperback) 978 1 4746 1771 0
ISBN (eBook) 978 1 4746 1529 7

Typeset by Input Data Services Ltd, Somerset
Printed in Great Britain by Clays Ltd, Elcograf S.p.A.

MIX
Paper | Supporting
responsible forestry
FSC® C104740

www.weidenfeldandnicolson.co.uk
www.orionbooks.co.uk

CONTENTS

AUTHOR'S NOTE

When I was ill, Gabrielle Crawford sorted through those of my intimate diaries that were written in English and transcribed them over
a two-year period. She scanned the pages of text and the drawings, and without her there would have been many times I would
have given up on the project. I thank her for her boundless enthusiasm and her kindness. It's not for nothing that Serge called her the
'Angel Gabrielle'.

I also wish to thank Erin Floyd, who assisted me with the transla-
tion back into English of many extracts from the French diaries.

The names and characteristics of some of the people mentioned
in this book have been changed.

Jane Birkin

PREFACE

I wrote my diary from the age of eleven, addressed to Munkey, my confidant, a soft toy monkey dressed as a jockey that my uncle had won in a tombola and given to me. He slept by my side, sharing the sadness of boarding school, hospital beds and my life with John, Serge and Jacques. He witnessed all the joys and all the unhappiness. He had a magic power; we took no planes, stayed in no hospitals without him being by our side.

Father said, 'Maybe when we get to heaven it'll be your monkey that welcomes us with open arms!'

Kate, Charlotte and Lou had his sacred clothes, without which travel was unthinkable. Serge kept Munkey's jeans in his attaché case until the day he died. Faced with my children's grief, I put Munkey beside Serge in his coffin, where he lay like a pharaoh. My monkey was there to protect him in the afterlife.

On reading my diaries it seems to me that one doesn't change. What I was at twelve, I am still today. The lack of confidence, the jealousy, wanting to please . . . I understand better why my loves couldn't last. The reader will be surprised, as I was, to see how little I talk about my professional life. I hardly mention the films, the plays – not even the songs. When people die, I talk about it months later – the happy times I was too busy living.

The diaries are, of course, unfair. You show your hand and complain, and there are different sides to everything, but here there is just mine. In principle, I have changed nothing – and believe me, I would have preferred to have reactions that were more mature or wiser than those that I had.

I've left out things that could have been wounding, but very few. I myself have remained very childish. It seems to me tiringly so. There are years that are missing, lost notebooks, people that aren't there. The stories are as arbitrary as the photos that may have been taken, or not, like spools of undeveloped film or the absence of a camera that day, that year – like a selective memory, I have sifted through.

I decided to do a sort of autobiography with anecdotes of things that have come to mind in reading these diaries. Commentaries, too. And I've talked about people who had been so important that were missing, so we've done a sort of mixture of diaries of the time, with the memories of today.

I wanted to publish nearly everything, and I've had a long life so I needed two volumes. The first, from boarding school to the separation with Serge and waiting for Lou; the second book from the birth of Lou until the death of my daughter Kate.

I stopped writing my diary at that moment.

There was a last entry in Besançon on 11 December 2013, then nothing more. I entered into a phase during which I lived a parallel life.

'You're there but not there,' said Lou's son Marlowe, and he was right. I had no more to say, as if I had lost the right to express myself. With Kate, my diary came to an end.

I was born on 14 December 1946, very premature at seven and a half months, at the London Clinic. They put me in a little box on the radiator, together with a little boy, both covered with a damp cloth. Incubators didn't exist.

Mama had begun to lose me just after breakfast, she said. They opened her up for a caesarian from top to bottom. She never complained; she said it was a relief. Not like the agony of the year before with my brother, born at home just after the war.

My father, David Birkin, was from an upper-middle-class family in Nottingham, the owners of Birkin Lace. His mother was a Russell, her clergyman father the youngest grandson of a duke. A sinus operation went wrong; the knife slipped and gave my father double vision and he was prone to bleeding lungs and constant fragility. When he was eighteen, his aunt prayed to God to spare him his plight and take him to heaven. After Cambridge he wanted to be a surgeon. Ironic.

He had many other operations that were catastrophic and left him convalescing in Switzerland, but when war was declared he came back to England. He tried everything to get into the services, without success, because of his health. His eldest brother was in the army, the second was a brilliant pilot. He, the youngest, with great persistence, finally got himself into the Royal Naval Volunteer Reserve. He spent a year doing a crash course in intelligence and navigation, starting as an ordinary sailor on a static training ship. He had never set foot on a boat before but was a gifted mathematician.

He learnt that there was a possibility for him to be the navigator of a boat that would make return trips between France and England, and he was soon entrusted with overnight missions from Dartmouth to the Brittany coast from Aber Wrac'h to Paimpol. It was his ship that picked up the Free French, the spies, and the English and Canadian pilots who had ditched in France and had been hidden by the French Resistance. His and the sister ship[1] had to wait for moonless nights to navigate in the ferocious waters. He was sea-sick, battered about in his tiny cabin – maps fell; they had no lights, no sonar. So many missions right under the Germans' noses and he didn't miss a single one.

Throughout his two years at war, my father had to hide his bleeding lungs from his superiors. He asked that someone stay by his side during his operations in case he talked under the anaesthetic because everything had to be kept secret for fear not only of risking the loss of the flotilla, but putting the French Resistance in danger.

Towards the end of the war my mother had said to him, phoning from a telephone box in London, 'I think I know what you're doing.'

A woman at a cocktail party had said that her son had come back from France by sea and not by air and my father replied that she should have kept her mouth shut.

After the war he never set foot on a boat again and because of the Official Secrets Act he only spoke about it all very late in life, around 1967. He got the Distinguished Service Cross but those who won his admiration were the French – the Bretons such as Joe Mainguy, a Resistance leader who refused to have a street named after him out of modesty, and Tanguy, the Lannilis garage owner who hid English airmen in his attic before putting them in a lorry, taking them to an island at low tide and hiding them under the seaweed for my father to pick them up at high tide.

One Christmas the airmen weren't on a certain rock as planned and my father and his crew had to go back to Dartmouth before daybreak. They all had a tremendous lot to drink, miserable not to have found anyone, then they received a message, something like, 'Jean-Pierre's shirts are ready at the cleaners' or 'the privet trees are in flower', and they had to get back that night and bring back the airmen safe and sound. It was he, or the sister ship navigated by Peter Williams,* that took François Mitterrand back from Dartmouth to Beg an Fry.

After my father died, my mother and I went along the Breton coast to scatter his ashes in every place at which his ship had docked during the war. Old Resistance members waited for us at each place and when we got to Bonaparte Beach we found Joe Mainguy. He took a handful of Papa and threw the ashes in the sea, saying, 'Adieu, David.'

My mother's mother was an actress. My grandfather, who was also an actor, came from a modest background in Norfolk and changed

---

* The missions were always done by two ships, one with my father navigating or the sister ship that Peter Williams navigated. He became my brother's godfather.

his name from Gamble to Campbell to get the part of a Scotsman. He and my grandmother wrote and performed melodramas and opened a theatre in Grantham which they changed into a cinema later, one of the first in the North of England. My mother, Judy, spent her days there. She said her culture came from all the films she'd seen on the usherette's knees. Another little girl who came from time to time to that cinema was Margaret Thatcher . . .

Mama shared a flat in London with two actress friends, Sarah Churchill[*] and Penelope Reed, who we called Pempie, my father's cousin. She was the reason that they met. Pempie had said to my mother, 'If only you knew my cousin, David, he's divine', and to my father, 'Oh if only you knew my friend, Judy, she's the most ravishing girl that exists.' Ma and he were married in 1944. It was filmed for the Pathé news, because my mother was really very well-known. They were so chic, Pa with a patch on one eye and Ma the film star, dressed by Victor Stiebel, my godfather, the greatest couturier of the time, with Sarah Churchill, my godmother, and Pempie. This marriage was great news for my father's family: my grandmother had had three sons and a husband who was always away at war (the First World War and even the Boer War) so to have a girl in the family was wonderful company for her. On the other hand it was a catastrophe for my mother's parents, who, after such a promising beginning, had hoped that their daughter would shine in the theatre. My father swore that she could go on as an actress, that he'd never get in the way. Promises, promises!

A year later Andrew was born and the year after, me. My little sister was born four years later. And Pa had taken us all off to a farm, his dream, and for us, a paradise, but just a little too far from London for Ma to perform in the theatre in the evenings. He then had

---

* Winston Churchill's daughter, actress and poetess, who had an unhappy life. Papa and I were in the crowd cheering Churchill for his last birthday and in 1965 for his funeral Andrew and I were there amongst the thousands. We climbed on top of dustbins to get a better view. What was so moving was to see the cranes bow their heads, one after the other, as the barge took his coffin down the Thames.

another farm at Henley-on-Thames and after that he had to have so many operations that we moved back to London. Maybe he felt that Ma should be closer to the theatres. So they bought a big Victorian house in Cheyne Gardens, Chelsea. I think that Andrew was sent to boarding school at the age of six, like lots of little boys from well-to-do families.

At the beginning he was only going to be a weekly boarder, as petrol was rationed, but my mother thought that he was having such a good time and in a hasty judgement they decided to let him stay as a full boarder, and then at around thirteen he was off to Harrow, a very expensive institution where members of my father's family went before Cambridge.

As small children, Linda and I went to a day school in Kensington. Mine was especially eccentric. Miss Ironside, the headmistress, could boast of having educated two prime ministers and a traitor and it was there I met two teachers who influenced me all my life, Miss Staynes and Miss Storey, who taught history, literature and English. I went back to them after boarding school and they took us off to Stratford-upon-Avon to see Shaw's *Saint Joan*; or to scrutinise diamonds at the British Museum in case we got offered one one day; to admire the step-cut diamond and the beautiful jewellery of Queen Elizabeth I; to cry with them at *Richard II* . . . But that's another story.

1957

30 April

Dear Munkey,

In the morning there was a great hassle. Andrew was going back to school and we had not packed his trunk. First we got all his clothes in – one white shirt had not turned up. Then we found his boiler suit was not packed, then also two pink ties, then four handkerchiefs, and so on. After a while we found everything except a few braces, then the trunk had to go and Andrew and I had to go to Thomas Cook travel agency on the way (we went on a bus). We got out at the wrong place, at Lower-Something-Street, not Higher-Something-Street. We had to walk all the way back to Lower-Something-Street (I say Something Street because I cannot remember what street it was). Luckily I had three pounds and ten shillings for Andrew and one pound and ten shillings for me. We got there at last and we got the form we wanted and went back by bus. At LAST, Andrew got off – not to my relief, but I thought he was late for the school train. When I say I luckily had three pounds. It was true but that meant we did not have to walk ALL the way from Lower-Something-Street to Higher-Something-Street. I waved goodbye to Andrew and went inside the house. I must stop now because the rest is rather dull.

30 October

On Wednesday, Linda and me played a game we made up. We pretended we were boys in a boarding school and it was rather a coincidence that Mama that evening talked about sending me to boarding school. We were thinking about sending me to one called Lady Eden's or one in the New Forest, one on the Downs, or one by the sea that my friend Jenny Sheridan is going to. Then I watched a thing about pigs on TV.

* * *

Finally my parents sent Linda and I to Upper Chine, a school for girls on the Isle of Wight. It was I who'd insisted because all my friends had gone to boarding school. I was delighted, I was twelve. There was the main building where Linda and the little ones slept, and we were all in separate houses, each one maintained by a nurse and her companion. Mine were Nurse Vanderban and Miss Thomas. We also had our heads of house, mine was Jane Welplay, I adored her. She was a few years older than me, with a great plait of hair that ran the length of her back. She was my idol and for nothing in the world would I disappoint her. If I had late marks, I was afraid to hear them say, 'Oh 99, you disappoint me so.' My number was 99 and my sister was 177. Our colour was green; every house had the name of an explorer; ours was Scott and I think that Linda's was Rhodes. Each girl belonged to a house with several dormitories that slept eight girls each.

When the bell rang, we had to put on our uniforms, which were not particularly pretty, but very precise. When Nurse saw me with my light brown shoes, not dark as required, she said, 'Tan is not a substitute for brown.' Then we had to rush from our house to the main building, crossing a little brook, the Chine, in fear of a late mark. If you got three late marks it became a disobedience mark and after many of those you got sent away; you were expelled. I felt as though I were responsible for my house, Scott, for my adored Jane Welplay, for Upper Chine school and eventually the ruin of England.

As Linda was small, she was allowed lots of things, like strawberries, whereas we were 'the bulk years" born after the war; there were too many of us, we were nearly adolescents, we had no charm. I left boarding school after what I thought was three years. My mother said it was only two, but out of luck or good fortune, my parents popped the question a bit vaguely: 'Would you like to leave boarding school?' And my mother said that I'd replied, seized by emotion, 'If you make me do one more term I'll die.' So they took me out and I was able to go back to my lovely little school in Kensington. Boarding school had been painful because we were only girls and the first few terms we weren't allowed out in case we didn't want to come back. Then after that we were allowed out on Sundays after chapel, and before chapel in the evenings. Our parents could take us out to the tea shop in the neighbouring village and then the last year it seems that it was possible sometimes to spend the night at my parents' cottage on the Isle of Wight. It had been their idea in sending us there; that they wouldn't be very far for Linda and me. Not so for Andrew.

From the age of five years old Andrew had been to pre-prep school, then prep school then Harrow. My parents took him out at the last minute before he was expelled for having seen *Splendor in the Grass* with Natalie Wood. He had got out in the dirty laundry basket but unfortunately for him he'd kept the cinema ticket. He was also suspected of having set fire to the old Japanese embassy while shooting his own film. It seemed to him that lighting a match and setting fire to a curtain would give a more dramatic effect! He was a boy who didn't disobey rules, because for him rules didn't exist. Years later in a plane, a man asked me if I was 'Birkin's sister'. I replied in the affirmative. and he told me that Andrew, who used to be beaten every Monday, was to be found one day under a car reading a book because it was raining instead of being at chapel, the famous chapel that Churchill and Lord Montgomery returned to visit.

---

* We were the post-war baby boom generation.

I went a few times on visitors' day to that chapel where Lord Montgomery said at the pulpit, 'God says,' and then added, '—and I agree with him'! I used to cry during the service, I was so moved by the backs of the little boys' necks in uniform, the little ones with their bum freezers,* and the big ones in tails. In those days every new boy was servant to an older one, who used to scream 'Fag!' and the new boy would have to run to bring him his toast. If you desperately wanted to be part of a group, you suffered terribly. My brother didn't care, he didn't want to be a part of any group. At his previous school they tended to warn boys on a Friday that they would be beaten on the following Monday – that way they could think about it all weekend. Andrew was eccentric for Harrow, a school where it was better to shine in sport as my father had done. Andrew, with an originality that finally won over his seniors, even if they had to beat him often, preferred that to having to wait for a bad school report that would be sent to my father, and to see his disappointment. It was always the case.

It is only fair to point out that Andrew's recollection of his school years is different from my own, and he regards mine as charming and perfectly incorrect, 'a wonderful melange of facts'!

I, his little sister, on the other hand had reports that said, 'Jane is such a good pupil, she tries so hard, what a pity it's so difficult for her, but someone has to be last.' Maybe they didn't say the final bit, but that's what I thought. Linda, with her little gang, was up to mischief. She was very secretive, but had lots of friends. She had curly dark hair like my mother and a cupid's bow lip. She was my playmate during the holidays on the Isle of Wight or in Nottingham; but after boarding school we couldn't see each other much because we were far apart, and we weren't in the same classes, and I wasn't allowed to kiss her goodnight. To have some peace from the other girls my age, I used to stay late in senior prep, to write my diary . . .

---

* Small boys at Eton and Harrow wore little short jackets.

1959

December

Dear Munkey,

I hate school today, I feel like a sack (dead). I know that if any-body annoys me or if anybody tells on me or if anything goes wrong, I will scream. I wish I were home. Thank God it's only a few more days till I am, I can't wait to see Father and Mama. Everybody is so nice but I am just catty in return. I feel awful about it, I was crying in chapel last night, I have done everything wrong, I have approached everything in the wrong way. I feel fed up.

Goodbye for now, I am sorry I have bored you by writing how I feel. It's the only way I can express it.

Love,

Jane Birkin

* * *

My parents took a very long time to choose my name, searching for originality. My mother was very taken by 'Georgiana', a name that nobody knew, a distant duchess of Bedford. My father found that a little bit snobbish and said, 'Why not Jane, like the sexy strip cartoon in the *Mirror*?' He liked simple things, so my mother put everything into my second name, Mallory, which she invented. It was the name of Sir Thomas Malory, who had written King Arthur. She also thought vaguely that it was the name of a flower, but that's 'mallow'. In any case it seems to me that Jane Mallory was the perfect name for an actress but I thought of it too late. I was already well-known and my father had already had to put up with *Blow-Up* and 'Je T'Aime . . . Moi Non Plus' and so I kept Birkin, out of loyalty. In French it's much prettier, people say 'Jeanne Birkine', 'James Biquin', 'Jeanne Bikini', rather more fun than 'Birkin' which sounds a bit German, which it is; it means 'little birch tree'.

1960

19 January

How strange it feels to:

A) Have only one granny and B) to be back at school. Miss Thomas and Nurse are being very nice.

* * *

Granny Campbell, my mother's mother, had just died at hospital, and the father of my mother died when I was born, or just about. The same year Granny Birkin died as well as my father's dog Clover, which was more important to him than anything else. My father said, 'All we need now is Churchill dying!'

* * *

Wednesday, 20 January

Checking and unpacking in progress. I am missing one coat hanger and one pair of black pants.* Now I must put all my clothes into drawers. It's a jolly nice dormitory I'm in, will write again this evening.

_____

* At boarding school we wore knickers like everyone else, but on top of that we had over-pants in black flannel in case we tripped over and showed our underpants under our skirts, which were precisely three centimetres under the knee!

Sunday

I have just come back from going out with Ma and Pa; they were so nice about me not having a friend. Susan is so nice, everyone is. I think everyone was thinking I went to Granny's funeral. I hope not. I do so want a good report, I hope I can manage to keep my last one up. I forgot to tell Nurse I was going out. I hope I can be enrolled soon. I must learn the laws. I think they are these:

1. A guide's honour is to be trusted
2. A guide is a friend to all and the sister to every other guide
3. A guide is courteous
4. A guide is a friend to animals
5. A guide is pure in thought, word and deed
6. A guide is loyal
7. A guide obeys laws
8. A guide is thrifty
9. Trusted, loyal and helpful, pure as the rustling wind.

Monday

I am very upset I haven't finished my prep. I am now in the sewing room. Made Sylvia an apple pie bed but she found out. Diary is such a useful book, I am so pleased Linda gave it to me! I must learn to revise my notes and extra French now. I will write again later.

Wednesday

Mr Standfast is such a boring book! I suppose that's because I haven't got further than the first page so I'm not in a suitable position to criticise.

I must work. Copy out all my French and master my Latin grammar. The latter is impossible to do. Nearly time to go and change for tea.

Andrew has sent me and Linda lots of the Harrovian papers,* very nice of him, also coloured postcards of roses. Mama has written a very private letter about friends, etc. It's a great comfort to me. Father has also sent a postcard of ship saying my St Christopher† is nearly ready and it will be sent, isn't that lovely? Andrew has an idea about Capt. Cruickshank‡ as a play for Pa and Ma. It would be a good idea, also other ideas, another treat for them, a smashing box of Aero, Toblerone, Smarties, mint chocolates and other favourites. It's lovely to get letters.§ Ma and Pa and Andrew write so many, and so great is the joy when I get one. So today I got a parcel, a letter, and two lovely coloured postcards. I must do my prep now.

Thursday

Today is Thursday, good, only one more day till Saturday, good. What happened today in our dorm I would be glad to get rid of. B. came in and found Susan lying on her bed reading. I asked where the others were, she said she did not know. I lay on my bed admiring my St Christopher (which had just been sent). I saw the wardrobe curtain move and a giggle came from behind it. They all jumped out and said, 'Boo!' Awful noise and Nurse came in. 'What is this? What are you doing?' 'Hiding from Jane,' they said. Nurse turned to me. 'Have you anything to do with this?' she said. 'No,' I said truthfully. 'You are meant to be tired, you're supposed to be having rest.'

Friday

Have been to Guides, have passed my promises, law and motto. I am a Guide (nearly). I'm not allowed to wear my uniform yet, Linda

---

* For the Harrow review, not to be confused with the journal my brother kept during prep school which was very critical but true, which was even read by the teachers.

† My father's medallion.

‡ Captain Cruickshank was invented by my father, a terrifying character that resembled Hook in *Peter Pan*.

§ Of course, there was no phone.

can wear hers. It's jolly unfair. She will be able to wear wings, I am not allowed to as I wasn't a Brownie. Everything is fine, so easy-going with Linda, it's just going wrong with me. The work is horribly difficult but Linda's is easy. I wish I came here when I was Linda's age, she gets all the fun. I'm going to chapel, by myself, now I feel very unhappy.

Saturday

Mrs Ryder has given me permission to paint in the art studio for the Scott poster (she is very nice). I will do it in form time and break. Mrs Ryder has given me the key to the art room. I feel much better now after a good cry last night. I now feel I have a friend. I have done extra geometry so I will get a high mark and they are near even if they're not right! I'm longing to see Ma and Pa. I'll have a break soon. I'm beginning to like *Mr Standfast*, I'm on page 20. I have done my picture; I am not satisfied with it.

Sunday

I am unhappy again. I expect I'll get another C+. I went into the cloakroom and I saw people clambering on the lockers. I have nothing to do so I did the same as them. JW closed on me and said, 'You're not playing with us.'

Linda is allowed to see the secret garden. She says it's wonderful but I'm not allowed to see it. The loo is the only quiet place to cry, that's what I'm doing. I hate school, if I don't get higher marks I'll . . .

Tuesday

Another ordinary day, miserable yet fun. Sylvia's terribly nice, I like her. I am going to bed early, they all have to go to bed as an order, a continuation of the last punishment. I haven't had any supper I don't feel hungry, I have been crying again, I am a horrid cry-baby.

Wednesday

I wonder, am I really alive? Is this all a dream? Have I ever woken up since this morning or did I ever wake up? Am I in my dream? Susan's dream? Or perhaps God's? The bell is about to go and I haven't drunk my hot milk yet. I am still in bed, but that thought still troubles me.

Saturday

Everybody is horrid in my dorm. Diana is being beastly, she said she would ring the bell at half term and now she blames me for not ringing it. They are all so nasty dissing me, always butting into conversations. Diana is always trying to turn Susan against me, if she reads this it's her fault, she shouldn't pry.

Wednesday

Dull dull, very dull.

Thursday

A nature film, a woodpecker one, how they get their food, get married and get children.

Sunday

Go out with Ma and Pa. Had a smashing time, went to a hotel. Lovely lunch. Ma's play opens in London.

Horrid to be back at school after such a lovely time with Ma and Pa.

Friday

Queen has a baby boy! Born at 4 o'clock in the afternoon on 19 February! May be called Albert, I hope not. Cheers from the whole school. Hurray, all over the blackboards is written, 'It's a boy, it's a boy'.

HURRAY
allover the Black bds
written ITS A BOY
IT'S A BOY
GARÇON

Sunday

The Rev preached the sermon. He was sweet, in his sermon, he said, 'A very young member of the school asked what was the Holy Ghost.' I know he meant Angela, his child, because she is the youngest in the school. The hymn makes me cry.

Monday

What's the use of trying if you don't get anywhere?

Tuesday

I'm in prep; Maggie copied all my work, she's a terrible cheat. School is one heap of unfairness.

In fact she is really very nice, I found this out when she said, 'Love your neighbour as yourself'.

Saturday

Nothing much happened today, I feel fed up, I don't want to dance, don't want to do anything. It's horrid, everything is horrid. I feel like a lump of coal on the side of the road, a very busy road.

Linda was wearing lipstick and powder tonight. I tried to lick a red Smarty to make it look like lipstick but it was no good.

I wish I could get up-to-date with my preps.

Sunday

A normal Sunday. I am worried about Pa's eye. Very worried, I do hope all goes well. It's so unfair, why has he got it all? I want it, I wish God would give me a bad eye and not Pa. Every time I wish, I wish the same old wish 'let everyone be happy'. I invented a hospital yesterday: the private rooms would have roses on the wallpaper, and Pa's eye could be massaged every day and Ma could be physiothera-pied and they would feel top of the world.

I learnt today about God. I wonder about that subject, He must be such a strange person, is He a man? Has He a body? If not, is He a void? And if He's a void how can He grant our wishes?

I feel so much more grown-up now I have bought a lipstick and I have grown a bosom at last. I work harder and my mind is different. I have stockings* and juniors have crushes on me.

* * *

I found my tennis shoes cleaned by invisible hands and little notes

---

* Opaque 60 denier stockings. And if you laddered them, there was a great technique in darning them – I still know how to do it.

in my locker. I'd done the same when I first went to boarding school for Jane Welplay, our head girl. I held her in my arms an afternoon during senior dancing, I remember it was Elvis Presley's 'Are You Lonseome Tonight'. JW was going to leave the school and I slid the heart of a tree into her pocket. At least it was sold to me as such. No doubt it was a bean in the form of a heart. I'd wrapped it up lovingly in a piece of loo paper, without signing of course. Today she's a vet somewhere in Canada with lots of children. In the 1970s she came to take part in a TV programme about me. She was very surprised to learn that I'd loved her. I don't even know if she wasn't a little embarrassed nor whether she remembered me.

* * *

I feel very queer, I think it's growing up? A nice feeling, maybe. My mind thinks about other things, I wonder about God. I suppose everyone does this at sometimes. My wireless is playing 'The Blue Danube', it's excitingly romantic. I will write a poem or a book maybe.

No date

So much has happened since I last wrote. A lapse of approximately four weeks. I have fallen off a horse and been in bed for three weeks because of it. My leg in plaster. And I have to have my tonsils out tomorrow.

* * *

I was sent by train from the Isle of Wight to the Saint Thomas hospital with my leg in plaster. The archbishop signed on my plaster and put a little cross after his name. And the porter who helped me get into the train signed it too, writing 'BR' for British Rail.

* * *

Tonsils out (letter for the class)

Dear all,

I miss you a lot. I had my operation today. Firstly, I had hardly any breakfast and then I had an injection. I was meant to go to sleep but I couldn't. I was in a white linen backless gown. And white football socks. It was very exciting, I just laid down maybe a little frightened and then sat up to see if I was still awake. Half an hour passed and a trolley came. Two nurses and a porter wheeled me to the operating theatre and then into the little room where they all waited in green with masks and little knives. I had a prick in my elbow and this time I knew nothing more until I woke up. I had a shock when I saw a great patch of blood on my gown. They changed my gory clothes and put on another gown. What a beastly taste of blood. I've still got a horrid sore throat and can't speak or eat much. A very young doctor came to see me and explained how a stethoscope worked. I listened to his arm and heard a very distant noise which was the heart pumping blood. He came again yesterday and asked if I was still at school.

My leg is out of plaster and I have to have physiotherapy. I am very, very near Big Ben and can see it if I get up and look out of the window. It makes a lovely noise, it is striking at the moment.

An American boy has just come in who is having his tonsils out today. He is nervous and I have to tell him about it and say it's all great fun.

Monday

Organ broke, still sang and clapped without it! Yes we did!

Saturday

UNCLE JOHN* ENGAGED. He is going to be married to Elizabeth Jackson, a mathematician, jolly good.

I've been in chapel most of the time. I love being quiet and by myself.

Tuesday

Marks and remarks. Mine = behaviour good, tries very hard, I win Guide cup.

Friday we break up. Nice break-up breakfast.

Father meets us at Waterloo and is pleased about my cup. Andrew and Ma in Paris, France.

Tuesday

Solomon and Sheba, it is wonderful. Yul Brynner and Gina Lollobrigida. She looked wonderful when she was being stoned, she was wearing light blue against a yellowy gold stone. Black hair (she was

---

* My mother's brother.

Sheba, needless to say). God's voice was American! When I went out of the cinema there was a crack of thunder (firework display for Charles de Gaulle). Yul Brynner had a wig. He looked so beautiful, his own beard and such a soft voice.

Ma and Andrew back.

Saturday

We see Aunt Madge.* She is very ill, last week she nearly died. We took her grapes and some flowers, a lovely tea.

When Andrew and Ma came back from Paris, Andrew gave me a little statue, rather ghostly.† They had been locked up in the Marie-Antoinette garden and they had to climb scaffolding to get out. They visited the dairy where she pretended to be a milkmaid, the man showing them round took a liking to Andrew and Ma, so he showed them it and said no one else has ever seen it, it was a secret place in the Palace of Versailles.

Sunday

Linda and I go to church. It is Palm Sunday, we feel uncomfortable and we were about the only people singing.

Pinny might die, I hope she doesn't, I'll write to her.

* * *

Pinny, I suppose, is Marjory Russell, the sister of Olive Isabel Russell, my father's mother. She had six brothers and sisters. Her brother was Sir Thomas Wentworth Russell, more well-known under

---

* Aunt Madge was my mother's aunt, she lived in a crazy house with her budgerigars and her companion Nell.

† A gargoyle from Notre Dame in plaster of Paris for tourists that I still have. It's funny because when Andrew and I went to Paris in '68 with Kate, for the film *Slogan*, we were in a hotel opposite Notre Dame.

the name of Russell Pasha. He had a grey parrot, very chic, it used to scream 'Thomaaaas!' all day long and lived with my grandmother with Polly, a green parrot that I inherited after my grandmother's death. All the Russell children had been brought up by their father the reverend Henry Charles Russell, their mother having died very young. He had the church and the Wollaton presbytery. His elder brother had inherited Wollaton Hall that one can visit today and by which we much were taken as children. It was there that my grandmother was born by accident during her parents' visit to the older brother.

* * *

I am waiting for the Portsmouth car ferry. We have missed it. It's full up. Finally we caught the Southampton Cowes ferry. In the pouring rain, Ma's watches stopped, both of them, that is why we had missed the ferry. We rang Pa up at Southampton and he was very nice about it.

Tuesday

We went to the beach in the morning and Linda and I brought back an explosive thing saying on it, 'Danger! If found do not handle or move', IN RED! We will take it back soon. Pa very kindly said he would. My St Christopher's safety chain has bust.

* * *

I lost my father's St Christopher medallion when I was with Serge. I had put it on a little chain round my ankle. God knows why my legs were sticking out of the taxi window on our way back from a night-club. When I got home I saw that the St Christopher was no longer there. It was the medallion that my father had kept throughout the war – on one side it was written 'Church of England' so that one

knew how to bury him – and I'd lost it on a whim, trying to look cute.
I didn't dare tell my father. During the filming of *Death on the Nile*,
Pa and I shared the same duplex with Serge, and I wore fur moon
boots in spite of the 42-degree heat so that he wouldn't notice.
When I saw him after in London I said, 'I've got a terrible thing to
own up to,' and he said, 'Of course, you've lost your St Christopher.'
So he knew all along!

* * *

Sunday

We see *I'm All Right Jack* in a very nice cinema. The manager
showed us the control room, it looked like somewhere on Mars! He
also gave us pamphlets and papers and advertisements and sticky
posters about films, etc.

All trunks to be packed tonight. Ma found her best Malta weave
cushion with Valspar on it. No one knows whodunit. It hasn't come
out. It's very horrid because although Ma said, 'forget about it',
everyone is kind of 'under suspicion'. I owned up about spilling ink
on the carpet in Linda's room. I really felt I had to it and I feel much
better now. I hope because I owned up late about that they won't
think that I did this too.

Friday

Telephone call. Granny is terribly ill. She had got pneumonia, she had a fall two days ago and Father has got to go straight
away. Oh gosh, I'm going to offer to go with him. From the sound
of Uncle Michael's voice she may die. Oh dear, here I am, crying
and praying. How weak in thought I am, Granny and Pin are
so brave.

Oh, everyone is speaking about death, 'nearly dead'. Father has gone to Cowes with Ma driving him. Pin is, I think, the same. And Granny's handwriting on the letter she wrote to Ma is very feeble. Andrew is a great comfort to both Linda and myself. He is keeping outwardly cheerful but on the other hand not evidently so.

The most terrible thing has happened. Granny is dead. I now have no grandparents and Father and Ma have no parents. Death happens so quickly. Just think, I'll never go down to the town with her ever again. I hope she is in the heaven she wanted. Father didn't get there in time. She died at 3 o'clock, she was unconscious and died peacefully. I always thought she was so strong. Granny just fell (according to her last letter) and her glasses flew three feet in front of her. She went to call, and her foot caught in the carpet, and she fell. I think she may have been unconscious. When I heard, I cried for hours. Poor Pin and Pa. Thank God for Mrs Griffiths. Granny said she thought that God had sent her in her need. Both Pin and she were so brave; they will be an everlasting example.

Wednesday

Granny's funeral, very sad. And when we drove through Wollaton Park on the way in the Rolls-Royce I have never seen so many flowers. They were as a carpet on the ground. There were cloths on the furniture. We went to Wilfred Hill cemetery and Cannon Giles's and Cannon Ingles's robes were blowing in the wind. I could see their trousers.

Tuesday

Today is a bad day, very bad, what's more I feel bad. I have got 2/10 for Latin that I don't feel I deserve. I've got to have an early supper I can't get my prep finished. I wish I could start afresh, but I have to muddle on and on, getting worse and worse. I want to give up Latin, French, English language, English literature, vocabulary, geometry, algebra, arithmetic and almost life, certainly school. I hate school, I loathe, loathe, loathe it.

Summer

First day of our hols, but not Andrew's. We didn't do much, went to see Aunt Madge which was lovely and she gave Linda and me a packet of sixpences.

We go to *Oliver Twist* after heavenly early supper, sausage and Spam then greengages and plums with Coca-Cola. *Oliver* was wonderful, the boy who played him was terribly good. I think the orphans were good too and Fagin was one of the best!

Friday

Ma makes me a dress, she has been doing it for a day or two and she also bought me some white and silver shoes. A lovely dance at East Grinstead, I danced with very nice boys, all terribly sweet. None of them could dance which made the situation rather uncomfortable for me who couldn't either!

* * *

Ma had made me this dress because I was a bridesmaid to my uncle and because I was presented to the Queen when she visited my grandfather's lace factory in Nottingham. The Duke of Edinburgh stooped towards me and said, 'Did you grow the flowers yourself?' It's probably what he said to all the little girls who gave him flowers. For the Agatha Christie films I'd been presented along with the entire cast to Queen Elizabeth. I remember that the heroine of the film, Lois Chiles, panicked because she didn't realise one should wear long gloves, so I took off my left glove and turned it inside out. That way we both had two right arms and Lois was able to shake the Queen's hand. I saw the Queen again at a dinner at the

Elysée where she made an extraordinarily funny speech about the Entente Cordiale. I don't know if it was on that occasion or another that I found myself next to Lady Diana. She had a way of blushing that was terribly attractive. I said to come and live in Paris, that the press would leave her alone . . .

* * *

I go to the ballet in the evening at the Festival Hall. It was very good. Beautiful costumes and I liked the Prince Igor. There was a dance with the ballet dancers in pink against black background and it was beautiful.

Saturday

Andrew to Nottingham where he finds an old newspaper from 1719, very interesting. Linda and I go to *Saint Joan* in the evening, terribly good and I cried a lot.

Tuesday

Went swimming and then to the National Gallery with Lillian,* some good Turners and Constables, then we went to see the Jewels.

Thursday, *in Nottingham*

Went into the town to buy some plimsolls and some jeans. No shop had any real jeans, not even Marks & Spencer. Eventually we found some and a very pretty petticoat. We played in the garden and went back to Lincoln House, to Aunt Gertrude's† for tea. Played hide

---

* Our au pair. Ma chose the most beautiful girls so that Pa could paint them. I remember two French girls, Renée and Jacqueline. I still have their portraits. The only thing that was demanded of them was that they liked Pekineses.

† One of my father's aunts.

and seek in the garden. Father hides and we seek. He has to give us a hint. We dashed to the greenhouse and find Father under a bench in the second greenhouse. We looked for worms in the garden but the birds have eaten them all. Played in the garden and helped May* clean the stairs. Went to Pin's old house and peeped through a hole in the wall to see the blacksmith at work.

That afternoon, Sarah Churchill (my godmother) came to lunch. Ma took a cine film of us against the passionflower. We had another game with Pa and this time I found him crouched behind a glass door.

Saturday

We go to Wollaton Hall with Lillian. I made out a family tree in my head. The house should belong to Pa if the Middletons are not the main side (Russell).

We saw all the big rooms, which were very interesting, and the animals and birds† and eggs (a vast collection, Andrew was very interested), lots of biology and botany.

There was a fair going on, Institute of National Railwaymen.

* * *

Someone told me that my grandfather reserved a carriage coming down from Nottingham on British Railways. I think he was a shareholder. He used to stay in their hotel at St Pancras. He didn't like to go into town and only went to visit my father during his eye operations. He found the best surgeon, Bedford Russell – unhappily, because that was to be the cause of all my father's troubles with his eyes. The evening of the first operation my father went out on the

---

* One of my grandmother's maids.

† My great-grandfather, the Reverend Russell, used to change the heads on the bodies of the stuffed animals and underneath these creatures he wrote, 'Such are the wonders of the good Lord.'

quiet with a nurse by the fire escape. He was nineteen and when they came back he had a temperature but he didn't want to own up to the fact that he'd been out because of the nurse. The doctors thought, therefore, that there'd been a serious problem and they opened up his eye again. The famous surgeon's scalpel slipped and cut through my father's optic nerves, which caused his double vision. I don't know how many operations he went on to have. A piece of his hip was even grafted into the socket. That's why my father had such a romantic patch on his eye when he got married and the bleeding lungs were caused through too many anaesthetics and lasted all his life.

* * *

It has been decided that Lincoln House will be knocked down and sold for flats and the oak trees too. This is the last time we will see it before the sale. It has to go. We don't know who is going to inhabit the place and there was no alternative to selling. It would only get £2000 as a house, whereas if it was going to be flats it would bring £5000.

Sunday

Andrew, Linda and I all go to Wollaton Church.

Pa's eye is really bad and very, very painful, poor thing! He's going to have yet another operation. We went to see where Granny and Pin and Aunt Sheila used to live. We spoke to Cannon Giles who showed us round the churchyard and we went to Wollaton cemetery to see Pin's grave. It hasn't got a tombstone yet. We went to Pin's house and Ma found a large straw hat for me with a bow.

Father threw away some letters of Granny's. I pulled two of them out and they have proved to be valuable, with Robert Browning writing one.

All the chickens were killed by Wally.* Everything's going today. The rooms are being used as storerooms. I have a writing desk and some Copenhagen china, a paper box and another box, both with birds on them. I have a book of art and a diary that has never been used for next year.

Monday

Cat club, ideas. First meeting of the summer hols.

Present. Andrew, Jane, Linda.

Collect wildflower bunches and sell them.

Sell mushrooms (if any).

Collect blackberries and raspberries.

Odd jobs.

End of meeting.

Honorary member, David Birkin, suggests we collect for another committee as we have collected a total of £8.10 shillings for the PDSA.

End.

Tuesday

Went to see the place where Pa was born, it had a copper dome with Grecian windows and monster gardens. It is now a school.

Thursday

We play in the garden and go to the greenhouses, as they are the best places to hide. We play the ladder game in the loft. It broke and Andrew came hurtling down on top of me. He would have killed himself, but luckily there was a sack to stop him cracking his head open.

---

* Wally was the chauffeur, married to Mavis. They lived opposite my grandmother's and we were very intrigued because they didn't have any children. Wally used to come and pick us up from the station when we arrived. He used to take us shopping or to the beach.

Friday

In the evening, when it was all dark the guy that Andrew and Linda had made beside the incinerator was set on fire. Pa got the fire extinguisher to try it out; it contained a sort of powder, but it didn't work and didn't put the fire out.

Saturday

Ma and Andrew load up the car, they are going back to the Isle of Wight ahead of us. Linda and I go to church. A muddling, but good, sermon.

Monday

Linda and I do all the cooking, the shopping too. Mrs Clark at the shop said I should put Polly (parrot) in a wooden box and carry her that way. At the house, Pa gave us Granny and Grandpa's crash helmets and a bullet strap from the Boer War.

Thursday, Friday, Saturday, Sunday, Monday, Tuesday, Wednesday, *Wight*

On Wednesday we went down to the beach. We went on bikes to Compton. We collected shells, crabs, seaweed and rocks for the idea I had to have a show of things we found about the sea. We got our shoes wet, as the sea was not as low as it might have been. We found a vast yellow plastic ball which we took home. It weighed a ton. My bike went wonky so I rang up and said we will be late, so Andrew and Linda went on bikes and I followed on foot. Pa said the yellow ball might be a lobster marker or mooring marker. Ma said it might be a buoy. After lunch we repeated our actions. On the way back we saw a myxomatosis rabbit; it had maggots and it was still alive. It seemed to be wet and damp and also had pneumonia. Andrew killed it quickly against the fence. We were late again – and we had rabbit for lunch!

Pa is drawing me at the moment and the sun has come out.

Andrew's friend is coming to stay. Linda and I went to the beach and after trembling at the brink we swam. We went to get the milk from Hooky and then we went home. Andrew and his friend have not arrived. After lunch we ask Andrew if we can swim and we did for a long time. I remember wondering if his watch was right, wouldn't it be awful if it wasn't? I got out of the sea and Linda followed. Andrew was calling us from the cliffs and we dressed quickly and got on our bikes.

Linda suddenly said, 'Your watch is wrong! Mine says seven and I set it by the kitchen clock. It's not twenty-five to.' We panicked at once and asked a crotchety old man who was just getting into his car what the time was. 'Just after seven,' he said. I went to the telephone box. 'Can I have some money?' I asked Andrew. 'I haven't got any,' he replied. 'Reverse the charges,' he said, so we did. Father answered and told us to come quickly so we did.

Monday

Ma, Linda and I to see the Roman villa, very interesting. It's funny to think that a Roman walked on the land that you can still see. Ma and Pa thought of doing a little film with our seashells.

Tuesday

In the evening we got ready for the midnight picnic. It was wonderful and afterwards we hurled burning wood into the sea and it fizzled.

Here is the story we're going to film:

Pa is the smuggling smuggler. He is found by Linda and I in a shack. I climb on the roof with Linda and out comes Pa. We hide and he goes away. But then he catches Linda and I see him come back. I bonk him on the head and fetch help. The end is not fixed.

Clover* has been very ill. We looked after her, but at last we rang up the vet. He was in the cinema so Pa had a slide flashed onto the screen. He came and gave a prescription and a vastly painful injection.

Today is 6 October

I hope Pa's eye is all right. It seems so unfair to have it for one's life. I just prayed all would be well.

Tuesday

Pa is out of hospital. Rejoice!

Thursday, *Upper Chine*

Pa is better, I think. I forgot to ask him for his stitches. I must write and ask him now.

Sylvia and Susan got a diso (disobedience mark) each for treading on the garden to get fallen apples.

Good night.

Sunday

I go out, and Mama tells me that Clover is dead. She died peacefully after a bad attack. In the morning Pa put his hand on her and she breathed, but gradually it got slower and slower, and then she gave a flutter and she died. They put her in her basket. Tracy† sent around some red roses and some white carnations and was terribly

---

* My father's Pekinese, who was sixteen.

† Pempie's daughter.

sweet. Ma and Pa drove her to the Isle of Wight and wrapped her in Mama's white shawl and Pa's copper-coloured jersey, both of which she knew so well. Mr Barnes dug a deep hole and put her in. He said, 'I won't scatter the earth too spiteful.'

Pa said she looked more beautiful than ever before. Her ears back, her big eyes closed and a wet nose. Beautiful fluffy white chest, just as if she was asleep. A stone is being made simply saying 'Clover at rest'. Everyone is so upset. It was better than if she was run over or something. Ma, Pa and Andrew are the people who are the most miserable about her. Poor Andrew, it must be hard to hear by telephone.

Monday, 11 December

Such a long time since I wrote last. I almost feel older as I take up my pen to write. Too much has happened. I will write it down briefly and comment on each in turn.

Pa's birthday. Got him a brush and two pencils.

London. Went home and had a gorgeous two days. Couldn't find my brace when I came back, very worried. Finally I found it under my chair.

Susan's birthday party. I gave her talcum powder and records. Everyone swooning!

Andrew's birthday. Sent two cards and a letter. Present in the hols.

My party. Wonderful fun. Small fruitcake, doughnuts, egg sandwiches, fruit salad, mousse, bridge rolls. Orange squash, lemon squash and ginger nuts.

Lovely preparing it, got Linda to help.

Hols!

Christmas presents bought. Mama, slippers and sweets. Pa, two drawing books, a rubber and charcoal pencils. Linda, two doll's outfits. Andrew, Giles cartoon book.

Christmas Day

Gorgeous cooking, Ma.

Ma and Pa gave me what I'VE ALWAYS WANTED, a transistor radio. Andrew gave me a record 'You've got a face like an angel face, h-h-how about that' and four bars of chocolate. Linda gave me crayons and pencils with my name on in gold.

Christmas trees are a silver one on the landing, a green one in the sitting room and a golden one on the dining-room table.

I wore my Scottish dress with a velvet collar. I used my Woodlanders crayons – they are splendid – and I ate all Andrew's chocolates.

Tuesday

Did a play. Andrew's scenery was very good and Ma did Papa's make-up, which was wonderful. I was very worried it would be a flop as it was my idea, but was OK, with Andrew helping with the scenery and Nigel* on lights and Linda learning her lines so swiftly and coming so often for fittings.

It was very funny when I said, 'It's beginning to snow' and a handful of paper confetti (handmade) was cast asunder and Andrew's hand shot out, casting snow on the floor. 'It's not a turkey but a condor!' said Andrew and he began to flap his hands and put on a face. It made me laugh. The turkey was meant to say, 'Fainter fainter grows the maiden's breath and night will bring a frosted death.' But instead there was a dead silence.

We went to Aunt Madge for tea; she shoved a bag of sixpences into our hands and when we said she mustn't she whispered, 'I've pinched them, I pinched them all for you!' Aunt Madge smothered us in kisses. When we went home Andrew took vast branches of greenery for the scenery and asked if he could take Ma's cloak for the woodcutter and we did our play the following evening.

---

* Nigel was the son of our GP. He died a few years later in the plane crash at Orly.

Isle of Wight

Pa has ordered flying squirrels* and promises a puppy in the spring. But if Ma and Pa went abroad for a while it could be a problem. I'm certain it would do Pa's eye good, it is very sore. Poor Pa, he had a nosebleed and it was a piece of the skin graft that came away.

I've got the marvellous attic room. I look through my telescope every morning (Pa has given me his). I watched three pheasants for a long time.

Wednesday, *back at school*

I have a great many preps to do. I hear Mr Toomey talking in strong grammatical Old English next door. Elocution to learn, a vast chunk from Shakespeare. Pretty, actually, all about Oberon in a wax with the Queen.

---

* He had this idea because he was so depressed when Clover died. In the end, they bought another Pekinese.

1961

May, *Upper Chine*

I got a very funny letter from Andrew about the statue he is making called 'Isabella in the waterhole'. Ma and Pa wrote yesterday and told all their news. Pa is going to buy a dinghy. He asked Captain Watts about it, and he's having his studio painted. They are off to Venice for a month. I am very sad, but others are boarders for two years without seeing their parents.

I got an A for my geography map! I took a long time over it so I'm very glad.

Must go now. Perhaps it's because it's the thirteenth everything is going wrong.

Jane xxx

Friday night

Everyone was telling stories after lights. I'm trying to block my ears but you know how it is. I was sure Nurse would come in halfway through and give us disos. You know how it is when you're very tired – and I was, after finding my average was B, and not understanding the algebra graphs. I was on the point of tears; and as for being 'fresh' for the weekend, the idea depressed me even more, so I went down the bed and cried. Suddenly there was an awful smell of egg; it was Veet, everyone was remarking on it! I flopped down on the bed, as the poof above was terrific.

John sent me a letter, wooing me again! He gave me a choice of present, i.e., soap, etc. Pa told me to say it was his choice, Ma said to ask him for a souvenir of Switzerland. I think I will ask for a pressed flower, the most beautiful he has ever seen in Switzerland, as well as a photo of him.

I came second in the potato race. I have a new home dress, which I wore when I went out. Mrs Sanderson has given me two disobedience marks now. I am going to do really well and not get any bad marks to please Pa and Ma. Must go now to say goodnight to Linda.

Wednesday

Last night I watched my alarm clock from 9.30 to 10 o'clock. I thought: Ma will just about to be ready to start her play on television. Today all the staff commented on how good she was. I felt so pleased. Her name was top of the lot. Judy Campbell is Mrs Skeffington, and then all the rest. I was purring with admiration. I sent a letter with a red rose to Ma for congratulations.

Today the sun is shining, everyone is laughing and playing in the garden, and I am feeling in the mood to write a story; but I would rather describe and use words than think of the story as such and write it down.

Wednesday

Ma and Pa arrived last Saturday in France and are going by train to Venice to stay in a village just outside the city. I hope it helps Pa's health.

Saw the school photo. I think I look foul. The backrow, standing on a chair. I suppose it couldn't be worse than last year. I put curlers in my hair last night and it was quite nice one side, but the other curled up the wrong way.

Art today. I got an A for last week's open-day painting and I'm doing figure drawing now. I've got to draw Mimi at the art exhibition. I'm the only one parents are going to come round and watch paint. How embarrassing. All the same I'm quite pleased.

It's been raining in Venice!

Thursday

We have had a lecture, terribly interesting. I have almost made up my mind what I'm going to be. She lectured about nursing and hospitals and physiotherapy. Apparently being an air hostess is not such fun. I asked a question, which I had never done before! Whether being a probation officer in a prison was a good thing for a girl. She said they didn't have girls under twenty-one as a rule and it was better to work in the youth centre. I am really going to find out what I have to pass for GCE, as I would really love to be a welfare officer, someone who helps prisoners. Perhaps it's a dream the idea of helping those who are in trouble or any other adversity. I have dreams at night where there is some poor wretched creature that needs help or advice and how I helped him and how rewarding it was settling the thing that worried him. People laughed when I said it, and pointed out an incident where I might be with a sex maniac.

* * *

My father volunteered as a probation officer, acting as a guarantor, helping to prevent young people going to prison for a first offence. There was a pyromaniac called Tom who lived in Battersea. Linda and I visited him with my father. There was a corpse on the table in the kitchen, and another arrived in a wheelbarrow, because Tom's mother laid people out. Tom was in his bedroom where he touched himself up all day long. Pa whispered to us that he'd do the same if he was him. We saw the rats' tails slithering between the floorboards. Tom's mother clasped her hands together in wonderful ecstasy, exclaiming, 'Oh Mr Birkin, when the terrible day comes, I'll make a lovely job of you!' She was so relieved that Tom didn't finish his days behind bars. He'd never been able to resist the urge to set fire to anything labelled 'Her Majesty's Property'.

* * *

I can so much easier express myself in my diary now, how it feels to be growing up. Things that did not occur to me before matter now. I'm feeling more responsible and yet scared of getting older and having to earn my own living. I try so hard not to read books like *Peyton Place*, or *Return to Peyton Place*, yet something attracts me to them. I wish it wouldn't, as I feel very coarse and common and horrid when I do. I wonder if most people wear tight skirts and stockings, and eyeshadow and lipstick. All the seniors do and, although I thought it was horrid to do that, I sometimes wonder if I'm wrong and I am babyish not to.

What is wrong with me? All I can do is write and sing; my memory cannot take anything in although I want to so badly. I try not to give up, thinking it will come right tomorrow, but nothing improves, my spelling, verbs, even music, which I love above everything. Poetry, I cannot learn; I try to, I begin to, but it just ends up in crying. I must have a block in my brain or something. I want so much to remember the beautiful things in life, the sky in the evening, the sun in the morning. I choke back tears every night; I cry for Father and the world and for the time when the sun does not shine any longer for me, when I am gone, my lights snuffed out.

I have been playing Scrabble and afterwards I talk to Mamma a bit about funerals. I don't like talking about when people die, because it frightens me, it really does, and it makes me cry to ever think of either Ma or Pa or Andrew or Linda or anyone dying, I suppose it's because I haven't enough faith. People who have a great faith in God and heaven are very calm about dying. I think Granny Birkin was always calm and truly believed in an afterlife. I don't think she ever doubted anything about it, but I do; I'm not certain although I am Christian and everything . . .

Friday, 30 June

I could ramble on and on about the happenings of yesterday and today. My mind, as a flustered hen, cannot take the strong tortures of its frail substance. Misery is not a thing to be forgotten, sad eyes and heart are not easily dismissed; in similar time it will be difficult to express the thoughts and sadness today has brought.

M and J are doing exercises, and I must do mine. 'I must I must increase my bust' exercise, one hundred times. They must improve. I feel so left out – whenever I'm enjoying myself someone always says, 'Oh you've got nothing on top or below, why are you trying?' Or some, 'You're a half-caste.' Or some, 'You're a boy not a girl.' Which seriously makes me feel out of it and different.

But I *am* different.

'Why do you wear a bra, you don't need one?'

Well, I don't know except I don't want to be the only one without one. I get teased enough and laughed about, in front and behind my back as it is, and the fault is my slow development. For instance, someone picked up an acorn, a very young one. 'What is it?' Someone said, 'An undeveloped acorn.' And she said, 'I know someone else who is undeveloped, an undeveloped human being!'

Fancy a girl of fourteen who has not *commencé* yet, with nothing on top or below. Laugh, laugh. Maybe it was a joke but it hurts.

Jane xx

Thursday

Latest news: Sylvia has caught the dreaded disease chickenpox. Latest number of victims seven! I'll be the next you bet!

20 July, *after the exams*

We break up tomorrow and I have got the ART PRIZE for the second year running!

Saturday, *last day*

Friday was the best I ever had at Upper Chine. I threw my black pants into the Solent. We saw *Twelfth Night* at the Old Vic, heavenly. I can't wait to see *Romeo and Juliet*. Saw *West Side Story*, cried a lot. It is the equivalent of *Romeo and Juliet* in American modern times.

Went to a friend's house, playing records, etc. We smoked a cig-arette but I didn't like it and stubbed it out quickly. Went to see *Romeo and Juliet*. Heavenly, I loved it. Andrew came too as he had broken up. The scene at the end in the vault was done so well with lights etc. Go to see *Stop the World – I Want to Get Off** with Rachel Gurney, Ma's friend.

Tuesday, *Isle of Wight*

Andrew finds a young seagull caught in the storm and brings it

---

* I told Serge this story, who then used the title of the film in his song, 'Quoi': 'Moi j'aim-erais que la terre s'arrête pour descendre.'

home. The seagull died. We took it out onto the lawn and it died in the sun. Andrew and I buried it on the beach as every time we threw it into the sea it came back on the waves.

Saw *The Alamo*. So bloodthirsty and too much tomato ketchup.

I do not understand myself. I hate being the age I am, neither a woman nor a child. I hate being told I'm too old for something but I hate 100,000 times more being called a child. I am not either. I am jealous of Linda for things like slip-on shoes which I never had till I was thirteen, and she has at eleven, and things like lipstick. I am not allowed to put it on; she will have it at thirteen. Why should I think this way? I have fits of depression when I cry and where I am told to grow up. Other people wear lipstick, tights and heels. I do not understand why I can't be the same as other girls of my age. I want to go out and see boys, go to dances and have a good time. I want to have these things other girls at fourteen have. To be allowed to grow up and stay out too, later than 9.30. Jenny goes home at 11 or 11.30, so why shouldn't I?

1962

Return to Cheyne Gardens and to Miss Ironside's school for young girls

Sunday, 11 February

I didn't get up early today on account of the day. I was absolutely dead. I really was. But Ma was up. Her play finished yesterday, *Heartbreak House*. It's daft, actually, they had masses of advance bookings but the Aubrey chap wants his play on, something about 'soup' which is losing money like crazy, so Ma's lot have got to move to let his soup thing in. Daft, as I said.

* * *

It was one of the rare times that I saw my mother on the stage, because really, most of her theatre appearances had been before our time. And when she went back to the theatre I was in France. At boarding school we were not allowed to go out. And I don't think my father ever took us to see her. I saw her lots of times after, when I was grown up, with Omar Sharif at Chichester, and playing lots of eccentric people such as those created by George Bernard Shaw, and to my joy after my father's death she went back to singing again, at eighty, in a tiny cabaret that was chock-a-block full every night with people in tears when she sang 'A Nightingale Sang in Berkeley Square'. She was so resourceful getting to her theatre in her little car, never a taxi, not respecting any rules – and when she was stopped by the police for going through a red light and the car wasn't even in her name, she invited them to tea! She had a ferocious loyalty, was opinionated, and terribly independent. It's extraordinary that she sacrificed so much for my father. In the sixties there was a very classy play at the Royal Court, by one of our best writers. They asked her to play a part but she had to say 'Fuck', so she refused because of my father's family. I remember that my parents had rented a little cottage in Wales, very simple, no electricity, and Andrew, Linda and I were hiding under the stairs and we witnessed an extraordinary fight: my mother was pouring milk on my father's head and my father was massaging butter into her hair. We didn't know what was going on. My brother started to giggle, and both of them turned on him. It turned out that Ma had just said, 'I'm going to the local hairdresser,' and my father had replied, 'What for? No one will see you here.' It was really rotten since my mother had just turned down a musical on Broadway because it was during the holidays. She told me later that she envied us a bit for being the stars who could bring our children along on films, who could have a second hotel room. She had had neither the status nor the means. For more than eight years, at over eighty years old, she could do exactly what she wanted, being with her theatre friends and her dear John Wood, my agent who became hers, and also became her friend. After my father's death my brother took her to Hollywood for the Oscars. She found all her actress friends; it was her dream. She went to New York after September 11 to sing 'A Nightingale Sang in Berkeley Square' at the Town Hall. They told me later how moved they'd been to see this lady, who had known the London Blitz, take the time to come to New York. Ma was in her element, having a whale of a time in the nightclubs.

* * *

I have breakfast and take Pa's tea up. There was a jay on our bird table. I thought it was a pigeon at first. By the way, I got an early

Valentine card from Simon, two to be exact (three shillings each). Jolly decent really. I don't know whether to send him one as it's not a leap year. I think he sent the second one by mistake but that one said 'I love you', so I'm jolly glad.

I started on 29 January (my period). I was so happy; it's made all the difference, it really has. Now I'm the same as everybody else. Pa was the only one in the house except Linda and he was so sweet it wasn't true. I really am so pleased: three years of praying come true! Well, I really must go now as it'll soon be lunch, bye.

Monday, 12 February

Poor Ma had three fillings and can't talk. Pa's eye is all red and Linda's got her entrance exam tomorrow, poor thing!

Well, I'd better stop now, bye.

Sunday, 18 February

I haven't written for simply ages, I know, sorry, but I had such a lot of prep. I hardly have any time to write. Yesterday I saw *As You Like It* with Vanessa Redgrave. It was simply wonderful, it really was; and we went round to see them afterwards. I like the shepherd, William, the best, he had a heavenly face.

* * *

Vanessa was barely twenty and very pregnant. Our mothers had been friends. I was very fond of her and we crossed paths all our lives, but not on *Blow-Up*. I loved her brother Corin, too, Vanessa and he could always count on my mother for their various causes. Later, we both went to Sarajevo, and at the demonstrations she was much more eloquent than me and much more daring, and radical, even putting her career in peril.

* * *

Linda and Pa have gone to the round pond to sail the boats. I would have loved to go but I have prep. Pa says I'm a bore about it and I spend too long on it. I can't help that; I don't spend time just for the hell of it. God, it makes me sick. Missed *Juke Box Jury* yesterday because of it all.

I had forgotten to ask to change my music lesson tomorrow because of the dentist. There will be a hell of an eruption. I'm not kidding. Stupid of me, I admit, but by gum, I'll pay for it. I'll have a firing squad at home and at school, no doubt, bet your hat on it! Told Ma I had fixed up the lesson, I never thought I could be such a blithering idiot, I really didn't. However, I paid for it dearly when I had to pluck up the courage to say I lied and HADN'T fixed my music lesson. But honestly, she was so kind when I told her, I swear to God I couldn't sleep with that darn lie on my brain. I never can, it's my conscience you see. Bye.

April

Today everything has gone wrong.

I've been writing letters and took them downstairs to show Ma and Pa plus the one for the lost property office (Ma's lost umbrella). They went on and on about how they couldn't read my writing, how ghastly, what appalling spelling, how I couldn't remember any addresses but Linda can. Linda's quite remarkable, Linda even knows the lost property address, and Aunt Madge's. This was said in front of everyone. God, I felt like crying. I just couldn't stick it. They're always running me down and praising Linda until I'm just about ready to scream. When I said I thought it was 30 Durand Gardens to Pa after Linda had said it, he said she was so good, clever, bright and brilliant and he said snubs to me. I felt everyone laughing. I have heard Ma talking about how my writing is now illegible; really I just feel miserable. And when Pa asks me what's wrong I just read

the *TV Times* and say nothing, although I feel like the whole blasted
world is wrong. It must be me, I suppose. They used to criticise me
and I never used to mind but now it hurts like hell, it really does.
They're sweet, really; they don't know what they're doing. I just can't
take any more criticism. I just wish I had someone I could cry to and
I could just be a baby again and not the way I am. A place where I
could be quiet for a while and think things over without going red-
faced. Linda made the lovely jelly lunch. Ma kept on about her being
so good as a housekeeper, etc., and praising her for it. I don't know
if it just happened that way. 'Well done. Thank you, Linda, congratulations.' A mumbled 'thanks' from Pa for me, which was jolly nice,
but nothing from Ma. Only for Linda – and I had cleared the table.
Gosh, I can't stick it any more. One more comment on me doing
things wrong and Linda doing it better and how rotten I am, I really
think I'll blub. The thing that gets me is I must've changed. Let me
say as quick as lightning it is not anyone else's fault, not Ma's nor Pa's
nor Andrew's nor Linda's. Just me. And that makes me depressed as
hell.

Easter Sunday

Went to pick up Marilyn from King's Cross and went with the
Williams to Battersea. Was very sick, miserable but Simon is sweet
and feeling rotten too.

* * *

Simon Williams was my brother's best friend and he became my
first boyfriend. His sister Pollyanna was Andrew's girlfriend. We did
a film together. Andrew, who was about fifteen years old, was the
director and wrote the script. Simon and I played the lovers and I
was to die of tuberculosis on the cliffs at Brighton. There was a kissing scene on the lake in Battersea, which was censored by Harrow
where Andrew showed the film and wrote 'censored' on the poster.

* * *

1 May

Going to Scotland with Pa in a sleeper. Millions of different electric lights in the morning. I heard the porter speaking Scottish and I knew we were over the border. Ma and Andrew saw us off from King's Cross. Poor Linda was crying and I had to promise to kiss the postcards we send to cheer her up, and give her two of my ulcer pills.

No date

We filmed, yes, and the entire absolute film (me as heroine! and Simon as hero). It was such fun. Battersea boating lake, the American embassy, cafés and everything. It is a love story. I enclose a script. Andrew was the producer. Andrew and I go to Sussex. I have never enjoyed a weekend so much. We did filming, of course. On the Downs, in the sea (I had to die in inches of sea water on the rocks in Brighton in the pouring rain almost crying). Then we all went to see *The Nun's Story*. Simon was absolutely sweet and lent me his coat and said my hair was smelling nice and was so kind and trying to cheer me up after my being soaked in the beach scene.

We played Murder in the Dark at their house as their parents were out. Bill was a very good detective. Simon was ill the next day and was a bit sore about his parents or something so we left for London in the late afternoon after being on the Downs all morning.

August 1962, *trip to France*

On Thursday I had my hair done in a very swish place in Sloane

Street.* I have some bumps on my head, which stung like crazy when
I had the perm and the pins burned holes in my head as I drank my
tea under the dryer. All worthwhile, though, as their hairstyle was
simply heavenly. That night I was very excited; I went to my room
to pack and made lists. I adore getting ready for things, it gives me a
gingery feeling in my bottom!

I woke at four-thirty and then at five, then we all got up. I wore
my pleated blouse and turquoise skirt. Pa drove us to Kensington
where we waited in a modern room for the coaches to take us to
London airport. I cried a little (to myself, of course), when we left
Pa, but he said he would meet us in Paris. Ma met a friend who was
very nice, who went with us to London airport (by this time I was
sustaining the gingery feeling with all my might). We boarded the
aeroplane and I found a window seat. My ears went pop and I was
very nearly sick to the point of having to hold a sick bag. When we
landed in Paris we were met by French-speaking people (I was so
happy I could've smothered Ma in kisses). We spent the day in Paris
and it rained a little. Andrew had to go to collect the bag he had left
at the airport. He went to the wrong one and had to come all the way
back to us and then off to the other one. All while we were eating
very expensive breakfast! We saw the Arc de Triomphe with a vast
flag, as it was Liberty Day.† There was boastful old Bonaparte being
crowned with glory and the stone of the Unknown Warrior with the
flame. The police told Linda to get off it. It was all heavenly and then
we went to a very expensive café and a record shop.

Then to the sleeper, a wonderful surprise. It was so old but it was
so cosy. I felt like a soldier going to war. There was a mother and a
little girl who were French in our sleeping car. Ma gasped in dismay
at how we and they were going to fit in, but we did. Andrew gave
his only blanket to an Australian and flopped to sleep before me or
Linda had supper.

---

* Vidal Sassoon.
† For the commemoration of the Liberation of Paris, no doubt.

We arrived at the station and then went to the village Aix sur Mer. The tenants were still there, so we went for a swim in the sea and bought a parasol and a chair from a very good-looking young man. I got stung by a jellyfish. We spent most of the day on the beach and then had dinner in a sweet restaurant with a grapevine climbing through the window. We played on the jukebox, which was very nice, and we twisted. On Monday we all got very sunburnt, especially Linda, and found a new beach with great rocks which some boys were diving from, so I did! On the way back we found an old newspaper with pictures of Princess Margaret and Marilyn Monroe.*

Tuesday

The train stopped so I have time to catch up with just a little news, I am on a journey to the IOW from Essex.

Friday, *Isle of Wight*

Went down to the beach again and saw Noelle's friends, all went to swim, surprisingly warm. Such fun. I've never got in so fast, never wavered, but I flashed into the water in my pink checked bikini; we were considered heroes by the boys who shivered on the edge. We splashed on the raft, me trying my hardest to look alluring, like a mermaid. When I got out, my hair was in rat's tails, I didn't want to wear a cap, it would have spoiled the effect!

That evening there was a party at Peter and John's house. I drank a teeny bit of cider, no more, as I won't get a car if I drink, and refused beer and strong stuff and drank orange and lemon juice. Rosemary got dead drunk, which was embarrassing; I was so glad I took Ma and Pa's advice, she was so peculiar and merry. Anyway, I was talking to about four boys at once, David knew everywhere

---

* It was on opening these newspapers that I learnt of Marilyn's death.

in Nottingham that I knew, it was such good fun chatting about it.
Peter's cousin, John's brother, talked to me about child psychology
and he wanted to read our comics and hear about my dreams; I
told him and we talked for ages, very interesting. John tried to tell
me cider was non-alcoholic and kept trying to fill my glass which I
poured back every time into his. He wanted to hear a poem I made
up and I told him I'd write him one. I was very pleased when I saw
the brown boy looking at me looking into a candle. He looked even
more good-looking, which is God-like. Rosemary, by this time, had
collapsed and everyone was trying to sober her up with black coffee.
She had drunk six glasses of cider and one of ale, which nearly
popped her off.

Bolshoi Ballet (undated)

Yesterday I went to the Bolshoi Ballet, it was heavenly and there
was a girl clapping for half an hour. I saw Dame Ninette de Valois,

who is sweet; she said I was too tall for a ballet dancer but I have dancer's feet.

Everything is wonderful with Alan ('Arty Type'). I've been to his house, I drank red wine. He kissed me on my neck just before I reached the door. I really do love him; I think about him day and night, it is such a marvellous thing to love someone so much. He has told me he feels the same. God, it is awful not being able to think anyone else, not even Cliff Richard, it's really a bore.

* * *

Alan was the neighbour who lived opposite us in Cheyne Gardens. In the summer I couldn't see him very well because of the leaves, but in winter, because my room was a floor above his, I pretended to be a ballerina with my parrot on my shoulder. My sister Linda and I had a code to say whether he was on the balcony. 'It's raining' would mean that he was there. One sunny day, Linda said that it was raining so I went out to the Embankment with a sketchbook to pretend to be drawing the pretty lamp posts. He was suddenly there and I heard his voice for the first time. He had a New Zealand accent. On turning round, I saw he was about forty years old. For the first time I went over to his place. Pa said it was OK because he could survey all from the balcony. What he didn't see was that Alan was able to give me a kiss behind the front door. The next year Alan had moved house. He invited me to his place, a basement; I'd had too much red wine to drink for dinner – he drank whisky and we ate ratatouille. He lay beside me and tried to get on top of me. I said it was the wrong time of the month, and he said it didn't matter. I found that a bit disgusting and I ran away. I got home much too late and I hadn't called Pa as I'd promised. When I got home, I climbed the staircase trying not to make any noise, but Pa was waiting on the landing, and said, 'It's at this time of night that you get home?' 'Sorry, Pa,' I said, and he replied, 'Sorry is not enough.' So I went up to my room and swallowed all the Junior Aspirin that I'd saved just in case. My sister found me at four in the morning, deathly pale. She told Ma. Stomach-pump. Ma slapped me and was right to do so. Ever since I've always hated whisky and ratatouille.

* * *

When I am very old, forty or something, with hundreds of children and things, I may be a little sad at reading something so young. When I'm lame, I may cry a little at my past activity, and maybe weep at my young bones and ideals, so in view of those days to come I will tell something of national interest.

A man has gone round the earth, Gagarin, Shepard and many others. There is a 'Telstar' for television. Marilyn Monroe is dead, thirty-something, poor beautiful creature. Suicide, some think, empty bottle of aspirin in her hands.

My love? I don't know. I like Simon a lot and I love Brough, although I haven't seen him after he stayed in IOW last year, but Cliff Richard to me is perfect, and I do love him – not only as a fan, I shouldn't like to think that at all. I would marry him like a shot if he asked me, but he wouldn't . . . but I really love him, very, very much, more than anyone, any boy, I love him.

*

Poems

Suicide lost

Do you know the way to another place
Can you tell me how to go?
Can you show the way to snuff out fast?
Tell me, I've got to know.
I'm a coward, a terrible coward, it's true,

I'm a child who's frightened to live
I'm a person who can't find a way out
and yet, please try to forgive.

For my sparks have filtered
And have long snuffed out,
My aims are lousy and low
I've lost my way to heavenly place
Please tell me which way to go.

*

Jealousy

I cried for something I would never have
I cried for a hope long gone
I prayed for a night with the turquoise star
And a day with the Moon that shone
I was bitter for the thing another had
I was dead to the thing I adored
And I smiled to the fate of another day
And the hours of another world.
I dreamed of a dream that would never come true
But I thought and hoped it would.
But I cried, for my dream tied to another
Died, as I knew it could.
Oh little thing on my solid heart
O sun that is willing to shine
Bring that small thing my jealousy bites
And tell me it could be mine.

1963

Pa decided to send me to France to Madame P, because of his affection for the French. There were six of us English girls living with Madame P and in the daytime we would take a bus or the Metro to Place des États-Unis to Mademoiselle Anita's, a plainclothes nun who showed us how to make chocolate truffles, and a bit of French, and we visited the Musée de l'Homme (a museum of anthropology). We were all goggle-eyed at what was on show. The idea was that on coming back to England I'd be a debutante and get married.

* * *

I arrived in Paris two days ago by aeroplane, to stay with Mme P. who lives on the fifth and top floor of 67 Bld. Lannes. When we rang the doorbell she said: 'Who are you?' But she soon realised and, as we were the first to arrive, we had the choice of four rooms. I chose a noisy but airy room facing the Bois de Boulogne. It has a very nice view and I share it with another girl. After some tea we unpacked and Mme P's fat son brought up our cases. He's not as bad as all that; he has a good sense of humour and hates Général de Gaulle. EVERYONE seems to. I can't think why they don't kill him, apparently they don't want him to look like a martyr, but there is half the youth population in prison for rioting against him.

The food is very good here (except everything is stuffed with garlic so I chomp millions of peppermints).

Yesterday we went to the Eiffel Tower, wine vaults built by the monks and deserted when the monastery was burnt down in the revolution. We all had a glass of white wine from the owner of the two restaurants on the Eiffel Tower.

Robert,* a boy who was nice to me while I was being sick on the ship between the Greek islands, is going to ring me tomorrow. The English news is on the wireless, it makes me feel very sad and homesick.

Saturday

Went out rowing in the Bois de Boulogne with Bertrand.† Oh it was lovely that day, the sun shone for a while too, then it began to rain so we ran to the car and back to the old park of Paris, full of beatniks and arty types, it was such fun walking through the little streets full of questionable dark strangers. We had an English cup of tea in a fashionable tea place.

He drove me back past the Arc de Triomphe – my goodness, Paris looked beautiful! It was so nice being with Bertrand. He was like a brother; you could talk frankly about love and he told me about his girlfriends, and I wasn't worried about leading him on and thinking 'God, I hope he won't get fresh, and what will I do if he kisses me?' We may see *55 Days in Peking* on Thursday.

Sunday

Went to a very high-class Catholic church. The outside very impressive but when we got in, no windows; it's the biggest in the world with no windows and what was horrid, the congregation took NO part in the service, not so much as an Amen. Some sat, some stood, some grovelled on the ground, some genuflected and one yawned. The priest kept ringing three bells and flinging incense around. The whole thing could have been beautiful but I thought it long and boring and I'm glad I'm an Anglican.

---

* During a visit to the Greek islands with Ma, she'd been pursued by a millionaire and I by a French author, Robert Quatrepoint, who wandered around with a guitar. He sent me letters with pressed flowers, then his book, *Journal d'un Être Humain*.
† Obviously a very kind boy.

That afternoon I wanted to be by myself to write by the Bois but Mme P said it was dangerous and wouldn't let anyone go. Then I went to the place Pa and I went that year before. I nearly cried, I missed him so and I wanted to talk to him.

Monday

This afternoon met the school party at a flea market. It was heavenly, but one kept being followed by rather dirty old men. However it was fun, masses and masses of stalls. I wandered around not buying anything but got separated and was worried as two horrid sex men were following me and talking to me. I just walked fast and tried not to listen, and as it started to rain I put my spotted hanky on my head and ran to the Metro where our chaperone was waiting; girls were missing so she was a bit in a flap.

Wednesday

Nasty *dictée*; the teacher surprised us by asking us to WRITE down the verbs, i.e., no helpful whispers!

This afternoon to the Jeu de Paume, to see the French Impressionists. They were heavenly ... that statue of the Degas dancer doing nothing, putting her rather ugly face up but in the most beautiful position with a real net skirt on her bronze figure. I love Degas' dancers when they are doing up their laces. I love Gauguin's colour but most of his people are so ugly. I like poor Toulouse-Lautrec. He's sad and the vulgarity and patchiness of life comes out in his painting. I like Renoir but not his very fat, pink, nude ladies – talk about spare tyres!

Thursday

Bertrand picked me up to go to Versailles. He drove all the way and we talked about affairs before you're married. I think he is very sensible about everything and right too. By the gates there had been an accident. Blood on the road, poor B tried to convince me it was oil, but oil is not that red. Versailles is the most beautiful place, all the green parks and white steps and unexpected ruins and lakes. Dear Charles (Général de Gaulle) is supposed to be taking up residence here.

This evening I went to *The Longest Day* and it jolly well was long.

I bought a bra at Eno's which was open at 9 o'clock at night! I had to carry it in my pocket, unwrapped; I was so scared that it would drop out in the cinema. I changed in the cinema too – the bra had a very funny shape, all bumpy.

Friday

Came back for lunch to find the longest queue outside our house, we knew Edith Piaf lived there, so we imagined it had something to do with her. We went in, beaming and laughing and everything, and I thought it was super. Then a cameraman said, 'No cheese.' I said, 'No cheese, j'ai pas de fromage, non, non,' and he tried not to laugh and another cameraman said, 'Shhh.' A bit mystified we went up in the lift. Someone said that she (Edith Piaf) was dead. Wasn't it awful, we had been laughing? We felt awful. After lunch the crowds had grown.

We went to Delacroix's collection in the Louvre; it was very good but too much sex.

Saturday

The crowds outside our house so large, police everywhere. This afternoon I tried to get out of the house and a silly lady cried, 'Françoise Hardy' (one of France's top singers).* I suppose I do look a bit like her and they conclude that if I came out of the same door

---

* I'd just bought her record, *Tous les Garçons et les Filles de Mon Âge*. She was on the cover with an umbrella.

as E. Piaf, I was a film star. Yves Montand and BB, who were friends of hers, had come to see her. It was fun for a bit, but after a while it was ghastly, reporters and men with cameras rushed up to me saying, 'Françoise Hardy?' And wouldn't believe I wasn't!

Sunday

Crashed our way through crowds to the British Embassy church. Very nice service and good sermon but such a gathering of snobs and debs: millions of girls and three men! Got out of the vicar's tea party.

On my way back I met a queue of thousands, Edith Piaf's body is 'on show', isn't it ghastly? After fighting a hostile queue (who thought I was queue barging to see her body), I arrived within yards of the front door. Policemen took hold of my jersey and dragged me back.

'J'habite ici!' ('I live here!') I yelled, really taken aback.

'NON,' he retorted and said 'allez vous en.'

I pulled out my identity card and forced it in front of his nose and he let me go angrily.

All the body regarders went in by the side door and out by the front door. All they see of her, apparently, is that she looks very old and mothy with a nose already rotten.

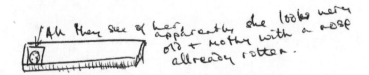

Monday

Went to the Louvre to see Greek and Roman statues, very beautiful but one of the ones which I thought was pretty was a copy!

Edith Piaf was buried today in the morning. We saw all the wreaths and flowers outside the door. And there was a great black curtain at the house door. In the evening there were only a few watchers and about two policemen.

Tuesday

Place du Tertre was a place full of super artists, two in particular who I was followed by. I should like to live in Montmartre. There was a sweet man who wanted to paint my portrait. I would have let him but I didn't have the time, I didn't quite know whether he wanted me to pay for it!

By the way, I have had two marvellous letters from Sam. And believe it or not, that simply sweet author (Bertrand) wrote back to me and also sent me his book *Journal d'un Être Humain* which I didn't understand a word of but I'm very pleased to have it and one day I may even understand it.

A star fell from the sky last night. 'Une étoile été tombé par la ciel il y a une nuit.'

1964

London

I arrived at Waterloo at about five thirty. It felt very strange being in London again, the grey buildings and towering brick. I felt very small and insignificant in my school uniform and I couldn't wait to rush home and tear it all off. I got a taxi to Chelsea; the King's Road looked the same, and the funny feeling of home was creeping on as I saw Chelsea Town Hall and the swimming pool to the right. 'Down the bottom and on the right' and there it stood, home at last. Elda answered the door and covered me with kisses.

* * *

Elda was our lady au pair, always dressed in black, a magnificent character. Years later, I found her again, when I was in Milan, and took her out with Serge. We had dinner at Harry's Bar. A woman of the world looked at her with disdain because she had a safety pin holding up her skirt, so I introduced her as my mother. Serge was sweet to her. When we were young she used to prepare sabayon with egg yolk and Marsala for Linda and I before we left for school. 'Very good for the health, darling,' she used to say. She used to come for the summer, arriving with an enormous empty suitcase and leaving with it full of colour supplements from the newspapers. She didn't walk in the middle of the pavement, but glided along next to the walls like a shadow.

* * *

'Darling,' she cried, and called upstairs to Mama and Father. They hadn't changed a bit. They still disapproved of me getting older, which I suppose should have touched me deeply with them getting older and everything. After dinner, I went up to my room. After taking a look in the looking glass, I realised how dowdy I looked, so I cut great chunks of hair, and formed a kind of fringe; it was an improvement and I felt very pleased.

The following day I went for a walk down the King's Road, bought all the things like mascara, and lipstick, although I don't like lipstick; I mean, it destroys the tragic 'I've been up all night thinking of you' thing. I whizzed up to the ladies' in Peter Jones and plastered on the stuff. I thought it looked pretty good, a vast improvement anyhow. Up in my bedroom, I really got going with a striped matelot jersey and very tight jeans. At least they jolly well should have been – I sat in a boiling bath in them for two and a half hours. Mama and Father weren't full of the approving exclamations I had expected, so I acted the martyr at lunch, not eating any peaches and cream. They didn't change, so I did, and came back soon looking pretty sober, but still with the eye make-up on. Father exclaimed, 'You look like bloody Cleopatra and a tart.' That hurt; he didn't know it, but I did.

I left the house for a walk by the river; my pride was hurt. I had thought that I had looked super and was determined to go on thinking it. By the river, life was better. The Thames, still its smelly, green, beautiful self, rolled on. I ran up to where I used to stand when I was so much younger, 'the children must not play on these steps'.

Ahead I saw a black shadow which was long and thin, it was a man about thirty-seven.* I'd never seen anyone quite so good-looking in all my life, and in one of those mad moments which come, I wanted him to follow me. It was very strange. I should have been shocked but I wasn't, just so mad about the figure I'd seen. I made quite a bit of noise so as to attract his attention and quickly fed

---

* This story is inspired by Alan, the neighbour opposite on whom I had a crush for years.

the seagulls. I felt the hot feeling inside when I knew he was looking. He came, as I felt pretty sure he would.

'Hello, what are you doing alone?'

'Oh.' I pretended to be surprised, which was not very convincing as I had been staring very hard before he came.

'I like it here and I love seagulls.'

'So do I.'

'Are you an artist?'

'Sort of.'

'What do you paint?'

'Anything I like.'

'Oh.'

'What do you usually do in the weekend?'

'Go to films. Do you like films?'

'Kitchen-sink kinds,' I said, which, rather than being brilliant, was just right for our conversation.

'What ones have you seen?'

'*A Kind of Loving*, d'you know . . .'

'Think so, what it's about?'

'A girl . . . A boy.'

'I've seen it.'

I laughed, didn't know whether it was a joke or not, but being extremely nervous it helped to relieve the tension. I only had seen three X films, so I bawled out: *The L-Shaped Room*, *The Apartment*.

1965

After my return from Paris, I went to Italy for a month with my father. We visited Venice and Florence and in Rome we stayed with Carol Reed and his wife Pempie because Carol was filming *The Agony and the Ecstasy* with Charlton Heston, a film about Michelangelo. On a visit to the film set, which was spectacular, I asked Carol whether he thought I had a chance as an actress. And he said, 'That depends if the camera falls in love with you.'

I suppose, therefore, that I did have an idea of following in the steps of my mother as an actress but not daring to say so, because my father wanted me to go to art school not far from home. Ma knew about plays looking for new faces through her theatre friends. It was with her that I learnt the text of *The Lady's Not for Burning* by Christopher Fry. We rehearsed in Battersea Park. I arrived for the audition in a little dress that my mother had bought for the Italian holiday. Pa had pinned a rose on the front for good luck. When I arrived at the theatre I sat with a lot of other girls waiting for my turn. They were all wearing T-shirts and jeans, chewing gum, and when my turn came, I went on stage and forgot all the text. The director said, 'That was very short,' and he asked me how much I weighed. A fragile young man came and lifted me up and said I was very light. They said that was a good thing because I'd gone up for a part of a deaf-and-dumb girl who, after being seduced by a doctor is squashed by a bus and left for dead under the statue of God that the actor Sir Ralph Richardson was sculpting. The author of the play, *Carving a Statue*, was Graham Greene, my favourite writer thanks to the Carol Reed film of *The Third Man* and *The End of the Affair* and *The Fallen Idol*. He was there. His eyes were so blue that it felt as if one was looking through a blue sky through a skull. I got the part. I was seventeen.

I started in Brighton and then at the Haymarket Theatre, one of the most beautiful in London, under the fire of critics who were outraged that Sir Ralph Richardson could be chiselling God's intimate parts. I suppose as it was in the West End where I was performing that I bought, in Berwick Street Market, the basket that would become so well-known one day. Actors like Michael Crawford* came to see me; he took me out to the Pickwick Club, where I met Gabrielle, disc jockey and actress, his future fiancée.

I know it was at the Ad Lib Club, a place that was very in vogue, that I met Roman Polanski and his producer Gene Gutowski, who told me auditions were soon starting for a musical comedy called *Passion Flower Hotel*. The composer was John Barry. I got the role and they wrote me a funny little song, 'I must, I must, I must increase my bust'. I was still seventeen then and John Barry was thirty. He had already created the John Barry Seven, a very famous group; he had composed the theme for James Bond and the music for *Dr. No, From Russia with Love* and *Goldfinger*. He was the greatest film composer of his time and he was terribly attractive.

He very quickly asked me to marry him. My father wanted to go to court to forbid it because I was still a minor. There were discussions in my parents' garden in Chelsea, filmed by Andrew. You can see my father trying to postpone the date, you see John Barry winning, Andrew grimacing, and me following John Barry through the house to his Jaguar E-Type, getting in, with my basket. Three months later I was eighteen, and we were man and wife.

* * *

---

* Michael was the man of the moment, star of *The Knack* in which I had a tiny part and that won the Grand Prix at Cannes. He went on to be star in Hollywood and of course created the character of Frank Spencer in *Some Mothers Do 'Ave 'Em*, and Erik, the phantom in *The Phantom of the Opera*. He was married to Gabrielle for many years, and had two daughters, Emma and Lucy. We went out together as a foursome the whole time I was married to John Barry in London. Gabrielle became a lifelong friend.

August, *wedding John Barry*

I am going to be married in seven weeks, it seems long but really it is so soon. I am marrying John Barry, a composer. He did all the James Bond movies and *Séance on a Wet Afternoon* and masses of films. We met in February at Roman Polanski's party at the Ad Lib. John, Gene Gutowski and I were in the lift together, and we were all very early, so I spent ages in the loo. Eventually we sat down. John and Gene asked if I could sing and dance, I said yes (proud fool) so they said why didn't I try for a part in *Passion Flower Hotel*. I asked John a few foolish questions like, 'How do you compose?' He says now he didn't think much of me! He was writing the music to *The Knack* and I said I was in it, rather boastfully. He said when he saw *The Knack* and my tiny part, he thought 'what a boastful girl'. Then I didn't see him again for ages. Until the audition for *Passion Flower Hotel*.

When I saw him again, I thought he was very good-looking. I passed him on the stairs and I thought I would die if he spoke to me. He told me about a singing teacher, I nearly fainted – and then he had to go.

November

I am at the recording studios at CTS; John is recording *Thunderball* the film. I have been married nearly four weeks, now it feels very funny when I think a bit. I only knew him for six months before but I know it's right. He's been married before and had a baby who is sweet, very blonde and pretty; we took her out when I first knew him and I tried to pretend she was mine.

He also had the Swedish girlfriend who sounds so beautiful. I find it difficult to understand how he could love me after her and he had a baby with her. She is also marvellous and very blonde and small, only about two. I think she must be sad that he can't see her grow up. I mean day by day, hour by hour. Every time you see a photograph of her, she is two feet bigger. I think he's very pleased with them both. I hope so, I know I would be. I'm not a bit sad he's been through all that, he told me about it after I'd only known him five hours, so I sort of accepted it like a child accepts everything as normal. The fact that one was born out of marriage seems to be quite normal now.

He's much older than me, which is wonderful; he is thirty-two and I'm eighteen, and he is so kind to me. I get a bit sulky sometimes because I love him so much and I can't see enough of him. All day I look forward to seeing him and when, in the evening, I come back from working like a lunatic on beastly *Passion Flower Hotel* (I get back at eleven thirty), I am so happy to see him. I suddenly have energy and he hasn't, poor thing, and he tells me to be quiet and then I cry and I am stupid but it's only that I can't see him enough which I suppose is a good omen.

18 November

Today started off so badly. I had a matinee and felt cold and terrible. I looked forward to ringing John and when there was no reply, I was sad. John said he would ring up, or be there, so I changed fast like a lunatic and waited about half an hour. Two PCs were on duty in the theatre, same as Monday night when J never picked me up either. I waited for hours in the cold, think they were kidding me saying, 'Ho ho ho, not blissful like it was before, no car to pick you up, he's out, etc.'

No, no, he had rung up, I said, but no call at all, so I caught a taxi and asked him to drive very fast. I called and everything, no reply, so I changed into sexy clothes like last night, black stockings, etc., and wiggled around, listening for the whiz of the lift so I could be waiting when J came home. Half an hour later, still no John. I rang the Popote restaurant and they said John had left one hour ago. I got worried; I waited on the balcony and I got cross as I was feeling so lonely and sick. I scrubbed my make-up off and sat on the bed.

I had rung the Popote in the break between shows and they said J had ordered a table for two at nine and he still isn't there or at home.

At last, when I was nearly in tears, I heard the door slam and J came into the bathroom, very pissed. 'Where have you been?' I said. 'I've been out with a lady,' he said. I thought he was joking, and so I said it again; I was so amazed I nearly cried. 'You don't want me to lie, do you?' he said. I was crying and feeling so sorry for myself. All evening I was waiting to hear from him and he was having a super time with another woman. 'I'm sorry I didn't notice the time' made it worse. Didn't notice the fucking time, four blasted hours. He said I didn't know the circumstances and I was stupid to cry so I perked up and thought perhaps he was joking all the time and it was his mother or his secretary, then he said it was Edina Ronay, a super blonde Brigitte Bardot type who used to go out with Michael Caine.

He said he had planned to have dinner with Nick and Edina, but Nick was out so he ended up taking Edina out and then took her home. I can't explain what a slap on the face it was for me. I didn't suspect John of being unfaithful, it wasn't really that, it was just that there I was, dying with cold and crying when he was giving a dinner. J told me to shut up crying and go to bed.

I got out of bed and walked straight into the door frame. I now have a black eye and a screaming in my heart. I went down the corridor and I was so mad I smashed raw eggs into the sink and scratched my legs till they bled; blood was running down my legs. I was so sore. I climbed back into bed.

'Stop.' John told me to go to sleep, for God's sake, and stop making so much noise crying. I wanted to talk to John, explained that I was dying for company. I went and drank cherry brandy and porto from the cupboard in the hope that I would get drunk. At that moment John burst in and yelled at me to come to bed, he was tired and just wanted to sleep. I suppose I fell asleep. I cannot explain last night's madness, except that I was so sad and miserable.

Morning after

On my way to the theatre. For me things are not back to normal and I feel like crying every moment. I have a session of photographs tomorrow at eleven and hope my bruised face will die down, my piggy eyes will open.

Today I am feeling so awful. I was sick all last night and shaking for John in the morning and was trying to sleep. I went to Dr Roberts today, which always embarrasses me. We just talked. He said he expected I was bleeding because I was a bit early but I said I felt ghastly and was crying and had a terrible week. He said I may have started a baby and I'm losing it.

December

Darling John,

I want to speak to you so much and you're asleep. I feel so strange and can't explain very well or else I would understand it myself and not be hurt myself. My mind is like a weed that has overgrown itself and I just want to cut free. I feel so capable of harming myself; I saw a glass and I knew I would break it and try to cut myself. It doesn't mean I tried to die; I don't want that because I love you and I have so much to live for, but sometimes when you are asleep and I haven't been able to tell you the way I feel, the only crap way I can comfort myself is to sink deep into my skin, so it hurts me and the pain seems to stop.

Been crying for a bit because of the pain of loneliness and being with you and yet still being lonely. Not being able to talk to you is the most painful thing. It sometimes seems to choke me. I wanted to sit in the loo and scream and scream until I break my lungs, and scratch my arms and legs until they are red. I am married, living with someone, but the lack of contact seems to be strangling me.

I can't tell you how much I want you, love you, need you. I sometimes love you so much I think it's better not to breathe, it hurts so much. I shouldn't care if you're not at home, or you've gone out or you don't see me or you don't talk to me, or you shout at me. I didn't use to mind when other people were like that, but with you, I mind about the smallest thing. I'm sorry I'm so impatient in my love; I want you so much and because you seem involved with other things it seems you don't mind being cut off from me.

I am trying, really I am. I say to myself: he's working, he must, he's committed, he's responsible and it will be over soon, but it's the silence of loneliness in the rebuke of the quietness of unanswered questions, I'm so easily hurt and so desperate to love that I have to cry and hurt myself, because, when in the dark there's only your breathing, I feel a panic of loneliness.

Darling John, I love you. I want to tell you, but I can't because the opportunity never comes and now I have to write it down or burst, so I've written it.

Undated

There's been talks of bringing back the death penalty after the apparent increase of crime in 1965. I have always felt and continue to feel very much against it. Pronouncing the death penalty in cold blood I know is basically and morally wrong. I do not believe an eye for an eye and a tooth for a tooth, that's the Old Testament. My father said something to me a long time ago: if you are not prepared to carry it out yourself, you should not shove the responsibility onto someone else.

* * *

My father and I had always campaigned against the death penalty, writing to the Home Office. Later, when I arrived in France with Serge, I carried on. I met Robert Badinter for the newspaper *France-Soir*, I wrote an article saying 'Bravo' to the jury of Troyes for the famous trial of Patrick Henry, thinking that that would be the end of the death penalty in France. Serge said that he didn't care a hoot and I think that it annoyed him, but still, he did help me by correcting the letter that I wrote to President Georges Pompidou.

* * *

Undated

All I want now is a baby. I haven't started one – small wonder as we don't go to bed more than three times a month. I am now feeling abnormal: to have to play with yourself when you're married is degrading and I'm beginning to be bitter. The feeling of being unwanted, undesired and unloved are beginning to strangle. John has always said before about Ulla, 'We tried to have a baby.' I think he did; I think he tried hard with her but not with me; but he hasn't the time for me, doesn't want a child as much as with Ulla, or I am just not inspiring the passion? I can never speak to him. I want to tell him that I'm lonely to the point of desperation, but every time I try and say what is in my mind, like tonight, he could not be bothered to listen – 'Some other time.' Well, I'm afraid if I don't speak soon it will be too late. I'm nineteen and I feel old. One bit of love-making, just one, can make me so happy, but he hasn't the time.

It is all becoming a pattern I never believed it would. I end up crying each night. Never am I forgiven, and if I do something wrong, never, 'Oh, I did stupid things when I was young, don't worry, I love you whatever you do.' Never a kiss of forgiveness. At the moment I am in another room, sleeping alone because I wake him with my crying, but no comfort from him, no hand, no kiss, just, 'Oh, for God's sake, shut up', and he turns over.

In the morning I will wake, say sorry – don't know why any more but my bloated eyes will tell me I have something to say sorry about – then he'll say 'Tea?' and I'll go to the kitchen and make it, bring the papers. After this, making love is forgotten; or rather, I have given up hoping because he is in a rush. Read papers, swap, read papers. I run his bath, he shaves, I have a bath then, see him off at the front door, nowadays in a permanent miserable way. He says 'cheer up!' and goes. I wave from the balcony, he disappears, I cry and cry. And then with nothing to look forward to, nothing to urge me, I get ready slowly. I have NOTHING to do all day, no job. Maybe a car driving lesson, or now I may visit a lonely person; maybe I spend money, buy food, provisions, but nothing is pressure, nothing is urgent. See Pa, maybe; he makes me laugh and he's usually alone too.

John says, 'I'll ring at lunch time, will you be in?' *Maybe I won't*, I think or even say but I always am because I love him and I want to hear him but I really don't think it would upset him if I wasn't in but it would upset me. I am tired and sad. All I can say now is that I love him and it hurts one's pride to love as much as that. Always you think, 'Does he love me as much as I love him?' Or even worse, 'As much as he did the others?'

Look, even now I am stabbing myself with confusion and words and he is asleep, he doesn't need me. I hoped he'd want me to sleep with him, but look, he doesn't. I know I will draw away into myself, become cold inside, frozen with hurt pride and squashed needs; my heart will betray me and show me naked to his will because I love him. But even one's heart can become solid with shattered hopes. I am becoming overdramatic but no, the situation calls for it, it's dangerous, this feeling; it breeds so many uncontrollable emotions and feelings; it must be stopped, and it is only John who can do it. But how will it ever happen while no contact is being made and while he has no time for feelings?

I need you so much, John, and love you so much; please don't let it dry away. John, I love you. I know I should not look at the present and only see the future – but which future? A job? Nothing very good, nothing I want as much as you, that's the point, but for the rest? I am afraid of loneliness, of hours and days of hollow minutes, uselessly ticking up my life away. I must be capable of better things; I have a mind, an imagination, feelings and I love people, but I must have an aim. With a child, I'd be fulfilled, I'd be so much nicer, anyway.

1966

Monday, 3 January

I finished *Passion Flower Hotel* on Saturday. It wasn't a tug at the heart; I am very glad I'm now doing nothing for a week as we leave for New York on the eleventh. I don't know what work to be doing next. I met Warren Beatty at a party and he said he'd seen me in Rome with John and likes me; he was very flattering and kept coming up to John and saying nice things about me. He seems to think I'm funny and interesting for his next film – he came to see the *Passion Flower Hotel* matinee on Saturday but mysteriously left in the interval. John was sweet because I thought it was all up and Warren had thought that I was terrible. John was so kind. Oh, and met Peter O'Toole – he's marvellous and so is his wife; we talked ages until three in the morning.

Sunday morning

Warren rang, he said he left in the interval to ring the director and producer who he at last found out were with Charlie Chaplin, so he joined them. Apparently, Charlie Chaplin was making very good remarks about me. They stayed there and didn't come to the second show, which was a good thing as we were all corpsing and mucking around. It was better he heard nice things from CC.

Friday, *Brighton*

I've just been to see Ma's play; she was so good, so real and mar-

vellous and I actually enjoyed the play, which I didn't think I would.
Sir Ralph was so wonderful and so touching. Ma and I walked by
the sea, it was so beautiful. I ran into the sea with my woolly black
stockings on, let the waves splash around my legs. I washed my face
in the seawater and talked to Ma till four in the morning. It was
lovely. Didn't feel tired, I never noticed the time. I do love her.

I have been through thinking everyone was against me, most of
all her. I thought she didn't love me and was jealous of my freedom
and the ease with which I seem to gain a position with really no
hard work behind me. I felt she resented my love for Father, and
the comparative favours I seemed to get from him. I wasn't very
thoughtful but now I realise how much I must've hurt her by my
blind self-pity. I must've made her feel so unloved and unneeded.
I didn't know how much she talked about me or cared about me, I
must have slapped her in the face, my coolness and my indifference.
I think she has such a terribly difficult life, she must so often feel
alone. I remember so often she stuck up for me wanting to be an
actress, and ever since Pa had said she had influenced me and forced
me to go into the theatre, she had to take the throwback of that
whilst I seemed to forget her existence, her love, her help, her need
to be involved with my life. She has so much pride. She never said all
that until she was nearly at breaking point when she spit out hates
and hurts which were destroying her. It takes very little to wound
someone who loves you so much. So that was all it was. I had just
thought I was paining her so terrible. Ma's in a grumpy mood, she's
been unfair to me, so I'll be cool, I always seem to do everything
wrong. Why can't she understand me? She had been so hurt when I
didn't ask her home. I'm so glad I stayed with her last night, I feel I
know her so well now, it's beautiful.

Ma said she had a telephone call in the morning from her director
who said to her, 'Was your daughter at the play last night?' Ma said
yes, he said, 'I thought so, I was sitting next to a very beautiful child
with funny black smoky eyes and long legs and black tights,' then
he said, 'I noticed she was wearing a wedding ring and I thought

this child is too young to be married,' then he said, 'I noticed she had the most enormous basket under the seat,' and after a while, 'I noticed that a ticking noise was coming from the basket. Curiouser and curiouser. A child who is married with a basket with a bomb in it,' and then he said, 'I realised who she was by your description of her, slightly mad, very young, with an enormous basket.'

Undated

Last night, I made such an ass of myself. Nick and John and I went to the Casserole for dinner. Somehow, the question of John's former girlfriends came up and I said, as I've often said, that I'd love to see a photograph of Ulla. John got furious and said that past was passed and in the end he said he didn't want me to see it. Nick said he was right and I was destroying things. John said where would all the curiosity end, I said I think it's normal, it's not as if I want to gloat or anything, I feel very sympathetic towards her. I'm sad I haven't got the figure that she had, but I may as well be different if I can't be as good.

I bet John would want to see a photograph of my boyfriend if I'd had one or if I'd had a baby with him, but anyway I said I would never mention it again, like a black-ribboned memory. Then John wouldn't speak to me for the rest of the evening. All I wanted was for John to tell me himself, 'I love you and don't worry about anything', but he didn't, he said he was tired and wanted to sleep and within seconds he was asleep. It was me mumbling, 'Do you love me? Do you understand?' But he fell asleep while I was explaining. The room is dark; a frozen moon has tactfully withdrawn to leave a grey mist in its place. My head is buzzing with the aches of tonight. I have lost my dream.

* * *

I'd heard through Tracy Reed, Carol and Pempie's daughter, that there was an audition for *Blow-Up* with Michelangelo Antonioni, in a studio near London. There was a big black wall and they gave me a piece of chalk and asked me to write my name on the wall and to turn profile every three letters to see if I was photogenic. I started therefore J-A-N, profile, E-B-I, profile, and an Italian came up to me saying, 'Bigger than that, write your name as big as you can,' so I started again. And the Italian came back saying, 'Oh so you think that's the way you'll get the part, that you're so great that you write your own name in huge letters everywhere?'

In my confusion I didn't know how to reply. I didn't know whether I was supposed to be a person with political convictions like Ban the Bomb?! The Italian went on saying, 'Is that the way you want to get the part, like that?' So I burst into tears. And another man, this time very elegant and suave, came towards me and said, 'That's all I wanted to know.' It was Antonioni. He gave me a few pages of the scenario and he said to go home and to think about it because he was going to ask me to be completely naked. I went home and told everything to John Barry who said I'd never dare because I used to turn the lights out when I had nothing on, but he did add that if I was going to take my clothes off for somebody, it might as well be for Antonioni. Antonioni was one of the greatest directors in the world, something that I didn't know. But John said that of course I wouldn't dare. Therefore I dared.

I had a few exquisite days with Gillian Hills. Antonioni couldn't find our costumes in Swinging London. He had our dresses hand-painted, and our shoes. He was an architect. He chose pink tights for her and green for me. He had my hair tinted blonde and her brunette. The filming took place in a tiny house with David Hemmings, who was an angel. And when I tried to hide myself from the cameras, and there were at least three, he said, 'It's rather from me that you should be hiding yourself.' Little boys were climbing up the lamp posts to try to see what was going on and to see the famous scene with Gillian and I amongst the coloured paper.

Antonioni was a great perfectionist. I remember how he blew up at the make-up girl because she didn't have the vaporiser to create a sweat effect. She thought that she could flick the water on David's face with her hand and Antonioni saw through it at once. He was cross in the same way when someone moved a piece of furniture. Nothing was left to chance. In fact, in *Blow-Up*, Gillian Hills and I were just a distraction, a way of creating tension whilst David Hemmings develops his photos.

There is an image from *Blow-Up* that has haunted me throughout my life: every time I cross a park at dusk, I find my eyes drawn to the top of the trees and, with the sound of the wind in the leaves, my eyes will drift down to the trunk of the tree, fearing the sight of Vanessa hunched over a body.

John Barry told me, to my great joy, that in New York there were queues to see the film that went all around Times Square. I heard the projectionist cut out the negatives to have bits of film with Gillian and I with nothing on. It was the first time, apparently, that one saw completely naked girls in a film. It was a big scandal in the newspapers. They called me Jane 'Blow-Up' Birkin, a nickname that followed me until it became Jane 'Je T'Aime' Birkin. But in 1967, when the film was shown at Cannes and it got the Palme D'Or, I was enormously pregnant with Kate. A bit scared of the rumours, I sent Ma off to see *Blow-Up* in the cinema on the King's Road. But she was great. 'You look like two children in a swimming pool, it was charming,' she said. A relief.

Nobody recognised me, it led to no other film part, no other role, but a few months later I had Kate.

* * *

California

Today I am sitting on the beach in California for the first time in five days because it is sunny. It was rainy before and distinctly smoggy, which apparently happens very often. I don't think I have a hope of getting brown but still it's quite fun. I think I'm going to fly home tomorrow. I miss John terribly; he says he is lovely and brown after only two days in Eastbourne or something, it's enough to kill you, grrr.

I did a screen test on Thursday for Tony Curtis, a film called *Don't Make Waves*. I don't know how it will turn out. They seem pleased with me, but I have a feeling they want a star, and a name means a lot to them. I may come out looking a little too young and they don't want any trouble about me looking sixteen and TC looking fourteen, which he is. So I don't know.

London

I had a lovely night with J last night, no quarrel or anything and I thought this lunchtime at least we'd be close. J is going away again on Thursday, a bit of a habit now, so I thought he'll be close this afternoon. I've hardly been seeing him, he's been working all out. Yesterday not so much as a cuddle, or a hello; he read and is now asleep. I'm alone and miserable. He will go away for at least a week, only five days after I've come back from America. I didn't think it would be as lonely as this.

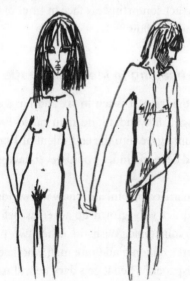

11 December

I am having a baby. It feels very strange, although I only had to wait nine months to start one I had a terrible feeling that I would never be a mother. I hoped so much for one and pretended to have one so often that I thought the only pregnancy I could have was a balloon under my dress, that I would have to admit it as a fake and take it out to have a bath.

When I was small I had to think for ages before sleeping. I would plan in advance what I would think about, usually the perfect house and seven children, their hair, their eyes and their incredible perfection. Ma used to say she did the same thing, she called them 'thinkums'. I was terrified with sleeping. My planned thoughts would be out of my control, my lovers would be murdered, my house would be haunted and my children become non-existent. When I see my stomach jumping, I have to touch it; it is so marvellous not to be continuing to make muscle twitch and fool myself, to get really fat and not to be me, sticking my tummy out. My bosoms hurt and I'm so pleased. It will be so strange having a baby. It was something I always used to act contorting my face in front of the looking glass and making real tears flow.

In the train, heading to Mercuès Castle

Now I'm in the train, it is ten to six and I'm supposed to arrive at about midnight. *Elle* had a kind man called François who took me to the station. I gave him the equivalent of 1 pound and he was stunned but he'd been so kind; I would never have got the right train without him.

I find being married helpful and show my wedding ring as much as possible and act very grown-up whereas before I used to go round looking vulnerable. Wish the other two passengers would come back, there's only me and one man who keeps looking from behind his newspaper. When it gets dark he will scare me, I know. I hate travelling alone. I wonder what being photographed will turn out. Ingrid's mother Enid is meeting me at the station. She is fashion editor for *Elle*, I think. So I'll know someone at least! I tried to ring Mme P but a sort of odd buzz went on so figured that they were out. I wonder if John really misses me; I miss him terribly, I took his vest to sleep in but didn't tell him because he'd just think I was soppy. It's marvellous knowing that you have a baby inside you. Even though it doesn't show yet, I know I have one so I'm sort of inwardly thinking: when things go wrong, oh well, it's in me and I love it. If I lost this baby I would die with unhappiness and misery. Even if it turns out a bit rough, I hope John will love it, if it is not looking like the two others . . .

1967

Kate's birth, Baby Book

She began at just before midnight on 7 April.

I had fallen in the King's Road on my way to see Ma & Pa for tea, and I think that it must have set her off. I had been going a bit fast so as to get away from a harmless old man who was very drunk and had been trying to talk to me in a very loud voice. I was very embarrassed as there were so many people around and I must have either skidded on my heel or got my shoe caught in a hole, which is what the old man suggested as I lay on the pavement, sprawled out for all to see. 'That's what did it, you ought to complain about this,' he said cursing and talking very loudly.

Two young men helped me up. They were scared stiff I'd start the baby there and then and sat me down and offered me tea, but I was so embarrassed about the whole thing, I couldn't get away fast enough. I finished the shopping and then got a taxi and went home to Ma & Pa's at about six to find John shaving his beard off and I made dinner and washed my hair. I felt a few irregular twinges during the evening, but the baby was so active so I didn't worry.

We went to bed quite early and John fell asleep like a log after taking sleeping pills. I couldn't sleep and got out Doctor Spock! My stomach kept going hard and I had slight pains which was like gastroenteritis or something. I wandered about from the loo to the bed and timed my pains on J's watch. I tried to wake him twice but he was very sleepy and I said I'd see what happened. The pains then started about every five minutes, and they were very regular, unlike the twinges, so I went upstairs and rang the London Clinic. It took a long time for me to pluck up courage and do it, because when the pains went they went so completely I forgot how strong they had been and thought I might just be making a terrible fuss. In the end, however, I spoke to a nurse on the maternity floor and I had a contraction whilst she found the matron who said they had to prepare my room.

I went downstairs, ironed my dress, put on some make-up so I didn't look like a monster, and woke John. He was dead and it took a lot of effort for him to even open an eye, but he got up and we set off with my suitcase and my monkey. I was so excited, setting off at the dead of night, that I wasn't even surprised to see a white car pulled up by ours. 'Oh they're trying to pinch our car,' I thought as I saw men hovering. They looked at me in amazement, a great blue lump contracting on the pavement, and they sped off. We noticed a hose coming out of our car to a petrol can – they had been pinching our petrol!

Poor J was so stunned anyway and he was now dumbfounded. I couldn't stop laughing. I had looked at the other car's number, hoping it would be an easy one to remember, and of course it was two rows of foreign numbers. We looked for the car after pouring our petrol back and there it was, hovering by the telephone box in Pont Street, so I took the number and we whizzed to Park Lane garage as we were empty and on to the clinic.

I had to get into bed. J helped me as the pains were getting quite strong, and the nurse felt my stomach and said, 'Oh yes, these are very good contractions.' She gave me four pills, then shaved me and I remember making faces at John because I've been dreading it and I giggled with embarrassment because he made such faces and I remember he had offered me his beard! By then the contractions were unbelievably strong, and my breathing was somewhat hysterical. John kept reminding me to do them, as I began to feel out of control and fear the next one. I timed them; they came in twos and threes and then a gap, until by the end they all seemed to merge together. The nurse had said to try to sleep in between contractions and gave me an injection, but I woke every 4½ minutes and woke poor J, who was staying by me, huddled in a chair, very tired and white. He could have gone and, for an awful moment I thought he might, as the sister seemed to be pushing him a bit, but the nurse said stay if you want, and he did. I was so happy; I couldn't have done it without him. I remember hearing my own breathing, very loud, and at each climax of a contraction it got wobbly and out of control and that frightened me. J held my hand and made me breathe or else I would have gone crazy. I felt the cramp of a new one start, the nurse felt it before me and told me they were 'very good and very strong'.

After that I only remember things vaguely. I didn't know the time, it was all hazy, but I remember saying, 'Goodbye, fatty', and the noise of my bed being wheeled and being rolled onto another bed. I suppose I was in the delivery room. I remember a tall, kind man as well as sweet Mr S, who was apparently the anaesthetist. I only remember the urge to push: it was the strongest physical feeling I have ever felt. I suppose it did hurt, but I only remember the pushing, like trying to go to the loo but a million times more, and you can't stop, the pain doesn't stop. I remember not being very brave. I think I yelled a bit and they said I had 'a good show'. I remembered Betty Parsons talking about that. At each contraction before I had desperately thought, 'I'm climbing my ladder; I'll never have to climb this step again; I'm getting higher', and it helped. I don't know, in my drugginess, whether I had this show in my own room before I was wheeled into the theatre. I remember groping at someone desperately and someone said (the anaesthetist) something about the baby's hair, I thought he said dark (he said he said fair!) and it was a girl. What I really remember was feeling very groggy and my face felt limp and Mr S said, 'Look who's here', and it was John, and I loved him terribly.

Kate* was 3.2 kilos which is nice and big; I had to have stitches as she was large. She was so sweet, with blackish hair in a fringe and

---

* John, being a good Irishman, wanted to call her Siobhan, I found that too complicated and he already had a daughter called Sian. I liked the name Kate because I had a cousin who was a bit mad called Kate on the Isle of Wight and there is a lovely scene in *Henry V* with Sir Laurence Olivier and Catherine, the daughter of the King of France, where he flirts with her. *Kiss Me Kate* is also the title of a musical by Cole Porter. I thought it was a romantic Christian name.

big blue eyes, the one on her right had a black line down from the pupil, which I said would be very attractive when she was older. She smiled so much, even when she was a week old (Pempie took her picture when she was laughing), and she fed marvellously and it was so nice for me, because I had so much milk! You wouldn't have believed it, three days or so after she was born John rang me to say he had won two Academy Awards!! Two!* I couldn't believe it. For *Born Free* score and best song.

John was allowed to take us out and he did on Friday – for dinner. He gave me such a kiss in the lips when I went back, my bosom came bursting through my dress.

I left the hospital with Kate on Saturday, or Sunday, she said 'OOOO' when she felt the air outside, I was so proud, I wanted to scream at everyone in the street 'I've had a baby, I've had a baby girl!'

She had the most beautiful hands; she did from the beginning, a little wrinkled then, but so beautiful. She was by far the prettiest baby they had there and made by far the most noise! Kate was wonderful in Majorca. We took Becky† but I wanted to look after Kate myself; I got so possessive. I stopped feeding her just under three months, so I could go to the *You Only Live Twice* premier with John in London. We returned the next day. She didn't smile at me when we got back; in fact, she screamed which worried and haunted me, and convinced me I wanted to look after Kate alone.

2 May

John is recording with Nancy Sinatra; I am just waiting for him to call me. A funny old day, I was scared of J meeting sexy old Nancy; John is a bit keen anyway and I know he will flirt like mad. He took a bootee of Kate's to wish him luck. I think he is scared of doing the song

---

* For *Born Free* by James Hill.

† Our au pair girl.

but I bet it will be marvellous and they will work very well together.

Majorca

I am sitting by the pool, the sun isn't shining much today but it's not cold. Kate is getting prettier and prettier and smiles, especially if you tickle her lips or her bosom. She is so sweet. Even at the hospital, she could hold her head very well and all the nurses said she had a great command of her neck and hands and legs. When she smiles now she really smiles at you; she's marvellous just to watch. Just to watch her fall asleep on my chest . . . I looked at her for hours, her mouth fell open and she sighed, but was so peaceful. She cried in her sleep, which worried me. It was quite remarkably sad to see her little face wrinkle up. When she cries, she goes completely mad, it makes me laugh. She's got a mad laugh; I think she's got it from Becky, but at two months, it's quite remarkable. Becky says she's never known a baby laugh so young. Her hands and feet are John's, so very long and elegant.

I'm sure she shall be artistic in some way. She's going to be chris-

tened in a private chapel here. All the godparents were supposed
to be Catholic, which is a joke because Andrew and Linda aren't;
maybe they might object to me as well, to the mother, not being
Catholic. And John, the only one amongst us who IS, is, to say at
least, somewhat lapsed. He is divorced, a child out of marriage (two
marriages both in registry office which they don't recognise), therefore Kate is not legitimate and we are living in sin. So according to
them, he has three illegitimate children. I only hope that the Count*
is right when he says Andrew and Linda don't have to say anything
in the service. He said he'll say we're all Catholics and not to breathe
a word to the contrary and if called upon, just to mumble.† I thought
Catholics would do anything to get another lamb into the fold but
apparently here in Majorca they're a bit strict.‡

Majorca

I feel so guilty. I've been awake for hours, crying, my eyes are
so horrid and bloated. I don't know who to talk to. John is asleep
and wouldn't understand and if I tell, I would be confiding private
thing; it seems so strange to think two years ago I was wishing boys
would love me for me and not always thinking of sex and now it is
reversed – someone does look at me for me but he doesn't desire
me and I want him. I sometimes lie awake and just wonder what
it would be like making love standing up or in the bath. People are
always talking about it and laughing; they all give knowing glances
and John does too, but I don't know. I never made love in a field
or by the sea. I've only ever in bed or on the floor. How sordid it
sounds, but I want to know, I want someone to want me so much he
can't wait to get home. What's it like in a car? I want to try it – but

---

* The Count of Cuellar had a house in Majorca that John rented during my time and after
my time, with Michael Crawford and their friends.
† Not to breathe a word to the contrary and just to mumble, later I realised this was completely false when I was the godmother with Patrice Chéreau. Murmuring was not enough!
‡ In fact Kate was never baptised, nor was Charlotte, nor Lou.

most of all want to be wanted. I don't want to suggest it, it's not for its sake, and I don't want to make the advances.

I'm fed up of feeling sexy and being left to feel sexy by myself, feel guilty, like now. I'm always willing; it makes me cheap, I feel so easy. I wish I was hard to get, but if I was I would never make love. Before I met John I was such a 'good girl', it makes me sick, good, good, good. If a man wanted me, I said no, I was so damn bloody good. I'd get into bed with one, and wanted him so bad I could cry, but I always stopped short because I was made to feel it would be wrong, so I left a poor man frustrated. When I think back, what a fool I was, how I wish now I had. How I want to love John in his own mature way. I do in many ways but I've got to get it out of my system. I want to do it with him, but he doesn't want to with me.

I remember every time we ever made love, I could tell you every time. I remember how it was the night I started Kate, those marvellous times in Manchester. He seemed to want me then: in the castle at the South Coast, at 69 Cadogan Street, in fact whilst I was in *Passion Flower*. What worries me is that this is the pattern: nearly every night I lie awake and think of it. I resent him sleeping, I resent his work – I don't really, I just resent the fact that he's doing those things and forgets me. Sometimes, when I walk past a boy and you know when they would like to sleep with you, I think, 'What would it be like to be seduced?' and this curiosity worries me. These six weeks were supposed to be half work, half holidays. He's written a symphony which is so marvellous and I'm so proud of him, but I'd sort of hoped it would be a bit of honeymoon and we've only been to bed three times and we go home the day after tomorrow and then he's back to work.

Mr Schneider said, last time I saw him, when he gave me some pills, it would mean laying off for two weeks and I said, 'Oh that doesn't matter.' Mr Schneider was all surprised and said, 'How about John? Ten days is a lot for a man, especially as you've been out of action for three months with the baby?' and I felt like saying, 'He doesn't mind, three weeks are nothing to him, he doesn't want me that much, you know . . .' But of course I didn't say that, it would have made him odd and cold and he's not, he's marvellous and I love him. So I said, 'Oh yes poor John,' and Mr Schneider laughed. 'Never mind, you'll make up for lost time.' I could have cried.

I adore John, that's why I find it so difficult to tell him he's married to a raver. I have Kate, who is marvellous. And I wouldn't be without her for anything, lovely, full of love and happiness. I do wish I didn't think about sex so much, but I'm only twenty and I've only been doing it for two years, a year of which I was pregnant and I've only done it with John and I bet he was like me before. But he's got it all out of his system with Ulla, which is a smack in the face for me because she was obviously tempting and sexy and I'm beginning to think I'm not. So then, of course, I hate her but I don't really, don't even know her, but I resent her having so much of him and him wanting her so much more than me. It's jealousy, that's what it is.

If he told me he'd been unfaithful, I'd die. I'd be so jealous of the damn girl, I'd kill her; oh yes, I'm sure I'd do that. I can't believe I'm a sex maniac, I'm sure I'm not the type, but it's beginning to be a 'thing' with me now. That's the last, the very last thing I'd want sex to be.

Monday

John is in Paris today, playing his theme of the sonata to Renatella Teraca[*], a classical guitarist who thinks she is the world's best. John will be seen in the film, playing and conducting. I'm in the garden, a hurricane blowing. Got a telephone from Ma this morning. Father is in hospital with a suspected burst ulcer in his stomach. I made up my mind to come home directly. John is staying with Kate and I have swapped tickets with Gloria[†] who doesn't want to go. Darling John is so marvellous and kind and said I was to ring and he would come home directly if needed. Apparently Pa was taken in on Friday.

---

[*] Renata Tarragó
[†] Gloria Broccoli, the wife of the producer of James Bond.

3 July

I have never been so constantly unhappy as I am these days; quite honestly, I have wanted to die so often that I wonder if I will do it one day. You would never believe how sad, disappointed and deflated I feel; never have I felt so unwanted by the man I love. I feel that my life is rotting and I don't know how long I can go on in this set-up – I only fear I will be more miserable outside it. My pride has been broken, both career and heart; he hasn't given me the chance he could because he doesn't believe in me. I swear to God, if things don't get better I am leaving for anyone who will have time for me, will want to discover me, who will need me and will bother even a bit about me, and for one second stop thinking about himself. I am beginning to hate him, I hate his selfishness.

I am growing up and he doesn't notice. I have to shut up and not speak; no appreciation, and appreciation makes you feel a woman and I want to feel a woman. I am quite desperate with loneliness. People DO want me, they find me exciting and I need it. I want to be desired and kissed. I want every bit of it, I WANT it all. But I really only want it from John because I love him and it seems he is destroying me as he has everybody else.

August, *leaving John*

Stood limp in the rain, suitcase in one hand and carrycot in the other, at twenty I felt more cold and alone than I have ever felt. I wished to God I was back home, warm and in love again as I was before. The square was dark. I walked towards the King's Road, looking the anguished heroine; I noticed running mascara and clogged hair in a car mirror as I plodded by. He'd be sorry if something happened to me, I thought, but I knew he'd be fast asleep, far from caring. Our quarrel had been such a futile one. I knew it would end this way. If only I had stepped down a bit, but I felt I had to be cold to make my point, he had been so remote from me, it was only fair.

* * *

What I wrote is like a little scenario: it was me who left home, which was a mistake. I'd just come back from Almeria where I'd joined Andrew on the film *Play Dirty* with Michael Caine, where he was location manager. For the sake of the anecdote, Brigitte Bardot was there too. She had just separated from Serge, inspiring the song, 'Initials BB', with the mention of Almeria. I came back to London because my father had phoned to tell me that John Barry was in Rome in the hotel where we had spent our honeymoon and no, he wasn't alone. I came back in haste with poor Kate, who was three months old. I'd broken all her bottles at the airport. Michael Caine had suggested that she drink from a cup, which she did perfectly. Getting home to Cadogan Square, I found John sitting in his armchair, imperious, and when I kicked up a fuss about Rome, he said, 'The time has come for us to go our separate ways.' I picked up Kate in her carrycot, and left the house forever.

I went back to live with my parents in Cheyne Gardens with Kate. I'd phoned them from the telephone box in Cadogan Square to tell them everything was over. They told me to come home straight away; they never said 'we told you so'. And they welcomed Kate with open arms.

* * *

Cheyne Gardens

Look what Andrew has brought back, a piece of the mantelpiece! Lincoln House[*] has been rebuilt, something that's never changed,

---

[*] Lincoln House was the immense Victorian house where my grandmother lived in Nottingham. The house had just been sold. It was knocked down to make apartments. They cut down the great oak tree in the garden, and Andrew, always curious and nostalgic, had come back to pick up some bits of the mantelpiece.

and that chunks of it should be lying around is unimaginable. My father's mother lived alone except for her Pekinese, two parrots and an aviary of canaries that she reared on hot water bottles and fed powdered Huntley & Palmers biscuits. Wally, her chauffeur, had a little house in the yard with his wife Mavis. I remember him picking us up from the station in his Rover with the Pekinese on the back seat and when we reached the vast white gates at the park the dogs would whine.

Undated

I am sending you a thorn in this letter so on opening it, you'll prick your finger

And have to think of me all day.

I want to waste your time as time has wasted me.

* * *

Poems

Kate & I

We were aloane at last
she and I
we ran along the beach
aloane together
against the tide
against the rain
we held hands and ran
running together
~~away from the~~
Far away were were
she and I
~~and she~~
he's was the only face I'll bue
~~heart~~ is the only thing that's mine
and I think I kissed her too much
and made her afraid,

Kate and I

We're all alone at last
She and I
We ran along the beach
Alone together
Against the tide
Against the rain
We held hands and ran
Far away we were

*

All we've got is a few virgin years
White, unlined untouched unknown
All to hope for, all to look for, all to find.
And then in finding them we'll have lost them
All.

*

Left nothing,
We have left nothing
Bred nothing.
Given breath to no one
Nothing remains of us
Not even a shell or a bone of what we had together
The web is broken and love once gone leaves no shadow.
We have left nothing for others to read or say
'What a love they had'
I have tears, which make a line
in a face I wore.

*

She and I

Hers was the only face I'll love
She is the only thing that's mine
And I think I kissed her too much
And made her afraid

*

He had a girl
No need to cry
We wrote nothing to prove that we clung in the night
Or that he once said that he loved me.
He did, for a little.
All we have left of photographs and they are lost or fading now
No one to remember with, to laugh, to say I remember
How the years have flown.
I have nothing left of you
Forgotten how it was with you
My dreams have faded now with the colour that was left of you.
We laughed I'm sure we did but nothing is left,
it was a time ago now and I am about
to lose his name which was the only thing
that was left of him.

*

Ghosts

Lie awake
And dream of stopping
Dream of ending
Dream of dying
And oh what fear of you

Ghosts ghosts
Oh what fear of you
Eyes awake
Ears awake
And think of deafness
Deafness knowing deafness coming
And oh what fear of you
Ghosts ghosts
Know what fear review.

Nerves awake
Blood alive
Dreams of clotting
Clotting veins
Clotting heart
And oh what fear of you
Ghosts ghosts
And oh what fear of you.

I lay awake
And thought of failing masonry of skin and blood
I lay awake
And screamed at stopping
Screamed at ending
And oh the fear of you my ghost
And oh the fear of you.

*

1968

When I was living with my parents, I heard about an audition that was going to take place in Hugh Hudson's studios for Pierre Grimblat's French film. I'd had lunch with Gabrielle at Alvaros on the King's Road and when I arrived I found myself with all the other promising young girls from Swinging London who were there for this audition. Apparently Just Jaeckin saw me and said that the girl he was looking for was me. Coming down the stairs for my audition, I made him laugh. I was wearing a mini skirt and he made a comment about my bandy legs and I replied that I'd pay for the operation to have them reset!! He asked me to come to Paris to do a screen test. I said that I really couldn't for the moment because I had a baby. Then in a few days, he said, and that's how I came to find myself in his apartment, greeted by his Chinese valet, and trying to learn three scenes in French.

In the car that took me to 50 Quai Point du Jour for the test, I longed for a tiny accident. Nothing too bad, but so I didn't have to do the test, not knowing a word of French. When I arrived in my dressing room, I heard those same phrases said perfectly by Marisa Berenson, the lovely actress in *Barry Lyndon*. When my turn came to come down the stairs and start the scene in front of the male lead, Serge Gainsbourg, he looked at me with such sarcasm, wondering who this silly English girl was in her ridiculous dress, mumbling the text in bad French, crying and mixing up her personal and professional life. I think he found it rather disgusting.

He did admit that I cried rather well and he whispered a bit of the text I'd forgotten. Cold, distant, but not exactly hostile. He could have refused me as his partner because he was the star, but he didn't. I went out with Pierre and his Porsche had been blown up in front of the Saint-Germain drug store: 1968 had started. When I got back to London I found out from a phone call that the role was mine, but I could no longer get back to Paris because there was a revolution. The airplane refused passengers but my suitcases came and went with Kate's nappies. Kate and I had to wait until June to go to Paris.

I went to Paris with my brother Andrew, who was doing a recce for Stanley Kubrick's film *Napoleon*. Andrew, Kate, Christine and I lived in the Hotel Esmeralda in the fifth arrondissement just near Shakespeare & Co. We used to wash Kate's nappies in the bidet and dry them on the windowsill, which gave the Hotel Esmeralda a Neapolitan allure. Serge Gainsbourg came to pick me up one evening and he saw a handsome English boy come out of the hotel and get into a convertible. He presumed that Andrew was my lover. After I started the filming of *Slogan*, I complained to Pierre about Serge's attitude. In one scene I'd been sitting naked on the edge of the bath and Serge was in the bath, wearing a vast bathing suit, red white and blue, looking at me with some hostility. Pierre said, 'He's not at all like that,' and he organised a dinner at Régine's I think, after the day's filming.

Grimblat disappeared after the dinner and I pulled Serge onto the dance floor. To my surprise, he walked on my feet and I realised he didn't know how to dance, which I thought was exquisite. I realised what I'd taken for arrogance and disdain was, in fact, just a camouflage for extraordinary shyness. After a few glasses, Serge took me off to Rasputin, a Russian nightclub. He had the orchestra play Sibelius' *Valse Triste* on the pavement when we were getting into a taxi to take us elsewhere. He pushed 100-franc notes into their violins, saying, 'They're on the game, like me!'

We arrived at another club, the Calvados. There, there were Mexican musicians and Serge played the guitar with them, and then played a four-hander with the wonderful black jazz musician Joe Turner. Then we went to Madame Arthur, an unimaginable, extraordinary drag club where gentlemen were dressed as ladies and disguised as chickens. They made eggs come out from under the arms of the enchanted spectators, screaming, 'Cluck cluck cluck!' They kissed Serge, crying 'Sergio!' He knew them all because his father had been a pianist at Madame Arthur for at least twenty years and he used to bring back the confetti and paper hats on New Year's morning for Serge and his sisters.

I think that dawn must have been breaking when we got to Les Halles. I think that butchers with bloody aprons drank champagne with Serge, but I've told this story so many times that maybe I'm mixing it up with *My Fair Lady*. But for sure, Serge got into a taxi with me and he suggested dropping me off at the Hotel Esmeralda. To my great surprise, I said no, thinking that he'd take me to his parents. I was amazed to see that we'd gone to the Hilton where the night porter said to Serge, 'Same room as usual, Mr Gainsbourg?'

In the lift I made faces to myself in the bronze panel with the floor buttons; I thought I was so fast. In the suite I rushed to the bathroom, hoping to gain time, and when I came out, Serge was asleep on his back. I was able to leave, wedging the door open with the Please Do Not Disturb sign, rush to the drugstore, buy the record *Yummy, Yummy, Yummy, I Got Love in My Tummy**, get back, and pop it between his toes. It had been the song to which I'd danced alone at Régine's nightclub, so I was able to go back to my hotel in all innocence, to my brother and baby.

At the end of the shoot for *Slogan*, which had been divine with Serge, who'd been so romantic, I decided to go back to London so as not to become the dependent wife that I had been with John Barry. We were staying at L'Hôtel Rue des Beaux-Arts where Oscar Wilde died.

Before I left, Serge had cried all night in silence in front of a lit candle, very Russian and dramatic, and the following evening, which was to be my last, during a dinner with him and Grimblat, my

---

* *Yummy, Yummy, Yummy* by Ohio Express.

good luck was that Jacques Deray had come to spy on me, thanks
to Pierre, to see whether I looked OK for the role of Penelope, Maurice Ronet's daughter in *La Piscine*, a film that was going to be
shot a few months later at Saint-Tropez with Alain Delon and Romy
Schneider. And that was how I was able, in all dignity, to stay in
France with Serge, moving with Kate to the Rue de Verneuil, to a
house that would be our home for the next ten years.

* * *

Monday, August??

I left Paris today to go to Saint-Tropez, to see if I am going to do
a film there or not. Such a lot has happened since I broke up with
John. I have just finished a film called *Slogan* in France. There is a
man in it whom I love and he is called Serge Gainsbourg. He is very
strange looking but I love him; he's so different from all I know –
and rather degenerate – but pure at the same time.

* * *

During the filming of *La Piscine*, Serge, Kate and I lived in the Hotel
Byblos in Saint-Tropez. Serge had had a colossal car take us from
Paris; strung on the roof was Kate's pram and baby stuff, which
rather spoiled the grandiose allure that Serge had hoped for. On
top of everything, this colossal car couldn't actually squeeze down
the tiny streets of Saint-Tropez and we had to take our luggage on
foot to the hotel, where we set up home for a month. My parents
joined us and, as their room wasn't yet ready, I'd said to my mother
to use our suite to refresh herself. She said that in the bathroom on
the mirror, she saw 'Je T'Aime Je T'Aime Je T'Aime Serge' ('I love
you I love you I love you Serge') written in lipstick with hearts. She'd
understood everything! In this same hotel, Demis Roussos prowled

around, a vast figure in a kaftan, a little hairy, who frightened tiny Kate near the pool with his gruff voice.

Our private life was completely separate from the film, where the ambience was exotic and heavy. One day Romy suggested that I bring Kate to play with her son, David, and Anthony, Delon's son. It seemed like a good idea; they were all the same age. So I brought Kate onto the set. Deray, the director, went mad, screaming at me, because I was supposed to be eighteen for the press and for the image of the film, so I shut myself up in the toilets with Kate, and it was Romy who came to see what was happening. I refused to come out and she said she'd send Jacques Deray to excuse himself, which he did.

Romy was a brick. During the intimate scene with Delon they'd put a crayon in my mouth to make me pronounce my words more distinctly. Humiliation. But it was totally compensated for by my friendship with the crew and especially the focus puller who, when I asked him why he was always measuring the distance between the camera and Delon with a tape measure, replied, 'Follow the money!' The star should always be in perfect focus.

I understood on this film – and for the rest of my life – that what was important to me were the technicians, their protection and their friendship. We made ourselves a club, the Tropeziens club, all eating Tarte Tropézienne together on Friday nights, and they put my photo on the inside of the camera. You could see it when they changed the film – very good for the morale.

There was a perfume, a smell, a heaviness even, in the images of *La Piscine* which doesn't resemble any other film that I've made, so present was the eroticism and a certain danger. At the end of the shoot Alain Delon's bodyguard was found dead in a plastic zip-up bag. Real detectives mixed with those in costume for Maurice Ronet's drowning scene. I felt like a child who had been granted permission to play with the grown-ups, not really comprehending the importance of my own part, just carried along by the others.

* * *

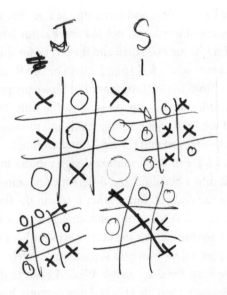

Tuesday

I have made a gentleman's agreement that I hope I can keep. He is terrified that I will go off like Bardot did in Almeria. He loves her and he wears her wedding ring, but on Saturday he took it off for the first time, for me. I've got involved much quicker than I wanted to. I wanted him, but I didn't want hearts to come into it, not hearts. And now he loves me and in a way I want that and I love him, but I also want the world because, through him, I began again and I wanted that. He did open a side of me I didn't know existed, the side of a lover which I had always been afraid of. I do love him. Yes, I do, but I look at all the people here and hope I can be strong.

Serge writes music, so it was strange to be back in that world again; not that I was really pining away for the bash of a piano but I was afraid of repeating for repeating's sake.

We were going to go on holiday, which I was looking forward to because all the time we have known each other we have been working; he says he is going to come and see me at the weekend. I want a flat so he can come and stay with me a bit. For the first time in my life I account to no one, not Ma and Pa, not John. I must be faithful to him (SG) or I will drift and it won't be for the better; *he* is the better. It's very odd, I feel younger than before Kate was born, it is as if I never lived the last two years, but I have my proof, Kate, so I know I've lived, and there are parts of my life with John where we have pressed too hard with our fingernails and the shadow rests on the slate even when you pull the tag a hundred times.

Serge says I have to draw another design around to camouflage it and turn it into a beautiful and different thing, more exotic and lovely, and in the end you forget what it was in the first place. I've nearly done that, and the erotic and strange design is Serge and what he has done for me. For the first time in my life I met a man; I danced with him; I slept with him almost immediately – and I didn't want to leave him, I was so happy. We had been to dinner at the King Club, Régine's, then the Hilton. I was nervous, but I wanted to be modern and free and prove it with a man who I found exciting and attractive.

Pigalle

'Oh, I want to go to a brothel,' I declared after two dozen oysters
and too much wine. It was so true; I had always hankered after an
experience like that and it seemed that it was right, as it were. Serge
guided the taxi towards a quiet street with a few ladies sauntering
in the doorway. Rather too respectable, I thought – after all, if you
go to a brothel you want the worst, don't you? Not a middle-of-the-
road hotel but the worst, the very worst, 'le plus mauvais,' I said.

So ten minutes later we were at the Pigalle. We walked towards a
dingy street; my heart was leaping, theory was becoming practice
and it was a bit thrilling in my black mini dress and kinky boots.
'*Arrache lui les yeux*,' screamed a ravaged broad and down the street
came four tarts, flaming in fury. It took not very long for me to com-
prehend aggression in a more than ugly form. The furious foursome
were getting rather close. Lucien* grabbed my hand and made off
towards the square, dragging me behind him muttering, 'Pourquoi
moi?' ('Why me?') in a tremendous voice. A crowd of Frenchmen
who, a moment before, had been trying to flog porn photos to us,
laughed and stamped, finding the plight drôle ('funny'), but Lucien
was not sharing their laughter. In the taxi he explained the horrid
scene – arrache ('tear out'), les yeux ('eyes'). Their aggression was
because I was getting more attention than they were on the beat and
they were furious, you see.

Another place. I couldn't face the same crowd again. We tried two
other streets, but they were not sordid enough, so one hour later we
returned to Pigalle, me shaken up like a turtle. This time we dived
into the seediest hotel, unmolested. I suppose our four friends were
otherwise occupied. Well, this hotel had to take the biscuit as the
most sordid and repulsive. We had to drink two cognacs in a nearby
strip joint for the courage to go in. It was, at first glance, a meeting
place, but 'hotel' in red letters told us it was what we wanted.

* Serge's real Christian name.

'Une chambre,' ('A room') said Lucien in a calm and organised voice as I whistled.

'Quel âge, la petite?' ('How old's the little one?') demanded a middle-aged man.

'She's majeure,' ('an adult') said Lucien.

I couldn't even look at the man, I was so embarrassed.

'Pas avec cette petite,' ('Not with the little one') the man said.

'She's twenty-one,' said poor Lucien, though he quavered a bit but was very firm.

'Identification,' the man demanded.

It was all getting very embarrassing. Four skinny men had joined us. I thought: any moment and it's the rape by force.

'Give him your passport,' said Lucien.

Oh dear, oh dear, worse and worse. I rummaged in my basket and wished myself elsewhere as the guy checked the English details. We all had to work out how old I was if I was born in 1947 and what year we were in now. I was hoping Her Majesty's protection held hard in Arab-brothels in Pigalle when Lucien nudged me to go upstairs after handing out some money.

The stairs were dark and creaky and I wondered how many prostitutes were having it away in the little rooms around us. Two flights up and to the right, the guy opened a door, took one last glance at me, the blonde victim, and left.

You'd never believe the room – dirty, base-grey dismal, a bright light glared over the bed, with a pathetic floral display in pink and green wrapped in dusty plastic with a net surrounding it. Lucien shoved the bouquet over the bare bulb to soften the light. I will never forget the criss-cross of the projection over the room and the swaying, so it made you feel dizzy.

'Act like a prostitute,' he said. So I whipped off the black stockings and suspenders. I was horrified to see that all there was in the blank room was a battered double bed and a bidet, not even a screen or anything; it just was against the wall, not even a basin for washing hands, just for washing *that*; it was very dirty and the tap dripped, drip, drip; it was the only sound.

However, this was what I wanted, to act like a sordid prostitute, so I lay on the bed. It was damp. I have never before been on a damp bed – you'd have to get pneumonia after a half hour. I attempted to look sexy and wondered if the mattress had ticks in it. I hadn't dared open the sheets in case I saw black things, like in the film *The L-Shaped Room*. So here I was, sprawled on the corner, being very vampish. Then we started off a bit; it was just beginning to get good when bang bang bang: 'Ouvre la porte!' ('Open the door!')

Oh Christ, I thought, they've come here to get us. I couldn't remember if it was against the law or not to be in a brothel. I dived under the cover, forgetting the potential insects and panted in the dark. Lucien had switched off all the lights two minutes before, so that we couldn't look at the bidet.

'Ouvre la porte!' the accented voice demanded again.

'No, I've paid my seven francs,' Lucien replied.

That sounded very professional and brutal and I was beginning to see myself as the beaten slave, when the footsteps died away and we were alone again.

The light was on and our surroundings seemed to me sordidly erotic in a way – the idea of a room just for *that*. We were just off again and I suppose I was feeling a bit in the role of a prostitute when bang bang bang. I was almost hysterical and Lucien was trembling horribly.

'Go away!' he said furiously.

'Open up!' a voice stormed.

I could hear many voices behind the door and their spokesman said: 'Open up or we'll break the door down.'

We waited in dead silence.

'Open up!'

We waited again.

'Get dressed!' Lucien hissed, hopping up off the bed and making for his trousers. Just then there was a crash and the door, plus four guys, came down on top of him. Lucien was yelling furious and terrified, envisaging rape and plunder of me by four men, but he was pretty squashed under the door:

'Don't let them touch you, kick!' he howled at me.

I must have been a picturesque sight, naked with black stockings and suspenders, trying to crouch behind the bed.

The leader came towards me.

'Tout est bien, petite?' ('Is everything all right, little one?') he asked with concern.

'Oui,' I said, grappling for a sheet.

'Would you mind leaving so we can put our clothes on?' said Lucien, naked and trembling.

They would not leave. I had to search for my panties under the eyes of four guys, feeling pretty embarrassed. We must have got out in two minutes. The poor man, almost desolate at the lack of blood and guts, couldn't believe I was unharmed. He wrung his hands, explaining he had put his life into building up this establishment and how another murder could ruin his good work.

'Murder!' I gasped.

Yes, true enough that a ghastly crime had taken place just a week before, across the corridor. He looked pretty sickened by the memory – who wouldn't? – and explained that my cries had disturbed his whole bar below, and he had at last been forced into action.

'But I love him,' I said, trying to make my position clear.

'You must understand my position,' he repeated. 'As soon as I saw la petite,' he said, 'I was afraid.'

We were hustled down the creepy black stairs and to the door, amazed Arabs regarding the notorious couple, bloodless and smiling, and we left like outcasts, probably the only lovers in love that had ever passed that door, thrown out because we had loved with passion, like it should be.

We ran away down the street towards the taxi rank at Pigalle to take us to our swish hotel where all is permitted.

1969*

At the beginning, when I met Serge, he was living with his parents on Avenue Bugead. I visited him there when he was giving an interview and he hadn't been able to resist playing his version of 'Je T'Aime . . . Moi Non Plus' with Bardot. Horribly embarrassed, I got my hand stuck in a tin of Japanese biscuits but Serge was so carried away by the success of his song that he didn't really care about me and was eyeing the beautiful Laurence, the wife of Yves Lefebvre who was interviewing him, lounging on the little bed, impeccable as all the French girls, with her Scottish kilt that was a tiny bit long, her white stockings and her little shoes with the gold chain, an Hermès scarf knotted on her Chanel bag. She had a velvet headband and she summed up everything that was Parisian chic and I saw that Serge found her exquisite. It was maybe later, when I was singing in the bathtub, that Serge asked if I would sing 'Je T'Aime . . . Moi Non Plus' with him.

'Oh yes, yes!' I said, not because I found it particularly pretty, but to imagine him shut up in a tiny cabin with a bombshell like Mireille Darc was a terrifying possibility. When he played me a melody on the piano, because I never wanted to hear the original again, it was so torrid, I sang it an octave higher naturally. Serge thought that was great because it gave the impression that I was a choirboy or something like that. We went off to London to the big studio at Marble Arch. Serge was a kilometre away from me, making signs with his

_____

* All of my diaries from 1969 were lost.

hand so that I didn't miss the high notes when I got carried away by the heavy breathing. Maybe it was there where I sang the Chopin prelude 'Jane B.' which, of course, I preferred. It was such a compliment to have a song written like the first page of one's passport; blue eyes, brown hair . . . and then back to Paris we came.

We were living at the hotel 'L'Hôtel' where the basement was a sort of dining room with lots of little alcoves where chic people would have dinner late at night. There was a disc jockey and a turntable and Serge slid 'Je T'Aime . . . Moi Non Plus' under the needle. The diners suddenly stopped eating, knives and forks suspended in the air, and Serge whispered in my ear, 'I think we've got a hit record.' A few days later I was sitting on the ground with my basket in Mr Meyerstein"s bureau at Phonogram. He listened to 'Je T'Aime . . . Moi Non Plus' and, after reflection, he said, 'Look, children, I'm ready to go to prison, but not for a single. Go back to London, and we'll bring it out as an LP under a cellophane cover.'

So off we trotted again to London to sing '69 Année Érotique', and a few other songs, to be able to bring out 'Je T'Aime . . . Moi Non Plus' and Serge, in his generosity, put me on the cover, alone. He wanted to make me a star. The song climbed up all the charts in Europe and was banned by the Pope. Serge says he's our press officer because immediately after it came out in *L'Osservatore Romano*, the Vatican newspaper, we sold records like hot cakes in South America and people brought back the banned record in Maria Callas sleeves. The BBC equally banned 'Je T'Aime. . . Moi Non Plus' and when we climbed the charts in England they had to play the orchestral version.

The song has since been sung as a spoof by wonderful French comics, Bourvil and Jacqueline Maillan. Serge thought that was so chic, and we were there during the recording. Last year the *Guardian* elected 'Je T'Aime . . . Moi Non Plus' as the sexiest song in the world. When I played it to my parents I lifted the needle every time

---

* Who ran Phonogram.

I started to breathe and, as they didn't understand the text, they thought the melody was very sweet. My brother arrived and put on the whole song. My parents were stoic. My father defended me in front of all his friends and my mother continued to say that it was the prettiest tune in the world.

The same year we made a film, *The Pleasure Pit (Les Chemins de Katmandou)*, directed by André Cayatte. I had the main role with Renaud Verley. Serge accepted a supporting role as the baddy. They put white powder in his hair to make him look older and a false moustache that was so badly made it froze his upper lip and he had to have his voice dubbed after! While we were in Kathmandu, I longed to smoke hash, which was illegal in Europe. At the market-place I saw a fellow who was selling something the size of a cricket ball with which I went running to the hotel, hoping for erotic nights. I was stopped by a little boy, who said, 'You've just been had, you've bought shoe polish!' Then he sold me a few little things that resembled camel shit. Many of the technicians and the actors had done exactly the same. Everybody wanted to try and I found them lying on the lawn completely stoned, looking at the facade of the hotel, trying to guess where their rooms and the loos were.

I said to Serge, 'I want the same thing; I want to be giggling like them,' and we went up to our room. I covered all the little lights with my red scarves to create a wonderful ambience. Serge emptied his Gitanes cigarette of all its tobacco and filled it up entirely with the camel shit that I'd bought. He'd never touched drugs before or after. At the first puff, the room seemed bizarre. I thought I had a spider climbing up my face and tore the corner of my mouth for fear of it going down my throat and Serge said I pushed his head into the toilet bowl to try and drown him.

Thank God our highs and lows were not synchronised and, in a moment of lucidity, I phoned the hotel doctor, who was really fed up with this French crew, all screaming for help. He arrived with his little doctor's bag and Serge accused me of shopping him to the

CIA. When the doctor brought out a syringe for an injection Serge screamed, 'For her!' pointing to me. And he took a few pills. The doctor stayed with us for some time and he said to me, 'You weren't in any danger, but he nearly died – he's got a fragile heart.'

At that time we were living in the Rue de Verneuil, first on camp beds. Serge had rented a big L-shaped room connected to kitchen for Kate and with a space hidden behind a screen for the au pair girl (first Christine, then Brenda). When she took a bath in our bathroom, she wasn't to leave any trace of her passage – like a sponge or bath cap; she had to be invisible. The agency in England said that, in these conditions, I could, naturally, not hope for first-class girls, who would want their own rooms, so no Swiss nurses in uniform. But for the most part we had really chic girls who were ready to share their room with Kate and then Charlotte.

　　Much later, when Charlotte had nightmares, it took a lot of courage for Kate to cross the kitchen and hall, passing in front of an 'écorché'* in the living room, climb up the stairs and along the passage, to tell us that Charlotte was once again dreaming of crocodiles. Later, when Kate and Charlotte wanted to *go pipi*, they'd have to go past the man with the cabbage head who seemed to look at them, so they stuck their bottoms out of the window into our next-door neighbour's garden.

When Charlotte was born, I swapped Kate's bed for a bunk bed, which I'd bought in mahogany so that I wouldn't offend his artistic eye, but Serge hadn't wanted anything to change. When I said that Charlotte's feet were sticking out of her cot, he said that I should 'just put socks on them'.

　　So living with Serge in his little house in Rue de Verneuil was delightful but complicated. It was rather like living in a museum: in

---

* A life-size anatomical papier maché model of a person without the skin to expose the organs and skeleton.

his salon every object had its place and the children weren't allowed to touch the piano. The cosiest room was the kitchen, simply tiny, where we'd have dinner in front of the telly on Sunday with a chicken on a spit.

When Kate and I moved in she had the long room on the ground floor; I had a little boudoir upstairs. There was a minuscule work-room for Serge with a bulletproof glass roof because of the conkers that would fall on it from the chestnut tree above, that could only contain one enormous armchair. Serge had a glass door made for our fridge so everything inside had to be put on tiny plates and look pretty. There was a bathroom with a very low bath and a Venetian chandelier. He'd been influenced by Salvador Dalí, whose apart-ment he'd seen when he was very young. There'd been a sheet in the bath that, after use, the maid would take away, and the walls were covered in black astrakhan. So the walls in the Rue de Verneuil were in fine black felt and the bedroom had an enormous low bed that you could fit four people in and it looked out onto a little balcony. At the end of the bed there was a Venetian mermaid. Serge's house is going to be opened up as a museum.

Serge taught the children very good manners: that they should leave their wrists on the table, not cross over their knives and forks. A very Victorian education, in strict contrast to when he hopped down the hotel corridors, jumping on all the shoes that the clients had left outside their rooms to be polished, pulling down his trou-sers a little bit and blowing raspberries!

1970

Fantastic January

Saturday. Serge and I were having lunch at Lipp's when he had the idea of going off to Deauville for the weekend with Kate. So we rushed home and rang the hotel and got a car (the telephone, which had been cut off for days, was miraculously working).

So here we were in the Normandy Hotel. A swish suite, Kate in one room in a vast bed with just her blonde head poking out, Serge reading in the sitting room, and me writing this diary in the other big room. We came to this hotel a year ago when we were filming *Slogan* and such a lot has happened since. Seven more films and so many countries and places.

Eighteen months ago it had just begun, Serge and I. We got back to Paris after that last week when we'd been here, and I slept in his parents' house. I remember that night now, how he tucked me up in his bed in a strange room and went off to sleep in another. I don't think I could love anyone more now. He was just the last person I imagined it would work with at first glance but now I can't imagine anyone else. I find him so beautiful; I never found him ugly, actually, just strange.

He is so gentle and soft and then so strong, and sensual and sexually marvellous – and yet I feel he is so much more than just a sexy man. He is so brilliant and so unique. If I lost him it would be more than anything I've lost before, because I've never felt so complete. Such a real love and I am so strong in myself. We just seem to complete one another, whereas John and I just seemed to destroy each other.

I have not written my diary for so long because I've been working so hard and so happily I never thought of it. But I suddenly realised so much is happening – and so many are really important thoughts – it might be a comfort to read some day.

We're off to America on Saturday to launch 'Je T'Aime'. It is so exciting to be going with someone that you love and for a reason that you both have in common. Even if it's a disaster, I'm sure we will laugh. *Slogan* is opening in New York as well; we'll do that too, for Columbia. I will send Kate to a student friend who is going to take over for a month while I find another nanny. Serge and I will go to London on the 13th, we'll try for the 14th, as it would be Friday the 13th. I go to hospital on the 14th. Ten days recovering, then I dub *May Morning*, the Italian film I did in Oxford, and Serge and I will go to France to finish *Cannabis*. There is a film with Guy Hamilton, which Serge and I may do in the summer in Yugoslavia. Kate could come and it couldn't be more perfect.

We're off to Trouville tomorrow. It sounds like a 'Noddy in Toyland' sort of town! There is a super fish restaurant that we went to the last time.

We took Kate to the casino tonight; she was so sweet and good in a little black velvet dress, Baby Dior, with white organza collar round the neck and she looks like a Little Lord Fauntleroy. To think of her being two and a half. There was a man playing violin who kept looking at her; he had such a long mad face with bulging eyes, it must have been like Fellini for her. Everybody looked at us, the scandalous couple with a tiny angel between us! The violinist was playing Russian music, Kate was swaying to the music; what a strange night for her! I wonder what she will remember of it.

I remember every detail of everything Serge and I have done together. The first night at the Hilton, Venice, Le Touquet, Deauville, Paris, L'Hôtel on Rue des Beaux-Arts, where we were a month, Saint-Tropez where we were for *La Piscine*. India and Kathmandu for the *Chemins de Katmandou*, Cannes, Oxford at the Bear Hotel*

---

* It was when we were at the Bear Hotel with Kate and Andrew that we heard about Sharon Tate's murder. That marked the end of innocence, Flower Power, and a time that seemed so free and gay. Poor Roman.

with the Italians where Serge spent all his time watching 'Je T'Aime' climbing up the English charts. Then *Cannabis* in Paris and after all that, moving into his Black House.

Christmas in London again, like last year, and New Year at Maxim's, like last year. What a success last year was! I'm now well-known because of 'Je T'Aime' and *Slogan*; we're the couple of the year. In a lifetime we couldn't say we had such fun. And what will this year bring ... America? What will that bring? Kate will be three and yet my life since her birth has changed so much. Leaving John and starting again it seems 100 years ago.

Back from Deauville

We had dinner with Serge's parents à la russe with Mr Hazan* and his wife and Serge's sister. Serge is very tired as he's been doing a radio programme all afternoon. He had to defend me, as a woman was attacking me for having done the new spread in *Lui*, saying it was porn. She said she'd seen it, so Serge said, 'Ah, so you read pornography!' And she said no no, my husband, so Serge said, 'Ah, de mieux en mieux!' ('Ah, better and better!') He was very funny; he said, 'You just touched the photos; I've got the real thing!'

Today I did more photos for Jeanloup Sieff, who says the cover photo that he did last week is very good, the Americans want me to do *Playboy* because they saw *Lui* and have heard the record.

---

* Louis Hazan and his wife Odile were Serge's greatest friends. He was Serge's boss at Phonogram. He'd been kidnapped in 1975. They were great connoisseurs of Gustave Mahler and I used to go and see German psychological dramas in the cinema of an afternoon with Odile. They stayed my friends until they died. Monsieur Hazan had started to translate my diaries in 1970. I was with him when he died.

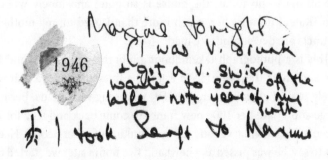

February

Bertrand Russell* is dead. Maxim's tonight (I was very drunk and got the very swish waiter to soak off the label). 1946 Dom Perignon, year of my birth! I took Serge to Maxim's Wednesday night. I do love taking him out for a change. I wanted the wine with my birth date on it! Until tactful waiter remarked that it was a rocky year for wine and a pity I wasn't born in 1947.

Still we drank the stuff. I was pissed and murmured, 'Oh gentille poussière' ('Oh nice dust') at the dust on the bottle, which they had probably just sprayed on with a dust gun.

I took Kate to see Serge's Ma and Pa for tea which was lovely, we took a mountain of chocolates. S's niece and nephew, Isabelle and Yves, were there and they played for hours.

After Maxim's we strolled off to Régine's.

Today is Saturday; we can't go to New York or Chicago until the fifth of March, after my operation, so Serge and I are off tomorrow to London. We went to the opening of Bernard Buffet's exhibition yesterday, lots of photographs. France Inter asked me what I thought of the paintings, as if I could say, two inches away from the earhole of B. Buffet's wife!

---

* A distant cousin of my father's.

Nothing to do today, the house is so quiet and lonely without poor Kate. I do miss her, much more than I used to; my motherly instincts are developing like mad.

This is a photograph taken about a month ago of Serge and his ma, and aren't they sweet? We went to a Russian restaurant, it was lovely with a gypsy singer, very fat, who sang just for us, because Serge and I gave her 1000 new francs to come back and sing for his parents. He is so marvellous, always thinking of other people. Needless to say, he was pissed as a newt and two hours later we started out for Raspoutine's with an autograph hunter in tow who stopped cars in the Champs-Élysées to get a pencil.

I'm off to Juliette Gréco now, to pick up Serge who is writing her two new songs. She is so beautiful and dark, I hope I'll be like her – you know, interesting and mysterious.

Undated

I am in the hospital having an operation* tomorrow morning. It seems so strange to be without Serge, lonely, so far back again.

Serge and I had a terrible scene a week ago. We were in Castel's on Saturday night; I can't really remember what happened, I think he was mentioning the name of some girl, actress or something. I slapped him, lightly and funnily, I thought, and he hit out at my left eye like mad so I hid my head for at least half an hour, my eyes running like a river. Then I made a grab for my basket and Serge turned it over; everything out, all over the floor at Castel's. Needless to say mad embarrassment. Then to pick everything up, furious, and jabbed at him with my cigarette still slightly alight. So he bashed me again and tore me down by my hair and slapped me again and left the nightclub. Didn't know what to do. Embarrassing, ugly and miserable. Stayed another half an hour whilst my next-door neighbours on my left filled me up with whisky and talked about me in French

---

* I'm not sure what operation.

which they thought I couldn't understand. I did. They said, 'Pity *France-Dimanche* isn't here.' I thought: time for me to be going and I thundered out.

What a scene! I left red-faced, even leaving my cape and my cookery book. I raced down the street to be turned down by the first taxi and taken by another to the Pont Royal hotel, opposite 5 bis.* I got out, sobbing, and I remember a man in a stationary car who had been watching my scramble for the taxi. I lurched forward to 5 bis, rang the bell and fell in. I remember very little else. Serge said he'd pushed the poor inquisitive man out then proceeded to drag an inert me upstairs. I remember pain but also nausea and being sick with myself. So I shut up and he put me in the bedroom and pulled off my clothes. Then I started to be sick all over the sheets, pillows, my hair. Serge was so kind and gentle. I felt so sick about myself. He held my head, my horrid sick head, told me to stick my fingers in my throat. He was an angel but a human too – he was sick too, on top of me, just to see me sick.

I slept in a sick bundle until eight then had a bath and washed my hair. We spent all day, Sunday, in bed. By then I'd discovered my eye was crimson. A bloke behind the desk at the drugstore said it would take twenty-four hours, very optimistic.

* * *

One night, when we were plastered, we started an argument at Castel's, the famous nightclub.

Serge had annoyed me to such a degree that I was terribly wound up, and, encouraged by the chic clients round the table, in a trice my hand was underneath a lemon pie that I threw at Serge's face. And I didn't miss. He stood up and, without wiping away the pie, went towards the door and the doorman let him pass. I was aghast by what I'd done and ran after him. I saw him turn right along the

---

* 5 bis, Rue de Verneuil.

Boulevard Saint-Germain with bits of pie falling left and right. At a safe distance I watched him turn onto Rue des Saints-Pères.

I said to myself that I'd better do something exceptionally dramatic before he turns left into the Rue de Verneuil, so I ran past him towards the banks of the Seine. I went down a few steps towards the river hoping to catch Serge's eye. He said later that he saw me wait for a few seconds behind a little tree, to be quite sure that he was coming down those very steps, before I threw myself into the Seine. I found myself somewhat overcome by the current. Serge was taking off his watch, which wasn't waterproof, to come to my aid, but the river patrol had already fished me out. On coming out of the water I saw that my Saint Laurent blouse had shrunk above my navel . . . too late, 'dry cleaning only'.

Serge and I went back to the Rue Verneuil, arm in arm, all was forgiven.

* * *

Oh, how I love him, his hair, his hands, his warmth. I want to kiss him and hold him until I cry with loving him, he's so beautiful. I'm under the influence of a sleeping pill and maybe dopy but I can think of no one but him, dashing Serge, how I want to marry him, to be with him all my life until I die. I want him and only him. They say when you die you have one man written in your heart. John is erased, eradicated, covered by the eccentricity and completeness of my love for Serge. It is not possible to love in another way, not to this perfection. Pray for his love.

It's now Sunday. Tomorrow, after my operation, I will be able to catch up completely these last few days. All I can see now is Ma, Pa, Andrew and Linda, their kindness, and the love for them could never be measured.

As for Serge, I want to change my religion to Judaism. I want to do everything to show him my love and that I will be faithfully his forever and, oh my God, whatever God you are, you cannot think me wrong for wanting it to last forever. Today is not enough to promise. I want to promise myself to him forever.

My darling little Kate, how I miss her, tiny thing. What would I do without her? She seems like so much a part of me, but a part which is so beautiful, so pure, so good. I cannot find that limb on me – she is better than anything of me, she is herself and already so proud of her, so proud of her character, beauty, for it is a nature character of such tenderness and goodness, how I love her.

The record is number 69 in the Hot 100 of Billboard. It came out before Christmas and then got to 89 and now has jumped twenty places. We are both very excited. We're off on Friday, Air France aeroplane Paris to Chicago, so excited.

Papa took me to the hospital today; how sweet he is, so kind, so brave. I realise how much Ma loves Kate. Said how much she wanted Kate to be with her and all of them for as long as I could. I'm so happy she can make them and Ma so happy. Andrew drew a funny and horrible cartoon on abortion to cheer me up. He's so funny. Linda looked so pretty, a beautiful dress she made herself; she is really inventive and original, she looked like a Pre-Raphaelite.'

I must stop now. Diary Munkey has returned by my side,[†] I have Papy's heart around my neck and Serge's ring and bracelet on my wrist. Oh I love that man, and how I miss him tonight, just to talk to or to touch or to kiss.

* * *

Afterwards I found him a sapphire heart and he gave me a little Victorian diamond, not at all flash, that I used to wear intertwined with my father's necklace. But years later, for Horovitz's play *Quelque Part dans Cette Vie*, I took it off because I had to play the maid but

---

[*] She always seemed far more original than me, as tall as my brother and mother, with long, dark curly hair. Barefoot on the King's Road, people used to turn round to look at her. I was pretty, she was beautiful. I was fashionable, she was original. And she stayed that way.
[†]As always I'd left Munkey by my father's side during his operation.

I didn't remember where I put it. During the night there was a fire at the theatre, which killed the real cat that was in the play with us, and I had to own up to Serge that I'd lost his diamond. Every Christmas he gave me a ring, one in sapphire, one in emerald, one in diamond, but I never put them on because I don't like my fingers. They look like sausages. He gave me a watch, a Dalí Cartier watch, and I had the romantic idea of breaking it the moment he gave it to me, a magnificent gesture at the Tour d'Argent restaurant. Serge took the watch back, explaining that the needles would fall out, and with all the rings and a few more diamonds, he had a little bracelet made, that I gave to Charlotte a few years ago when I thought I was going to die. He gave me a sapphire bracelet too; he threw it on the table at Raspoutine, in front of Bambou,* saying, 'I think I owe you this,' so I gave it to Lou at the same time. In fact, I have only one thing left: it's the diamond that Serge bought three days before dying. Fulbert, his butler, told me that Serge had gone off in a taxi with his little white shoes and that he'd chosen it in the window: a big diamond, he said, if ever life goes wrong. It was the last time that I had Serge on the phone, when he told me what he'd done, and I don't even know if I said thank you. I hope so.

* * *

Wednesday night

Telegram came from Serge, Ma, Pa and sister, all the people from Philips, *Vogue*, CMA. So many flowers, too, from Desmarty, Gene Gutowski, Carolyn Pfeiffer, Cider Films and kindly, kindly Juliette Gréco. Papy brought daffodils, Ma mimosa. Darling Serge brought chocolate rabbits – Father rabbit, a boy rabbit, a virgin rabbit with a veil. He sent dozens of red roses, so beautiful, and what he hoped

---

* Bambou was his last wife and the mother of his son Lulu.

would be lilac but was white enormous lilies. Serge comes with goodies every day, Easter cakes, honey like a bee.

Sunday

I've been home a week. Serge has been cooking all week. He promised I could do it tonight. I know it amuses him but last night he threw it at me that he's done the cooking all week and I quarrelled with him. I had a terrible quarrel with him about war. Ma, Pa and Linda were at dinner too. I was against Ma and Pa over the bombing of Dresden. I know nothing more about that than the next man except Andrew had told me from a colour supplement. Serge was with Ma and Pa on the side of the English, saying war is war. Must have been vicious or anti-him or it was his sucking up which got me because afterwards I said, 'You were always anti-English.' Which he is, unless it suits him better. He had been anti-English apropos of Dresden in a conversation with Andrew only last week, so to hear him jabbering away, pro-English as Jack Tar, I went mad then. For that has just an undertone for the next argument. I said all is not the same in war, the Germans and the Japanese did not behave the same way as the English. I'm not sticking up for England but we didn't torture by policy of the government.

We were all drinking the last of the wine so I was pretty smashed anyway and became sentimental and hysterical and weepy. Serge said: your torture is you drop a bomb, so I said I didn't think it was the same thing, I could drop a bomb given the war and having to win! Otherwise, naturally, I couldn't, but torture I could not. So Serge said I was a coward to which I said, 'Yes, maybe.' Anyway, I didn't relent, nor did he. Ma was on my side in the end and Serge said I was childish and romantic, etc., which got me very mad as I'm not. Secret police and pulling people's nails out whilst psychologically torturing them too, about their husbands or children? I would rather die in agony and I would judge other people by that.

Anyway, you get the scene. Ma and Pa and Linda going home. I'm in for something. I said, 'Thank you for dinner, can I help you with washing-up?' He said in French, 'Not much thanks you showed me for doing all the cooking, attacking me like that.' He was pointing a knife at me. 'Don't you poke that knife at me.' A night of fury all round, although I lugged a heater into Serge's room so he won't get cold and kissed him goodnight.

Anyway, that is to explain why tonight I was furious when he decided he was going to do dinner. Then he threw away the sauce he was making (it was disgusting) and said he was going to watch TV. So I went downstairs to make us some dinner (nothing in the house, of course). Serge comes down and says only bread and cheese for him. I was mad and threw the cookery books round the kitchen. Luckily he was out of the room, so he didn't witness me picking them up and putting all the bits of paper back into them. Anyway, bread and cheese it was, and junket. All goes well, then I say, 'Let's go and watch TV in my room', so he says OK and I say 'Good-oh, Mr Poop' and that gets him and he is very rude about me so I stomp off and say, 'Go away' to him so he goes downstairs again. Then I yell out, 'Come back, come back, come back!' until my lungs nearly fall out. No reply. So I stomp downstairs.

John Steiner rings up like he said he would, could he come round? OK. I go to say sorry to Serge. Not a bit of it. He is white with fury and playing some sonata. No good, so I let Steiner in as he's bashing on the door. Serge is as rude as he can be without actually putting the TV on. I go upstairs with John and chat about his getting married and work and Oxford and *May Morning*, Serge comes up half an hour later and switches off the television in front of our noses. John Steiner didn't want to involve himself in a fight and said it was time to be off. I put the TV on again. I can hear him, Serge, plonking through a million sonatas, too loud and dramatic. I don't want to say sorry again, I've done it so often. He always says it's my fault; it's always OK in that way, it is always me who says sorry. Now he's got an old record on full volume.

Tomorrow I'm working at 2 o'clock, dubbing *May Morning*, first day up, so I'll be leaving a note or else tomorrow won't be worth anyone's life. I hate having quarrels anyway. I'd much rather 'cuddle up and make up' as they say. So God bless, starry Munkey, whoever you are, wish us luck.

Love Jane

Chicago with Serge, promotion of 'Je T'Aime'

I am in Chicago now. I've just done the Cup Show and am now thanking radio programmes for promoting 'Je T'Aime' so greatly for us. We are staying at the Water Tower Hotel (not the same room, not allowed in America!) then we are off to New York. I did *Playboy* yesterday, which was something. I did get what I wanted, which was my choice of photos and more than three pages, so we did it my way.

New York. The first night we went to the Emmy Awards – only until 11.30 their time but for us it was 6 o'clock in the morning, John got the prize for *Midnight Cowboy*, which was a coincidence.

Serge and I were introduced as 'the girl who did *Blow-Up*'. I nearly fainted with embarrassment. Everyone was so kind – they are all mad for the record. We did *The Dick Cavett Show* and then *The Merv Griffin Show*, because they had seen me on the Cavett show. Very lucky because before that date they'd said no, no place; except then, after they saw the other one, they were phoning us saying, 'When can you do it?'! So I did that, and Serge and I did a mass of promotion on *Slogan*. Back to Orly.

13 July

Serge and I are in a Yugoslavian aeroplane on our way to Zagreb to do *Romance of a Horsethief* with Yul Brynner and Eli Wallach.

I am so excited and am longing to do it. The director is Abraham Polonsky, who did *Tell Them Willie Boy Is Here* and who is marvellous. Also Gene Gutowski, the producer who did *Passion Flower Hotel*, who has always been so kind. It is a sort of miracle film, in that Serge and I are together and yet not together like in *Slogan* or *Cannabis*. The boy who was in *Hair** will be my love interest, sweet Ruth† is doing the costumes. It's in Yugoslavia, which is a country I've always wanted to go to. It is set in 1905, a fantastic time, and the script, which I haven't read, is apparently so good. Kate is coming on Wednesday with a nanny; Ruth's baby will stay too. So perfect for me and perfect for love. Ma and Pa, Andrew – and maybe Linda – will come and see us, so it's almost too good to be true.

I am sitting on the aeroplane with Serge next to me. He is wearing a purple shirt with a white collar that I made him buy from Turnbull & Asser. He looks so beautiful and romantic and dandy and sinister – great! I think we are going to a hotel in Vukovar. I hope we can have a house because of Kate. I've got a case full of Kleenex and tampons as if we were going into the bush for a year, so I am expecting the most primitive and desolate of villages.

In a way I am so afraid of starting a new film, potential dangers lurking, like make-up girls and hairdressers and continuity girls, not to mention the blossoming, bosomy Italian starlet who Serge is going to embrace and thoroughly manipulate in his love scenes. I am sure a mixture of Bardot and Loren, the opposite of me at eighteen, i.e., watery black eyes (even blacker if she tries her luck with Serge!), hot-lipped and raven-haired, bosoms bursting like ripe peaches all over the place, UGH! It makes me wince at the prospect. God, to think each day will hold this or other possibilities of dangers. Think they will never end till we are seventy and too late.

---

* Oliver Tobias.
† Ruth Myers.

We arrive in Zagreb in fifteen minutes. I'm getting excited; it looks a bit cloudy and hazy but I expect it's very hot. I'll write again when more to tell. For the moment it's mission unknown and we could be going to Mars for all I know, to be met by lumpy green insects.

Saturday

Well, I last wrote my diary on the way to Zagreb in the airplane from Paris. I didn't know what awaited Serge and I, what it'd be like. Now that film is finished I can say what awaited us! We had a marvellous time on that film! We all – Yul Brynner, Eli Wallach, Lainie Kazan, Oliver Tobias and the Polonskys and Gutowskis – lived in a converted museum looking over the Danube. For the first three weeks we were in a rather cramped double room along a corridor of long cramped rooms with showers looking onto the car park! Yul Brynner's (he had not yet arrived) apartment was being readied and until his was finished, ours could not be started.

The poor museum owner (well, not owner as it was communist) but caretaker/head of that unit/compound sort of thing, who was called Suleiman, was constantly worried. I don't think I ever saw him smile all the time we were there! I suppose he was worried about weather. The whole thing was a good idea as they were having to put in bathroom furniture, chandeliers – everything at a vast cost and converting this, at one-time secluded, museum of Ilok, into the Beverly Hills Hotel! Our producer had convinced them that it would be a worthwhile investment for that communist community as a whole and guaranteed him a large sum of money and made him believe ALL films would be made in Ilok, that masses of American tourists would flood the place when it contained a category A hotel! I think doubts were creeping up on Suleiman as conferences of the communist area groups were being held in the garden and gabardine men in flat hats were clustering in dark places and maybe he

felt the boot may come if Big Brother decided it was all an unfortu-
nate investment!

Anyway, the day of Yul Brynner's expected arrival came closer
and closer, the dining room was full every night with spectators and
hopeful fans. No Yul Brynner! At last he came – like God – much
awaited and feared. And Serge and I were in our bedroom when he
arrived. I'll never forget peeping out through the mosquito net when
his great red American car drew up, a jungle of dogs, hat boxes,
his elegant mistress, soon to be wife, Jacqueline, in an American
cowboy hat, cases and boxes and fuss and whispering and shouting
all at once.

The staff had lined up in reverence and a small girl had been
trained, flowers in hand, to greet them. She gave the flowers to
Yul, Yul gave them to Jacqueline. At that time I just saw her elegant, beautiful bone structure. She had an aura of inbred calm and
composure, of knowing what to do in any situation. I saw her hat
and was sure it was Italian, her shoes were Villon and her trousers
sure to be cut by Balenciaga. Serge and I were giggling behind the
mosquito net, mocking that bowing and kowtowing, but he knew
I was scarlet inside, blushing and yet wishing it did not touch me
a jot, and very thankful for the mosquito net hiding my ridiculous
position, ducked down below the window.

For all our previous mockery we had ended up liking Yul enormously. I liked Jacqueline more than anyone and admired her in
everything she did. She was at home anywhere, the kitchen or
a dinner. She had learnt about the cinema so she could discuss it
with Yul's work friends. She interested herself in everything he was
interested in and yet remained tactful and dignified. Yul was as I
remembered him three years ago, kind and gentle with us, bursts
of temper whilst working: 'Come on, cocksucker, you're dragging
your cocks on the ground, you're stepping on your cocks!' Yelling
and shouting.

He even yelled at me once. I was in the garden waiting for a script
conference which was in five minutes BUT I was in the sun without

a hat. Yul wacked me over the head with a *New York Herald Tribune* (which he gets delivered every two days) and yelled at me I was an unprofessional, silly little girl. Was red with embarrassment (it was in front of everyone). Luckily I had enormous dark glasses because my eyes swelled with tears which WOULD not stop running down my cheeks. Kate was there and to my added embarrassment she came up and said, 'Naughty Mummy, why did this man hit you? Were you sitting in the sun?' That, and a furious argument about bullfighting, were the only arguments with him. But some of the others really got it. 'Cocksucker,' he screamed to Mort Shuman, our composer, when he backed his car up near Yul's caravan* and the exhaust bothered him. I felt so embarrassed to be even near the scene and Mort was as red as a tomato, poor fat thing.

There was one fantastic memory though! It was Serge's good idea. He thought of having a party but not an ordinary party, a fancy dress party: everyone dressed as someone from the circus. So you have never SEEN such industry! Jacqueline and her daughter in the garden, sewing away. Gutowski's nanny sewing up mosquito nets, Eli Wallach preparing things secretly in his room, Lainie Kazan drawing on T-shirts and her entourage sewing madly. At last the night arrived and we all got very excited. The Yugoslavians had a unit party that night which we had to go to or they would have been hurt. But Yul didn't go, he was too busy preparing himself, and nor did Serge.

Serge and I did up our bedroom with bunches of balloons. We'd spent hours in the supermarket finding party trumpets and whistles (all children's toys). I bought pyjamas to rip up and Serge bought a woman's royal-blue knitted dress and cloche hat! Oh, I've never seen anything as funny as him: terrible nylon socks, VIOLENT red baggy pyjamas cut above the knee like ghastly shorts, green and mauve stripes! Royal-blue knitted dress with one bosom, red-and-

---

* On our way to the set one day, we saw a gypsy camp at the bottom of hill. Yul bounded out of his car, his arms open, crying, 'My people!'

white striped collar on the dress, red-and-white spotty patch on his bottom (and on the bloomer bottom) and cloche hat, red cheeks and nose and hat pulled down so his ears poked out! Kate had her black bathing suit on and I sewed on a mosquito net like a ballet skirt and a red ribbon, black tights and my wreath of flowers (off my straw hat). She looked so pretty, like a tiny Columbine with red cheeks and lipstick! I had a tatty mosquito net as a veil and a boy's sleeveless vest with 'Ilok Circus' written on it and my hair in an enormous red ribbon, like Minnie Mouse's, on top of my head, and red cheeks and nose. Serge's enormous walking shoes and fluorescent blue socks with red trimmings were too much for us!

We made the room look like Christmas and Serge made Portuguese sangria, with red wine, cloves, peaches. At 9 o'clock people started coming; amongst the first came Yul. Fantastic what he had done. The professional clown (because he was a trapezist clown), wore light green trousers with braces over a white workman's vest bordered in black, baby-pink socks and baby-pink tie on elastic and a black hat which had a flower sticking sadly on top of it like Marceau. His face was transformed. Kate didn't even recognise him. His eyes had black lines in the corners to accentuate sadness or happiness, his mouth too; a ping-pong ball on his nose painted shiny red, and out of his black hat, red matted hair!! He had sent Jacqueline off to the tailor's to buy a suit which he then destroyed, and everything to the last detail was perfect!! His face was a mask and it was so sweet of him to go to all that TROUBLE, all that work; he was marvellous.

Jacqueline had made a Columbine costume for Sophie, her daughter, and a Pierrot costume for herself, even the pompons were made by her. Her face was painted white and she had made the hat, too. Eli Wallach and Lainie Kazan came as two country clowns. David Opatoshu came as the bearded woman with balloons in his dress and a black wig and rouge and lipstick and his beard! His wife was a boy clown!

Each entrance made more and more impact until Mort Shuman

came. The funniest of all. Mort Shuman is as fat as an elephant anyway and he had made a balloon skirt in a blue silk material like bloomers, vast and bulging – his fat belly overlapped it at the top, hairy and gross. He had a bikini top with two balloons in it, a blonde curly wig and lipstick and rouge. Everyone died of laughter. His wife came as a tattooed woman, covered in tattoos! Lainie Kazan's hairdresser came as a skinny weightlifter (two balloons on a stick and the bottom half of her leopard-skin bikini). Hank and Abraham Polonsky had painted on masks from South America and looked like the Tin Man from *The Wizard of Oz*, all brassy and shiny, shiny green and fluorescent. Oliver came as a clown and had made such a big ping-pong nose he had to take it off as he couldn't breathe! He had a shirt collar and tie and vest and baggy trousers that I had bought and braces and enormous long shoes!!

Everyone was like children, dressing up and doing acts, and it was almost sad to see the old actors' faces when too much attention was paid to someone else. Everyone was drunk on sangria and we ate poor little piggies (Serge couldn't as he'd seen them, pink and raw and empty being skewed into a baking tin like babies!). That whole thing went on till three in the morning, by which time Serge, Oliver and Yul did clown acts, SO funny. Then rushed off to the bathroom to prepare acts and we heard giggles and they pretended to pee on the carpet. Yul did. Kate rushed up and felt the wet patch, everyone was laughing. For Kate it must have been like a Fellini dream, even now she talks about it! 'D'you remember Yul as a clown and Serge!!'

We all moved down to the garden at about three and they started moving the band's instruments from the balcony and slowly the party dwindled away. I have never seen such an enormous success. Yul said he hadn't had such fun for ten years and I think he meant it. His eyes were shining, he was in his element! Abe Polonsky was playing the drums and even Sylvia – who doesn't like parties – was enjoying herself. What fun, and we talked about it for weeks!

Ilok became very cold by the end of the film, but it had been great fun. I had had to go back to London for an operation. This is what happened.

* * *

After my return trip to London, because I'd decided to have a baby and to see my gynaecologist, we did a second film in Yugoslavia in the mountains. We'd hired a tiny house with Kate, Brenda and my brother. The film was financed by the Communist Party, in honour of Tito, and set in the last war. It was called *19 Girls and a Sailor.* Serge, of course, was the sailor, and I was one of the nurses who, on going for a swim naked in a lake, attracted the attention of all the Nazis, which allowed Serge to rush round the back of them with a machine gun and kill them all. He twisted his ankle and I heard, 'Ayayay!'

In the cast of characters there was a traitor who was mad, and the Yugoslavian beauty queen. Serge wanted to make a film inspired by this movie, where half the Yugoslav actors turned up for their breakfast dressed as Nazis and where there were plots between the hairdresser and the crazy spy. The last take would have been a crane shot, where you understand that it's just a film shoot, isolated in the mountains. Serge asked to be paid in cash and he bought himself a Rolls-Royce. It gave him a giggle to pay for it with communist money. The two 'R's were in red because Mr Rolls and Mr Royce were still alive when the car was made. It was one of the first Rolls-Royces. He kept it at British Motors. We took it out from time to time with the chauffeur because Serge didn't have a driving licence.

One of the 'grandes sorties' ('great outings') of the great car was to take Serge and I to the Rothschild ball in the country. We sat, freezing in the back, with my hairpins falling out – the car had no suspension. The chauffeur sat, heated, in the front. It took hours to get there. We were so cold, and dressed in Proustian fancy dress. Cecil Beaton took the rather well-known photos. But when we got to the Rothschild estate a man directed us to a distant car park, so we had to walk the last 200 yards and no one saw our grandiose arrival, after which I think Serge was a little disappointed.

The car stayed cooped up in the Rolls-Royce garage. Serge took off the bonnet ornament sculpture, which inspired him for *Melody Nelson*. I think the car was sold a few years later.

1971

21 January

The last time I wrote was Yugoslavia and a lot has happened since then. I got back after Venice in winter (which was like a dream), so much more fragile than in summer when the sun is brighter on the over-elaborate St Mark's. In winter the colours are softened and wrapped in a haze of grey. We stayed at a wonderful hotel where Serge had already stayed for *Slogan*. After four months in Yugoslavia, the richness and splendour and history were breathtaking. There was a low mist when we got out of the boat and into the Danieli. Serge and I had a romantic three days in a blissful bedroom, whilst Kate and Brenda rushed about St Mark's and battered pigeons.

It was really the best way to get back to civilisation, but I'd been having the most horrid pain in my side during most of the drive from Dubrovnik to Venice. The driver (who Serge has taken to Venice and given one of the best rooms in the Danieli) was sweet and, like a child, keeping all the chits from the hotel to prove that he'd been there. He sat in St Mark's for four hours and said he has never in all his life seen anything so beautiful; he said he will bring his wife to Venice and show her everything. Serge gave him a tape recorder and wireless for his car and when he left, he was most embarrassed, overtaken by it all; it was really marvellous to see him so happy and loving it so. John (driver) said maybe my pain was appendix, so I laughed and said no, thinking it must be a cyst. In Paris, I went to a gynaecologist who said I was suffering from appendicitis. I couldn't believe it, then he made me take a pregnancy test and what should happen? Blood test, too many white corpuscles, therefore pregnant, yes!! Well, to have all that going on inside you is really a laugh, but then I received a frantic message from the doctor saying that as I was pregnant, maybe the baby was in my fallopian tube. Christ, I panicked.

'If it is in one of your tromps, it must be removed,' he said.

'How many tromps do I have?' I asked.

'Two,' he replied.

Well, I wasn't going to be 'tromped' by just anyone, so after a surgeon came forward I said I wanted to go to someone I knew and trusted: Mr Schneider. So I rang Mr Schneider, and he said to come over straight away. Serge and I left for the airport that night (because if the baby is in the fallopian tube, it's got to get out fast or you explode). The plane for London will not take off. I nearly died, crying and frightened. Serge and I went to have dinner at the restaurant in the airport – no chance of taking off, plane was being turned about in London and coming back.

At last we got off the following day, went straight to Ma and Pa's house, but they were away. Linda was there and, after tea, she sweetly ran me to Mr Schneider's. Examination, no baby in the fallopian tube but a baby all right, in the right place and maybe an acute appendix, which he said if I didn't want to risk the baby must come out straight away, like that night. So at 7.30 that night I was in a little room in the London Clinic with Linda, who was so comforting and kind, trying to telephone Serge in Paris. When at last I got him at his parents' I'd already had the first injection and was about to be wheeled away. He was divine and loving and we were chatting when the nurse came in and caught me on the telephone and said I must stop. I had got Ma and Pa on the telephone five minutes before and they were dashing back from Sussex, when Linda told them the news.

I am very dizzy now and waiting for final injection. I am so in love I could almost die now and I am so covered by sweet and loving people, Pa, Ma, Linda and Andrew – I am so lucky I wish I could kiss them all now. Sweet Kate, darling Serge: how I want your baby more than anything, please God, don't take it away. It's strange how desperate one gets about sending, writing last notes. I'm so afraid I haven't said enough about how I love Pa and Ma and my love for Linda who was so comforting and sweet to me today, and Andrew. It's at moments like this that I so want to tell them. And Serge – well, I don't think in a million years I could love anyone as much as I love him.

Thursday, 22 April, 8 o'clock in the morning

Joanna* came running into our bedroom saying Jacqueline was on the telephone. I was a bit dazed as it was so early, but Serge grabbed the telephone; he told me later he had a premonition that something was very wrong. As he spoke very softly, I knew something awful had happened by his voice. He said something about, 'straight away', and hung up. It was dark in our room but I saw his face, half of it, and tears were running down his face. He put on a baby's voice and said, 'Mon Papa est en train de mourir.' ('My Papa is dying.')

His face and voice were indescribable. I have never seen such pain so close because when my grandparents died, Pa and Ma were not with me so I didn't see the shock on their faces that I now saw on Serge's. Jacqueline had told him his father was dying. The reasons were confused and I didn't want to ask too much. I wanted to give hope – dying is not dead – and yet I saw, and Serge had said 'sans espoir' ('hopeless'). The doctor had told Jacqueline it was sure. There was no train at eleven but we did not want to wait and I suggested a taxi and that is what we did. S did not want me to come as I am pregnant but if you can't be close to someone you love, when they are in the depths of sadness, when can you help them? So I dressed fast and promised to keep in the background. We picked up Jacqueline and she sat with Serge in the back, two hours spent in tears and worry and panic of being too late.

We arrived at Houlgate at last. Serge and Jaqueline ran into the

---

* The au pair girl.

little house. Serge told me to wait in a café. I held onto Jacqueline's suitcase and sat on the doorstep. I waited for half an hour, trying to think of all the promises I would give him, of how I loved Serge and would love him forever, of the baby. Most of all, I wanted him to know of my love for him and my need to help Serge and be with him and take care of him forever.

Serge came round the corner, pale and slow. I ran up to ask how his father was. 'Mais il est mort, mort depuis ce matin.' ('But he is dead, he's been dead since this morning.') So the doctor was a kind man; when we heard at 8 o'clock it was already too late.

I wanted to go and see him but Serge made me promise not to. Serge's mother was huddled in a corner, white and shocked and tiny. Jaqueline was with her, frail but brave and supporting as I could never be. Over and over Serge's mother went over what had happened. They'd had a beautiful day on the beach. He had told her it was their second honeymoon. It was so lovely. She collected a little shellfish but by teatime they were tired and went back to the lodgings, ate the shellfish and he told her he was very gay but tired. So they decided not to go out for dinner. They had a gas ring so they made themselves a bit of supper and went to sleep. About midnight he woke up and was sick.

Serge's mother said she thought it was indigestion and he had eaten too much shellfish but she didn't worry. He said he felt very tired and went to sleep. She saw on the sheets, on the floor where he'd been sick. He'd coughed up blood. She wondered about a doctor but he said he was fine. At about 5 o'clock he woke up and violently vomited blood everywhere. He said, 'Go and get a doctor, quickly! My stomach hurts.' And she ran down to the owners to get the doctor.

When she got back up again he was on the floor in a pool of blood. She took his head on her lap and he said, 'Is the doctor coming?' and she said, 'Yes.' Then she panicked and slapped his face saying, 'You can't go like this! Say something.' But he never did again. He was dead in a few minutes. The doctor arrived too late.

Serge's father

I loved you, little man, I never had the time to show you, never had the time to say that I loved you little man.

Lying in a box so quiet.

I never had the time to promise things.

Can you hear?

My baby is moving inside me against your face.

What a calm after the panic, a terrible and lonely peace.

What are you doing in the ether.

17 May

We arrived in Japan on Monday morning after stopping for fuel in Moscow where I bought a doll for Kate. We arrived at Tokyo airport and we hadn't been able to sleep in the plane, so I look like a crumpled hanky over a melon. They weren't expecting me in that state but they were very kind and didn't openly curse it! A lot of photographers at the airport and a group of people bearing banners saying 'Welcome Mr Gainsbourg and Miss Birkin'. When we came out of the airport, there was a big black car with lacy covers on the seats. We crammed into the car, Serge and my basket, weighed down after all the goodies I had swiped from the plane. I had pink eyes (no make-up because I wasn't expecting such a turnout) and a crushed dress. We waved away, barely to be seen because of all the bouquets of flowers stuffed in my car on top of us.

Tokyo roads. What an awful jam. It took nearly an hour for a fifteen-minute drive. The red system was quite extraordinary, flyovers in intricate webbing upgrades that seemed to enter the tenth stories of skyscrapers and weave their way around others. It was like Batman's town in the year 2000. Maybe Trafalgar Square will be like it in ten years. People have said such dreadful things about Tokyo, how impersonal. No blue sky, just a haze of grey smog, and it is unlike anywhere else, utterly modern and financially booming; it has no history but, in a way, that gives it personality and character. Under the flyovers, very little houses where people exist and live, using little streets and alleys; delicious smells of cooking and then signs of posters and an American neon Coca-Cola sign. People are dashing about in millions of cars and yet women in kimonos salute each other in the street with love and respectful bows and greetings, as if they were in a Japanese painting.

Our hotel was very modern, near the Tokyo Tower, which is like an orange Eiffel Tower used for television transmission. Our room was high and they had got us a suite with a sitting room and the most enormous colour television. We had lunch with the publicity organiser for *Cannabis* who was to be our companion throughout our stay. Serge was swaying because of the time change and having not slept, and I was dipping forward onto the plate, feeling as if I was floating. So they tactfully said nothing was fixed to do until the day after, so we went off to sleep. I slept on until midnight and we ordered something called the midnight special sandwich and then went back to sleep till the morning. At 7 the girl was in the lobby to take us to the television programme – our appearance was from 7.30 until 7.50, very precise. They gave us presents afterwards, two kimonos saying 'I'm boss' in Japanese and we realised it was an old Japanese custom to give gifts at every occasion.

We were free until the press conference at 1 o'clock, so we went shopping in the arcade under the hotel; everything was Sony this and Sony that, at half the price of Paris. I looked around for a little radio for my ma and gadgets of any kind for Serge! We went to a Japanese restaurant and ate raw fish, very clean cooking – or rather, no cooking. I swallowed a ton of saki. We were taken to the press conference, a little doorway down some dark stairs; it was a nightclub and had fluorescent lights on the stairs. Everyone grasped me, so I wouldn't crash down the stairs and have to be rushed to Tokyo Gen Hospital. It was a club on two levels and a balcony. We were met by 'Je T'aime . . . Moi Non Plus' blaring out and downstairs they were projecting slides of scenes from *Cannabis*; it was all very organised.

From the balcony, I could see a mass of people but I didn't realise they were there for us. Hundreds of men and women were gathered and about thirty photographers at six or seven microphones. Then, after an introduction we began, questions questions questions, flash flash flash of cameras, but they were not aggressive. Our interpreters found it difficult to translate Serge's double-meaning, strange and funny replies.

After the press conference, we were followed by about thirty photographers around different Tokyo spots. I bought two turtles, which I had to carry about in cups. 'What do they eat? Yum Yum?' I said, miming. 'Not to eat,' said the Japanese, aghast, thinking mad English tourist who wants to eat turtles.

I've tried to feed them a bit of rice but they didn't want to eat it, then a bit of steak and they fell on it. From then on they lost all their charm for me: two tiny Oriental cannibals in our basin was some-how so different from the quaint green pets of the day before.

Then to Osaka by plane. They organised everything beautifully. Hotel room in airport, fat, fat artist, and more kimonos! Put turtles in sink whilst we tried to find a plastic bag for their journey. It was an hour by aeroplane. Then a car drive into Osaka. Very modern hotel. Turtles were given a red plastic bucket which made them appear even more unpleasant. Serge and I sampled all kinds of cooking: raw fish, etc., and found a bar with three gay barmen, all very will-ing and able and giggling. Serge spent every spare minute trying out all the sweet liquors; they were delighted. Then to the theatre, where *Cannabis* was having a horrible private showing. They said it might not be full as there was a strike of private train transport but it was full up. Terrifying. We had to say a few words before the film and give prizes of signed posters of *Cannabis* to some poor girl who had waited all night. But this time two little girls came up giggling and covering their mouths. They gave me presents for Kate: a kimono, a happy coat, a parasol and tiny painted wood sandals. I said I would send a Polaroid photograph of her wearing them. More flowers, then luckily, before the show of *Cannabis*, we hopped for Kyoto by car which was a two-day trip, just for our pleasure, so we can admire some of the old Japanese monuments.

Kyoto Hotel, again very modern. Turtles, in another bowl, made our two housemaids giggle. Next morning, bright and early, temples. Poor Serge, after two – and one Oriental tea garden – he pleaded it was too tiring, plus swollen feet and wearied limbs. At every teahouse, off with shoes and poof, the pong of his feet! We nearly collapsed from laughing. Tea service is taken very seriously; no crumpets, milk or sugar and coarse laughs – it is a time of meditation.

After, we went off as there was a carnival in town. We had to walk miles and then we came to a sort of green. So many children, one asleep on a motorbike, and little girls painted in Oriental style, but eight years old! My Polaroid let me down badly: two colour films wasted. I nearly cried – not one photograph, they all got stuck in the camera. It was so depressing and Serge got fed up of posing when two minutes later I would be cursing that the bloody thing didn't come out of the camera. After the fair we pleaded for rest, so we were taken to another teahouse and after six courses we realised that there had been a misunderstanding and she had understood dinner for four plus tea.

Flower arrangement, dancing, comics and puppets – it was what you would imagine and the fact Serge and I were being honoured by being used as samplers for the tea service. I really collapsed trying not to laugh. Serge ate my sacred biscuits and everyone laughed. We invited our two constant companions to dinner and we had Kobe beef, very good, but Serge and I had the best of all in Tokyo, all done in front of you on a vast hot plate table, and then a lid on it . . . so good.

The day after was our last day so we got out of temples and went to three department stores. I bought a baby carriage for the baby. I gave my turtles to our boy companion in a sickness bag as they would have been confiscated on entering France. I was very glad to see the back of them. We caught the Tokyo express train (the fastest in the world); there was even a telephone in the train. So our boy companion phoned to see if Serge could buy a stereo wireless in Tokyo. On one of our stops we were hailed with banners and cultured pearls for me, and a tiepin for Serge. They were from the head of Nippon Herald Films. We caught the plane that night and flew over the Pole.

Next morning we landed in Anchorage where I bought a polar bear and PCs made in California. Sealskin hats were for sale and horrid Eskimo dolls. Needless to say, I didn't buy them. Took photos of Serge on aeroplane steps, out of focus, and not even a mountain in sight, let alone a polar bear.

Arrived in Paris at 8 o'clock in the morning. Serge took one million photos of the North Pole and got very drunk with the hostesses and stewards, showing our photo album which our Nippon host had prepared.

Serge and I had dinner and went to a film show of *Death in Venice* with Guy Rothschild. They were very sweet and took us themselves. I sat next to him and Serge sat next to Marie-Hélène. Serge liked the film. The Rothschilds and I were a little bit wondering about it: divine to look at but a bit less subtle than the book because in the book he is just an admirer of beauty. Too much panting and lusting . . .

7 June

Kate is at last over her bronchitis and is all too lively, wiggling about everywhere today with a great bout of overexcitement.

Had a ghastly shock last Saturday morning. Serge and I had planned to go to Le Touquet for a quiet weekend. But on Friday evening Linda rang in a visibly shaken voice to say that Pa was ill and had shown, to everyone's surprise, a tumour that could be cancerous. Poor Linda was desperate and Pa had said not to call and panic me, but it was obvious that poor Linda had no one, and Andrew was working, and Ma in Cambridge with her play.

I was quite desperate and rang Dr Roberts in London and got his secretary who said he was uncontactable. I said who I was and that I was in a panic about Pa and would she get Dr Roberts to ring me from the country and reverse the charges. Dr Roberts rang back two hours later. It felt like an eternity. He said that Pa would not be operated on straight away but on Wednesday. He said it wasn't dangerous and not to worry. I said I wanted to fly back immediately and he said, 'Oh don't! It may worry him.' I said I wouldn't, made it clear I just wanted to cheer him up. Didn't sleep much, I was determined to go to London Saturday morning. Serge was marvellous and cancelled our weekend in Le Touquet and we left at 4.30 and arrived in Cheyne Gardens at 6.15.

Linda had told me how Pa had changed after his sleeping pills so I should have expected it. But somehow I didn't. He started to say such adorable things, with such depression, that I had to fight my emotion. He said that he wanted to see the baby. He wished it would be born this week in case he never saw it, like Serge's father. We hugged each other with such tenderness and I hid my face in his pyjamas so he wouldn't see my tears. I pinched myself to be strong.

The more the sleeping pills work this Saturday, the more sad he becomes. He began thanking me for all the pathetic small things I've done which have no comparison with the angelic, marvellous things he's done for me. He said that he had been physically ill when I got married and how it had led to his illness and ulcer and how we unwillingly hurt one's father. I didn't even know, and yet I've done it to the one person in the world I would've moved heaven and earth never to hurt. He said how he loved Serge and could he have a photograph of him by his bed. He said how lucky I was and how sweet of him it was to come. I was glad Pa loved him too and that he saw what I know I see in him. Serge has to go at four so I went with him to the airport. I hate him going without seeing him off. So sad to see the sweet thing go off. He's been such a comfort and tactful and gave Pa his watch, the beautiful one painted on wood, to keep him safe.

Linda drove me home in Cheyne Row* and I went to bed. I was fascinated by Serge's *Playboy* and *Penthouse*, etc. I sleep in his room when he's away.

11 June

We leave London tomorrow. I spoke to Pa yesterday and they operate on the 23rd so I hope he'll come down to the Isle of Wight for five days with us. Serge will join us Monday morning. I went to see Serge's ma yesterday. She looks better but is of course still lonely and sad. I don't think Serge will have much luck with bringing her to the Isle of Wight. She is adamant about staying in Paris. I love going round to see her. She is so sweet and I think she needs to be distracted, poor soul, so as not to think too much about Serge's pa.

Serge took me to dinner at Lucas Carton, very old-fashioned and distinguished. On the way home we stopped off at Maxim's to have a drink there. I had a basket of cherries. They were going to wash them discreetly and delicately in a silver bowl but I think they were much more delicious a little dirty, warm and dusty, and gobbled them up straight away from the wooden basket. Serge drank a bottle of champagne and was very drunk (in a nice way). Our violinist played the *Valse Triste* by Sibelius as usual for us. Serge told him that his father (who used to play the piano at Maxim's) had died a month and a half ago. The poor man was shattered; he plucked sadly at his violin and was close to tears. After, I thought of Serge's pa for the rest of the time, and how he would love to have been with us at Maxim's. He never came. We meant to fix the dinner with him and Serge's mother but we didn't know we had so little time. I was too shocked and sad to write about that miserable weekend nearly two months ago. It was so painful for poor Serge, a nightmare of horror

---

* John Barry had bought the end of a lease in Cheyne Row just near my parents for Kate and I. We used to live there during the Christmas holidays, with my brother in the basement.

and sadness, he was so brave and strong and a marvellous support to his mother and sisters who were all so shocked.

20 July, *Charlotte's birth*

I am sitting in the hospital, the cot is ready, now all I have to do is produce. Had lunch with Gabrielle Crawford and Andrew at a little restaurant in the King's Road. We talked about fidelity and husbands and it was all very depressing to realise how few are. Ran the length of King's Road to try and make the baby start naturally, but no, and Serge had to bring me down to the hospital.

We left the case at the clinic and went off to see Dr Boss in Harley Street for Serge's finger, which he had burnt with liquid nitrogen. Then we went to see Pa at Edward the Seventh hospital. He's leaving tomorrow, things having turned out wonderfully. We walked to my hospital; I waited for Mr Schneider to examine me. Mr Schneider said the baby's head was well down, all was very good and to go out and have a good dinner. So we went to a place called Le Petit Mont-martre, which was stuffed with Italian waiters. It was so cosy having Ma and Serge there. Back to the clinic; I've had two sleeping pills.

I love my baby so much already. Girl or boy, I am so longing to see it and tell it how much I wanted it and love and treasure it because I already do. I have never wanted anything more. Sweet Serge was very nervous. What an angel! He is worried in case it hurts me too much. I told him it is not the case when you want something so much. He has taken a pill and I hope he will sleep well. Please God, let my baby be all right.

Sweet Charlotte was born 21 July at 10.15. She weighed 7 lb 10 oz and had a mass of silky black hair. It was the most beautiful sight I have ever seen. She was still attached to me by a grey-pink cord. I watched them cut the cord that had joined us for so long and they handed her to me. What a tiny, beautiful little thing she was! I wanted Serge to come and see her still attached but he was outside the door with Andrew. He says he was so pleased she's a girl. Ma said he was delighted and Gabrielle, who had been with me on and off for my labour, said he was like in a dream. He was so happy. Serge and Andrew have gone off to celebrate!

* * *

Whilst I was giving birth, Serge was behind the door on all fours with a stethoscope to try and hear what was happening. He told me he didn't want to see anything or he'd never be able to sleep with me again. Andrew was by his side, and I think they'd drunk through the entire row of liqueurs of the hotel bar opposite, right to down to the banana one.

When I saw Charlotte, with her slanting eyes and all yellow, I thought it was because of our recent voyage to Japan. It seemed logical. In fact, she had jaundice. We called her Charlotte because Serge thought it was pretty. I wanted Lucy. We called her Charlotte Lucy. Later I sometimes called her Yoyotte, but Serge was right: Charlotte was as lovely in English as in French.

* * *

Sunday

Mr Schneider advises that we get a paediatrician to look at Charlotte. Her jaundice is escalating. They want to take her up to the Middlesex Hospital for a transfusion. Serge spent the night in a ghastly hotel opposite because he was so worried. Yul Brynner and Jacqueline came and saw Charlotte; he called her 'Charlotte aux abricots' because she was all yellow. He gave her a bracelet, as he is her godfather. They came with Charlotte for me to say goodbye. I thought my heart would break … she was so small and delicate, little yellow, beautiful face and black hair. Then they asked what religion* she was. I thought I'd die. Serge was white with tears running down his poor face, he took Charlotte with a nurse to the Middlesex Hospital. I rang Pa in panic and the sweet man came over in spite of his stitches. He was here when Serge came back; he was soaking wet, he'd walked back in the rain.

* * *

Serge often said that the happiest walk he had in all his life was when he was able to see Charlotte at the Middlesex Hospital. That hadn't been easy because she was registered as Baby Birkin and when Serge showed up to intensive care he might have had a rather strange look, a 5 o'clock shadow, anxious eyes, hair all over the place and maybe a slight whiff of banana liqueur. But they took pity on him and, in spite of the fact that a madman had killed a lot of premature babies in an English hospital a few days before, they let Serge look at tiny Charlotte, behind glass, after which he started to walk across London to Chelsea!

* * *

I can only write about this now because I know she is all right, I saw her today in a little room in the Middlesex Hospital. The reason for her jaundice is a mystery. I will go and feed her at 5.30 tomorrow.

Monday, 1 August

I leave the hospital today. How sad to take away the baby clothes and blankets with no baby, no bundle. Serge walked all the way home from the Middlesex Hospital to Chelsea: Oxford Street, Regent Street, Trafalgar Square and Buckingham Palace where he found a

---

* I remember Serge said, 'Your church! I don't want her to hate mine.' He therefore wrote 'Church of England'. I really think that he thought that they'd take greater care of her if she was English.

taxi for the last lap home. Next day he collected me, exhausted after his long walk home. He paid £250 worth of bills and we left. All Serge's French money is gone and no baby to show for it.

* * *

All the press photos of Serge and me as the happy parents, baby basket in hand, in front of Cheyne Row, look idyllic, but in fact the basket was empty because Charlotte was still in hospital but it was a secret.

* * *

We got home and watched the men walking on the moon. Kate came back from the park, I wonder if she is having any trauma against Serge or me.

I just rang the hospital and I am to go in at 10 o'clock in the morning. Dr Hart will be able to tell me when I can take Charlotte home. I hope Serge is all right on the night train and he has enough blankets. Spoke to Gabrielle tonight who's going to find out where I can get him a bull terrier. I'll get him one for Christmas. He says he doesn't want one for a little bit because of Charlotte.

* * *

Serge wanted a bull terrier and nothing else because he'd seen one when he was very young, next to a super chic Englishman at Fouquet's. He thought the dog's face was prehistoric and wonderful, and if one day he could afford it, he'd have a bull terrier.

* * *

Serge came back on Thursday. Kate had spent the day with Gabrielle's two children. I think she will be better in a year; she has always been alone for years. It will be good for her to have a companion, to have a children's world. It is so important for her. Serge came back with an English pram called a Silver Cross in navy blue. It was a fortune. He bought all those things. Instead of working for Roland Petit,* he went to a swish shop in the Avenue Victor Hugo. He said everyone said 'Félicitations'. He looked so sweet when I saw him coming off the big train carrying the cot, smiling. I felt proud of him feeling so fatherly.

Sunday, 15 August

We are all in Le Touquet.† Charlotte came out of the hospital on Wednesday. It was so good to have her home. Serge had booked Le Touquet for Friday. I had quite forgotten to put Charlotte on my passport so we had to rush around registering her. We got it all done and at 2.30 we got on the boat, a jolly gay family, Serge and I signing autographs – and half an hour later all being sick everywhere.

October

Autumn is here. Charlotte is three months old. Pa came to visit on Saturday; we went to visit Kate's class, the annual look-in. She seems up to standard and good at drawing. She's left-handed and writes backwards but otherwise good.

Pa, Kate and I, off to Serge's ma for tea. She is very well and we had a scrumptious tea, with Jacqueline, Yves and Isabelle. Pa loved

---

* He was working on a show that Roland Petit was putting on with Zizi Jeanmaire at the Casino de Paris. The costumes were done by Yves Saint-Laurent and the decor by Herté, lyrics and music by Serge Gainsbourg. It was for Zizi that he wrote 'Élisa'. She was dressed as a military nurse and there was a real train that came onto the stage with boys in blue singing 'Élisa Élisa the soldiers' girl,' and the train left the stage. There was King Kong's enormous hand with Zizi sitting in it. Serge adored Roland, and Roland and Zizi Jeanmaire were amongst our few friends.

† We went to Le Touquet because Serge wanted to take me to Flavio, the very chic casino restaurant where Serge had been the bar pianist when he was young. He asked for lobster and the best table because, in the old days, he'd had to eat in the kitchen.

Serge's ma, who was in great form, laughed and was very gay, apart from the occasional sadness over Serge's Papa.

Out to dinner at the Orangerie. Whom should I see but Francis Bacon! I nearly died, but I plucked up enough courage to ask him for an autograph. He was very sweet and said I was very pretty. He signed a 100-franc note for Serge and was putting his pen away when I said, 'And one for me!' So he did that. 'And one for my father!' He laughed and obliged.

* * *

I remember that, to fill up the time while he was signing the bank note and the piece of paper, I asked him where his exhibition was going to be held. He was very modest and shy, and he wouldn't say. So I said, 'Oh come on, I live on the Rue de Verneuil. Maybe your expo isn't far.' In the end he said, 'It's at the Grand Palais.' The poor man was very sad because a few days before, his lover, George Dyer, had taken his own life in his hotel on Rue des Saints-Pères.

* * *

Tuesday

Pa and I got up very late. I was depressed and so we made each other laugh. Put off going to the Monet exhibition, which was lucky because it was Monday and closed. We had a coffee at the Deux Magots. Went to the cinema, and met Serge who was depressed over work. Then we went to dinner at the Coupole. A man had a heart attack behind us whilst Pa and Serge were tucking into oysters. But he recovered after someone put a plastic bag over his face. No one took a blind bit of notice of him, sprawled out on the bench. I wouldn't like to have an attack at the Coupole, chances of 'secours' ('rescue') are very slim.

December

Serge is having a very swish party for my birthday, hundreds of pounds worth of plates, old Chinese and English, and glasses – £20 each, some of them – silver dishes, so beautiful. Yul and Jacqueline, M. and Mme Hazan, Zizi and Roland, and Yves Saint-Laurent and his male friend.

I took Kate to the zoo on Thursday and then to Saint-Laurent for a fitting for my dress for the Rothschilds' ball. Saint-Laurent designed it especially for Serge, for me. Poor Serge got to pay I don't know what for it. It's so sweet of him and all his idea.

* * *

We only really met Yves Saint-Laurent for the musical with Zizi. Serge and I used to go to his showroom, sitting on little gilt chairs, and Serge chose dresses in taffeta for fun. YSL had created a made-to-measure dress in lace for the famous Proustian Rothschild ball at Ferrières.

There had been a great dinner for Marie-Hélène's birthday where Serge and I had ordered three dozen white roses to be delivered. All the presents had been deposited on a vast table to be opened after dinner. We were very nervous that our roses were not there. Before dinner at the table Marie-Hélène opened her napkin and found, hidden inside, an emerald the size of a baby's fist. 'Oh how sweet,' she said to the Baron of Redé. I was sitting next to the great pianist Rubinstein who was fiddling on my knee. During the pudding I whispered to Serge, 'Hey, the fellow next to me is using my knee as a piano!' and Serge said, 'Let it go, Jeannette, he's a genius!'

* * *

Serge has just come in and found a marvellous title for Vannier's record: *Enfant Assassin des Mouches*. What a wonderful idea! Vannier gave him a very disconnected mixture of sounds and music and asked Serge to help him find the title. And he has done so brilliantly, 'The Child Fly-Killer', with the last track called 'Child on the Fly-paper' and just before that 'The Waltz of the Fly King'. That is Serge's genius ideas. People can be a good orchestrator but without the idea, it's nothing. Its greatest talents are the lyrics and then the music of *Melody Nelson*, the materialisation of the idea which was superb; his ideas are unforgettable.

* * *

Melody Nelson is considered Serge's greatest record. On the cover there's a photo by Tony Frank. I'm wearing a little red Carita wig. Serge had drawn freckles on my face and I couldn't really do up my jeans because, contrary to *Melody Nelson* I was not fourteen and was four months pregnant with Charlotte. So that it didn't show, I put my monkey in front of me. Melody dies in an airplane accident, trying to get to Sunderland. When I heard the record with Andrew – the orchestrations, the drums at the end after 'Cargo Culte' – I thought it was the greatest work I'd ever heard. Nobody had ever done an entire story in a record.

Andrew ran with the demo to all the pirate radios but no one was interested. Vannier's orchestrations were both Oriental and sublime, and Serge's poetry was the most stunning of all that he had written, with *L'homme à Tête de Chou* a few years later. Neither were best-sellers but today they're recognised at last. 'L'Hotel' was inspired by our rococo room in the hotel L'Hôtel on Rue des Beaux-Arts. The red hair was that of Lucy, Gabrielle's daughter, and there are shades of Nabokov's *Lolita*. It's funny to think that apart from 'Poupée de Cire, Poupée de Son'; 'Je T'Aime. . . Moi Non Plus', and 'Initials B.B.', Serge hadn't really been in the charts. And he had to wait until 1983 for *Melody Nelson* to become a gold disc. We'd already separated but Serge gave it to me, saying, 'At last we got it.' It was only with *Aux Armes, et Cætera*, the French national anthem to reggae music, and later *Love on the Beat* and *You're Under Arrest* that Serge became 'Gainsbarre', his alter ego who loved to drink and party, with a platinum record overnight. At sixty years old, he knew popular success.

* * *

14 December, *my birthday*

Serge gave me a gardenia and a beautiful party. Everyone arrived at 9 o'clock in evening dress, me in my dress from Saint-Laurent that Serge gave me. Serge was very nervous and kept running into the kitchen where Mamadou was wrestling with two 'pintades'!* All day we have been buying things, table knives and forks, a ton of caviar, a huge bottle of vodka, an enormous Stilton and a mass of mandarins, champagne and fine old port. A delicious dinner and so exciting. Saint-Laurent was sweet and timid: it was our first dinner at home.

* * *

Mamadou was Serge's butler, a lamb. He stayed with us for a long time and used to prepare the 'mafé', peanut stew, refusing to make up the au pair's bed and dreaming of opening the door to our chic guests, but we didn't have many guests. There was this fête, which was a dream for him, at which he could show off his talents. When we received insulting letters he had his own way of dealing with them in his room. Serge believed in his great gift of taking away the bad spells. When Charlotte was born he gave her a volume of *Apollinaire* in the Pléiade edition.

---

* Guinea fowl.

1972[*]

From this time maybe I influenced how Serge looked a tiny bit. If I did, I'm very proud, I thought that he looked too smooth when he shaved, too young, and shone a bit. I thought he looked a lot more attractive when he didn't shave for a few days. The stubble grew in funny places, a bit like a Tartar emperor, so from then on he bought an electric trimmer, so that he could keep his beard at that length. It became quite fashionable. I decorated him with jewels. I found him so refined because he wasn't a hairy man. I begged him to take off his socks as I've always found it sad, a man in socks. When I went to Repetto, the ballet shop, which belonged to Roland Petit's mother, there was a basket of ballet shoes in their sale. I paid for my own ballet shoes as usual and in the basket I saw a pair of white shoes that were as soft as socks and, as Serge had flat feet and didn't like walking, I took a pair home and they became his go-to shoes. He wore jeans, but I liked it when he wore a gentleman's pinstripe jacket that we found at the Chelsea antique market. It was a model for girls and had darts up the front. He looked so fine in it that I bought him a costume at Lanvin, just for the jacket, and he used to put on his little metal reading specs which made him look like a Russian professor – eccentric, with his hair rather too long.

I bought him an attaché case at Vuitton, all black, and I'd kicked it in one night out of jealousy because of a girl. He'd never had it repaired; he liked to see the scars. Inside he had wads of banknotes that reassured him, his Gitanes cigarettes, and my monkey's jeans. Also a few insulting letters that he rather loved: 'You who have eyes

---

[*] The notebooks from 1972 are missing.

like an electrocuted toad, you have cost me 1 franc, the price of this stamp.' Also letters from people from the Légion d'honneur, who asked him to take off his false decoration because they said he didn't deserve it and shouldn't have it. They were foolish not to have given it to him. If only they'd known how he would have respected it and been so proud. His Commander of the Order of Arts and Letters was on a place of honour on his low table. After I left he wore a lizard jacket. He said, 'Look Jeannette, they made me this overnight.' I said, 'And it looks like it!' I loved him looking elegant, but he had created Gainsbarre.

That year I filmed *Trop Jolies pour Être Honnêtes* by Richard Balducci with Bernadette Lafont, in a horrible little modern villa in Spain. Before leaving, Serge had asked his mother to come and look after Charlotte, who was a baby. At the end of the film, on arriving at the airport for our flight, with Serge, Kate, Charlotte and Serge's mama, I saw that I didn't have my monkey. Serge said it was far too dangerous to take the flight without him, so off I went with Charlotte in a taxi on a two-hour ride to find the villa, rummage around, and there amongst the rubbish on a conveyor belt, was my monkey, travelling towards the incinerator. I left Charlotte in the chauffeur's arms and ran to save him from the fire.

When I got back to the airport two hours later Serge's mother saw me brandishing Munkey and said, 'Quoi, c'est une peluche?' ('What, it's just a stuffed toy?') with her Russian accent. Serge blew up and explained the importance of Munkey. Our airplane had gone and Serge, who hated airplanes anyway, decided to hire a car, and we were off on our way to Ramatuelle.

That year Serge rented the Chateau Volterra, an enormous domain belonging to Suzy Volterra, at Cap Camarat. Every week we trotted into Saint-Tropez to get the cash out to hire this 'maison de luxe'. We'd invited our two families: Ma, Pa, Andrew, Linda, Serge's mother and his sisters, Liliane and Jacqueline, each with their children. Just after we'd arrived I received a phone call from Vadim who asked me to perform in *Don Juan* with Brigitte Bardot. Of course I said yes, so we were back in Paris a week later, leaving our families on the private beach. Just before the filming, for the scene with Bardot in bed, Serge and I had a violent fight over Vadim and I took refuge in the hotel opposite, the Pont-Royal. An assistant came to look for me early in the morning to do the scene with Bardot but I'd cried all night and my face was all swollen and I had such shiny eyelids that I couldn't be made up. That's why I'm so pretty in that scene, because for once, I wasn't covered up with the typical make-up of the sixties.

Bardot was a darling, extremely kind to me, and a girl who would rather drink a glass in the bar than do our scene. She had no ambition, unlike other actresses. The morning of our famous scene together she'd arrived looking sumptuous; it was incredible to see her in real life, just magnificent. When we were in bed, I looked at her from top to toe to try to find a little fault. There were none; even her feet were beautiful. I suggested that we should mix my legs with hers so one might think her foot was mine. When the scene started, Vadim just said, 'Go on,' and we didn't know what to do. Bardot proposed with a little smile that we should sing 'Je T'Aime. . . Moi Non Plus'. I suggested 'My Bonny Lies Over The Ocean'.

It's a charming moment in this film, in bed with Bardot. She stayed someone who's very dear. Every time I send a cheque of nothing at all for her animals, she sends me a little personal card to thank me. Serge was very faithful in friendship and he used to have lunch with her quite often. And after I left him he put all the enormous photos of her taken by Sam Levin back up in his living room. One day, when I was living in Rue de la Tour with Jacques Doillon, Serge rang and said, 'Bad news for you,' so I said, 'Say it quick.' He said, 'Brigitte has called and she wants to bring out the original version of "Je T'Aime" to find money for her animals.' He was right to have wanted to help her, and now the two versions coexist. I think Bardot considered him one of the loves of her life.

In November,* I went on a march for the first time. I'd met Delphine Seyrig at her apartment at Place des Vosges and Sami Frey made us boiled eggs to give us courage before we left for Bobigny. I thought that was rather chic as, on the Rue de Verneuil, I'd encountered some hostility. We'd been a little afraid that boys would come and break up our demonstration, which would have been a disaster as then the trial would have been held behind closed doors. I remember the pushing and pulling and how my basket fell under the barrier. There was a great camaraderie between girls that I'd never known before. Of course I had been for the legalisation of abortion, because chic girls could always go to England or Switzerland without any problem of conscience or money.

---

* A minor, a young girl, and the women who had helped her have an abortion were defended by Gisèle Halimi at a trial in Bobigny.

1973

After Serge's heart attack, I rented two little cottages in inland Brittany, as staying by the sea after a heart attack was said not to be a good idea. When Serge was at the American hospital, I was filming *Protection Privée*. I came back one evening and Mr and Mrs Hazan were in our sitting room. I thought that was very bizarre, and there I was told that Serge had had a heart attack. Gabrielle and I rushed to the hospital, to intensive care. Serge had unplugged all the monitors linking him up to the heart monitor, which was making a ghastly noise, and all the nurses were running towards him, and when we poked our head round the door, Serge went, 'Boo!' It was his idea of a joke.

He stopped smoking whilst he was in intensive care because he was scared it would blow something up, with the oxygen. But he'd had time to take ten packets of Gitanes with him when they'd taken him out to the ambulance on a chair. He'd declined the stretcher, and he took his Hermès blanket, ever the aesthete. When he was able to have a private room I thought that he'd stopped smoking and found it strange that he was always asking for Old Spice deodorant, but when they opened the drawer after his departure, they found hundreds of little corked pill bottles with a tiny drop of water and a stubbed-out Gitanes cigarette in each. One morning, to my surprise, I saw Serge on the front page of *France-Soir* newspaper. I went up the hospital's back stairs out of discretion when I bumped into the singer Enrico Macias, who was there to see his wife. I bounced into Serge's room crying, 'Oh the rotters!' and Serge blushed like a young girl, and said, 'It was me who called them. Nobody knew that I nearly died.'

17 July, *Brittany*

We have been in this tiny mill house since Thursday. I drove all the way in my little Volkswagen. It's our first time out. Seven hours with a lunch break to eat a very stiff 'rouget', have a row, a black coffee – and off again. Serge was very nervous of coming, and so was I of him coming! He kept yelling instructions and getting cross. We were both in foul moods. I was stopped by the police one hour out of Paris; they noticed that I kept stopping (my engine was making an awful row). They wanted to know why. I'd been told by my garage to go all the way in 'L' – well, apparently that's for mountains! I hadn't even realised you could change gear in an automatic. I was terrified the police would realise I was incompetent. The burning rubber smell and only seventy-five on the switch pad was apparently because of that. The police were really nice and let me go with only raised eyebrows! Anyway, we arrived at 9.30, followed by the chauffeur-driven Mercedes with Mme Raymonde* and the children in it. Poor Serge was very relieved to be here.

It is a little cottage on a stream, with an 'étang' ('pond'). Serge goes out like Jeremy Fisher to fish for fish, which he hasn't caught yet, and frogs, which whizz off at the sight of him. Serge rows off every day in a little boat that looks very sweet in the reeds with its anchor ready to cast.

* * *

I didn't know that he rowed out of sight to have a fag! Once I noticed a bit of tobacco in the chip in his front tooth and I said, 'That's

---

* Madame Raymonde was the children's new nanny and housekeeper. Serge was too scared to let me drive the children from Paris.

tobacco.' He said, 'No, it's pepper. I made myself a Bloody Mary but without the vodka!'

* * *

Today, with Kate and Mme Raymonde, he built a home of wood in the trees with ferns for a roof. It was very gay. I played with Charlotte, who likes to slap my face! She is really so sweet. 'Papa,' she yells whenever she sees Serge. And 'Ça pique, Papa!' ('It stings, Daddy!'), whenever he kisses her and she has a tantrum when I leave her alone.

Kate & Charlotte on the bike.

Kate is at a difficult age when, in comparison to Charlotte, she is always being ticked off. We had a scene in the loo as to whether she had touched the chain and made it overflow. She swore she hadn't touched it. Serge said she was lying and I took her side. Serge walked out. He said he had lost his dignity and command when I disputed his 'raisons' ('reasoning') in front of the children and that Kate and I were in cahoots against him. I thought it was too severe but I don't think Kate takes it too badly. She knows he's like that; he's just very concerned for the moment about his 'command' vis-à-vis Kate. He must always be right and I must always back him up in front of her.

I have often heard Ma and Pa quarrelling about the same thing, 'not in front of the children'. Anyway, all is well now and forgotten.

Serge is so much better, thank goodness, and is being very good about his diet. He walks Nana* for hours. She swims in the lake and looks like a prehistoric beast, just her ears and tiny eyes poking out of the water. The first time she dived in, poor Serge was very worried and raced out to save her in his boat. He lost the oar, but got her. Now she plops in every day and is fine munching the weeds. She seems to be a water dog.

Serge and I went to the market on Monday. It was so gay! Everyone recognised him and I was very proud. He looks very handsome in his gumboots. It seems incredible that only two months ago he was so ill and I was in such desperation. The children are asleep and Serge and I are in our room with a waterfall outside; it's so peaceful, no telephone, a real holiday, and Serge will be so much better for it. We are going to buy camping equipment so we can sleep in a tent. It's back to childhood!

Wednesday

Dear Munkey,

I think I know what perversion is! Serge must be the most perverted person possible. He wanted to play Ludo, with me throwing the dice for him and him throwing the dice for me and by my throw I make him eat me! It was the most horrible idea, very decadent, and I refused to continue to play!

I spoke to Ma tonight. Maybe she's going to Germany with Andrew to do *Madam Kitty*. She is in turmoil about whether Linda should do her nude photo for £100 a day with another 'Birkin' heading. Pa is somewhere on the North Brittany coast on someone's yacht so I should be getting an SOS soon. I do hope he's OK. He is very brave because I don't think he wanted to go. There was such a storm last

---

* Nana was the name of the bull terrier that I gave Serge.

night, I hope what's-his-name Nicholson drops him off somewhere near here so he can come and see us.

Thursday

We have just come back from the lunch with François de la Grange.

We had a frantic morning. There was a female yak who was having her baby and Serge, Charlotte, Kate and I went to watch, but the poor thing was exhausted after having been chased two hours (to catch it). The enormous stomach heaved and sighed – she was much too young to have one and the calf was too big for her. The vet had his arm right up to his shoulder to pull out the baby; at last hoofs appeared, so they tied cords around and then started to pull about (she was tied to a tree). The head came out – 'Don't go too fast!' – and at last it slipped, the mother was too exhausted to push. She just panted. The sun came out as the baby emerged, but it didn't move, it was dead.

Suddenly all the excitement and happiness of birth was clouded over. It started to rain on the little brown corpse which lay still in the grass. The mother never saw her baby; it was wheeled away in a wheelbarrow instead of being warm by its brave mother. We left her having an injection to put her to sleep. No wonder she will never have confidence in man. I suppose that in nature she would have died too. Kate was in tears and her first look at Wonderful Mother Nature had been a very sad experience.

21 July, *Charlotte's birthday!*

Charlotte's birthday went very well. Serge gave her a doll like Papy, with a pipe, I gave her a wheelbarrow and a doll who smiled on one side and cried on the other. Kate gave her a very flash bracelet with rubies and gold and a purse – very down to earth!

Nine children came to tea, bringing humble gifts and flowers. The children from the farm – a little girl and two boys – and four little girls belonging to the house's owners (three horrors and one beauty but all very nice). At tea, everyone ate the vast chocolate cake (I got it ordered from the village baker with 'Happy Birthday Charlotte' on it) and the ice cream, biscuits, etc., and then everyone went off to play – except the smallest farm boy who ate his ice cream at leisure. Mme Raymonde said he's never had ice cream before. The children played until 7 o'clock and Charlotte and Kate apparently flopped to bed. Pa, Serge and I went off to a restaurant near the zoo, it was a chateau-manoir and when we arrived wedding guests were pouring in in long dresses. The autograph hunters started to snoop so we crept out by the garden to avoid them.

Friday

I am in a depression, worried about Pa and his operation and Serge and his smoking. He told the doctor today that he would start smoking again in October. It has been such a ghastly year: Sean Kenny dead, Jack MacGowran and many more famous people like Noël Coward and Binkie Beaumont, Jack Hawkins and Picasso. I was talking to someone on the phone and they said, 'Make Serge hang on to life, it's the only thing worth fighting for.' I am so frightened of the full stop. I was so worried when Serge was in that blasted hospital and I thought people were lying and he would be dead. I remember screaming and worrying how many sleeping pills I had got. If Serge is dead, I want to die too.

Papy and Serge ... all this has given me such a jolt. That Serge could die at forty-five? It had never even entered my head.

Sunday

A hundred and fifty frogs! That's what Serge and I counted this afternoon whilst walking around the lake. We had dinner with the De La Granges last night, with the lady who talks too much. Serge was worried we'd have to make friends and invite them to Paris, so we did our duty here. Serge is so funny: he doesn't want any friends, it's his panic.

We are leaving here on Tuesday, just about time, too. Serge has just about done everything and is fed up with the frogs, so I think a change will be a good thing, although I don't know how he'll keep to a diet in the hotel. Apparently there's a sort of bungalow for two, apart, and Serge wants *us* to be in that and the children in the hotel.

Monday night

Went to Questembert market with Serge and bought food food food and signed lots of little bits of paper for children. Decided to start a baby, April or March, then I will have a winter baby and maybe it will be a boy. Thomas David Joe Gainsbourg, wouldn't that be nice!

Haven't heard from Papy but I presume all is well. There will be a telephone at the hotel so I can do all the telephoning I want to there.

Had a sweet 'sieste' with Serge, it was lovely.

Friday

Well, here we are, installed again! Thank goodness we are not in the ghastly hotel on the main road. But when we arrived at the cottage it was a relief to see a country lake and a little garden. Well, we have installed the children in the kitchen, we are in the bedroom, there's a bathroom for Nana and a loo – all we need.

We all had a barbecue last night in the garden. What fumes! Two sacks of 'charbon' and packets of firelighters. It said on the ad 'within minutes you will have glowing embers'. An hour later we had a sad glimpse of a flame, with Serge flapping at it with newspapers. But then bangers and chops and even roasted bananas. It turned out to be very good.

Serge on his bike! He goes off for bike riding with Nana trotting after.

We have dinner most nights at the hotel as the lady there is the one who fixed up the cottage for us. It's completely empty each night; her cooking is not exactly indicated for Serge! All salty and even if you ask for 'sans sel', it's exactly the same. She has had two heart attacks in four months and is terribly fat and eats everything. Serge and the children and I play in the bowling alley (Serge's idea of heaven). I have tried to telephone Paul-Émile each night but no luck. But I got him from the town and he's coming next week. That way he can watch Serge while I am in London.

* * *

Paul-Émile Seidmann and Ginette Spanier were an extraordinary couple. He was a French doctor and she was head of Balmain. He spoke Russian and played chess, and had literary and intellectual conversations with Serge that he couldn't have with me. They had a sense of humour that used to make us cry laughing. I think they lived in a vast apartment on Avenue Maurice. All the actors from the English theatre went to their cocktail parties – I met Sir Laurence Olivier and Sir John Gielgud there. During the war the couple had been denounced by the concierge for being Jewish and they went off on bikes across France. Ginette's little black dress shrank day by day. At the end of the war, Paul-Émile jumped off his bike saying, 'It's over!' and Ginette feared he'd lost his head but in fact he'd spotted a packet of Craven A cigarettes in a puddle and had understood that the English had passed by.

Poor Charlotte had her injection against tuberculosis today. Took the opportunity to take S's blood pressure: 12.8, wonderful! So he bought boudin, bacon and pork chops to celebrate! Now he's gone off biking and the children are asleep. He's looking good and is much less nervous, especially when I'm driving. There is a 'fête' this Sunday and Serge is giving the prizes. Should be fun.

Now I must be off to Locminé to buy a little 'négro' statue which Serge wants. He saw it in an underwear shop window as an advertisement for 'le petit négro culotte'.*

Kate and Charlotte watching a film with Grace Kelly on the TV, so silly. Really, when I think how many bad films are made, and even when they're good, what counts is living and keeping people that you love with you all the time. I won't be separated for anything and I will follow Serge everywhere. It's the only thing that counts.

Saturday

Had a picnic in the pouring rain. Serge and Mme Raymonde were giggling all morning – I thought they had got something under their sleeves. Cold boiled eggs, cider, even coffee in Coca-Cola bottles. And what happened? Rain! It poured and poured. We were in the middle of the field with Charlotte sitting under a red umbrella.

---

* Le petit négro was a plaster statue about a foot tall of a little black boy with two little dogs pulling at his knickers. It was an advertisement for the Petit Négro brand of underwear. It must have been about fifty years old.

Picnic in the Rain!

Monday

Another fairy tale yesterday. Serge wanted the little 'négro' in the linen shop window. He was going to pay 50 francs and he thought they would say yes. But no, the old Breton who had the shop said he couldn't sell him because he'd been with them for sixty years. And all the children and even the grown-ups stop to look at him in the window as they go by. And people buy the culottes 'petit négro' because of him. And now they don't make the little statues any more so they could never get another. I was so proud of him not wanting to sell his mascot to the rich Parisian. I asked if maybe one could write to the factory in Belgium and get another but he said, 'No, they haven't been made for years.' It's only because they are a very old shop – he's been there seventy years – that they have it. All the

shop records are taken down with dip pen and ink; it was like a
Dickens shop and they were so proud. BUT, Serge wanted that petit
négro, it had become a fixation. 'For 1000 francs!' he exclaimed.
Well, you should have seen the little Breton's face! 'Anciens?' ('Old
Francs?') he stuttered. 'Non, nouveaux.' ('No, new ones.')

The little man twitched and muttered. Serge wrote the price in old
and new francs on a piece of paper in front of the ogling old man
and his assistant (who does the accounts and sits all day in front of
the window with the petit négro!).

'Je vais demander au patron,' ('I'll have to ask the boss') said the
little man and shuffled at speed upstairs. I couldn't believe the price,
£100 for a plaster statue. But I was still sure they would say no. After
all, it was there to 'porter le bonheur' ('bring them luck'), and had
been in their window for years and years.

Well, the patron came down and, after a lot of whispering, the bar-
gaining began again. Serge thought for a mad moment he'd offered
£1000 in cash. Serge said 'oui' and they said 'oui'. Not too late to turn
back, I thought as they took him out of his place in the window. Not
too late to turn back, I thought as they laid him on the table. The old
man touched his plaster face and said, 'Au revoir, mon bonhomme,
ça fait longtemps qu'on se connaît.' ('Goodbye my little fellow, we've
known each other for a long time.')

Oh no! But yes, he wrapped him in newspaper and put him in a
shoebox with string. The old man said he must be in a 'beau paquet'
('be nicely wrapped') because he had never sold short in his life,
never owed anything to anyone. 'We Bretons can't be bought,' he
said as he knotted the string and we said goodbye. Serge gave two
500-franc notes, and a bit more for the three towels I had bought
and we walked away.

I was most terribly sad. I think even Serge was sad even though
he had won. He said, 'All men can be bought.' I had so wished it
had not been true. We passed the window on the way home in my
car, boxes of pants and dust but you, no, petit négro. He would
soon be on the grand piano in Paris. But has luck gone with their

'porte-bonheur' ('lucky mascot')? No more children's faces will look in the old shop window, faces the old man would never have seen if it hadn't been for the statue of the black boy with the two puppies tugging at his white knickers. Serge says I've read too many 'roman de gare' ('cheap novels') . . . Maybe, but I was sad all day. I will think of the man next week when they spend the 1000 francs that they couldn't turn down. They'll think that they sold their friend cheaply when they see no more faces at the window. I wanted to leave our address in case they had regrets. Maybe the man will die eating his banquet, maybe the woman too, and the poor man who writes the accounts so carefully. Where will you look, now there is nothing in the window? And the people will walk by.

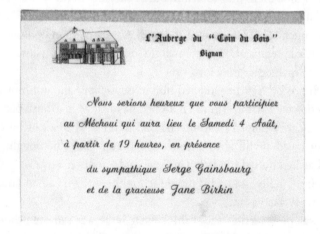

« LE COIN DU BOIS » - BIGNAN
SAMEDI 4 AOUT à partir de 19 heures
MÉCHOUI en la compagnie du sympatique
Serge GAINSBOURG et Jane BIRKIN

L'Auberge du " Coin du Bois "
Bignan

Nous serions heureux que vous participiez au Méchoui qui aura lieu le Samedi 4 Août, à partir de 19 heures, en présence

du sympathique Serge Gainsbourg et de la gracieuse Jane Birkin

I forgot Saturday last!! The invitation 'journalistique' for the 'grand méchoui' ('lamb on a spit')!! The local newspaper's invitation

for the grand méchoui' at 'table d'honneur' ('the table of honour')
with uneatable laaaamb!! All the guests looked at us as if we were
freaks and got very unpleasant when we didn't want to sing 'Di Doo
Dah' blared on the pick-up as publicity!

* * *

My first solo record, 'Di Doo Dah', which Serge wrote for me, was a
song about my flat chest, my father and my monkey. There were a
few songs inspired by my parents in Brighton. 'Mon Amour Baiser'
is one of Étienne Daho's favourite songs. In fact, it's very delicate
because it says, 'Baiser bouche, baiser doux, baiser tout . . . ' ('Kiss
the mouth, sweet kiss, kiss everything'). In the songs he describes
a young, easy-going girl who sleeps around, innocently and without pleasure, followed by these bad boys right up to her apartment
door. She opens the door and one of them is still there. Serge made
up this character, who was a little bit sad, a little bit funny. He asked
me to sing in a whisper right into the microphone and he was proud
that I sang so high.

We sang a song called 'La Décadanse' that I found even more
beautiful than 'Je T'Aime', and Serge invented a dance where you
hold the girl from the back, having turned her round, a bit exhibition-
ist. I sang it like a hymn.

* * *

Sunday, *Josselin*

We set off at 11.30 in 'cortège' (in 'a procession'). The lady from Le
Coin* with all the suitcases, me following in my car with Kate and
Charlotte and toys, and Serge following with Paul-Émile.

---

* Le Coin was her café.

7 o'clock

So here we are. Serge and Paul-Émile are playing chess, the children have gone off looking for the local village with Madame R., sniffing! I have made a Lancashire hotpot (with no salt for PE who has pâté with no salt, no meat, and no fat, so what's the point?!). It's Swiss, of course . . .

The dog is very happy, she has her own bed in the sitting room, an old Breton 'berceau' ('cot'). Serge and I have a little room down the stairs. We have arranged it to look very pretty with my straw hat and the chess set and bottles and things. The children upstairs in a little room with four beds. And PE is in the room upstairs with six suits of Huntsman tweeds! When will he wear them?! He's so sweet and funny with his suitcase full of saltless conserves and honey biscuits, even 'sardines sans sel' ('sardines without salt')!

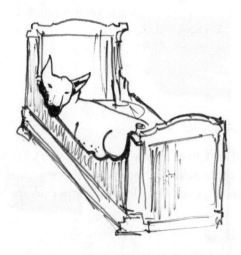

Monday

Serge and I had a snuggly 'sieste', which was lovely. I do love him
so. What would I do without him? When I think of what it might
have been . . . Well, I just can't, and it wasn't.

PE, Serge and I played Dada* until midnight. PE does make me
laugh. I gave him a toasted marshmallow, hot from the gas fire, and
asked him if he liked it. He went bright purple and said it reminded
him of the poor villagers in *Andrei Roublev* when the Mongols
poured molten lead down their throats! Serge and he cry with
laughter in Russian and it really is a jolly sight!! PE hates Dada and
when Serge – furious at being called a cheat (which he was) – said,
'Alors on joue plus' ('I'm not playing any more'), his face lit up and
said, 'Vraiment?' ('Really?') in a voice full of hope and emotion.

---

* Dada is a child's game with a die and little horses.

14 August, Tuesday, teatime

'L'événement de l'année!' ('The event of the year!') Serge has a bath!! The first for three months (his last one was 13 May!!) I can't say he had it willingly or without resistance, but he had it.

* * *

Serge was the most immaculate person that I've ever met. He used to wash himself by little bits at a time, discreetly, in the bidet. He didn't sweat and I never noticed the slightest odour. When I asked him how he managed it he said, 'I'm a pure spirit.' Never did he wander around naked and I never saw him standing up with no clothes. He always used to wear his velvet dressing gown. The children used to watch out but they never saw anything.

* * *

Did my shopping with PE as Serge felt too hot and tired. Goodness me! We bought a lot; we galloped about, getting potatoes and onions for Serge's Irish stew as all the stores will be shut tomorrow. Serge got a card from Papy – a reply for Serge's Breton lady (one of those awful cards with material and lace and the skirt in Breton costume) where he had told Papy that maybe if he lifted her skirt he might see something exciting!

Wednesday, 15 August

Last night the poor old farmer had to come and help us to find a button for the electricity as it had gone out. There had been such a storm and Serge was very cross because he'd thought there was a switch on the electricity pole in front of the house (in a field). I was screaming 'No, no!' He was all wet and I didn't want him electrocuted. PE wanted to watch a film about a straw boat that went to

South America. Serge plodded off into the rain, getting crosser and crosser. I laughed because he was a bit scared and kept coming back. At last he made me go with him as proof that there was no disconnection on the pole.

And then we went to our humble neighbour's house, which was full of light, to see if he knew where the button was. He was plastered, but managed to say that the electricity stuff had all been put underground! Serge had inspiration and darted into the house and pressed a button by the bathroom which said 'lumière' and, lo and behold, there was light! We offered a glass of beer to our drunk pal who was very red in the face and proud as he was under the impression that it was he who solved the light switch problem. I noticed he had a very nasty-looking bandage; a cow, he explained, had kicked him. The poor thing was so drunk and confused he said it had happened six days ago and he should have reported it to the Sécurité Sociale. And now it was too late to be reimbursed. The bandage was filthy. I called PE, who was watching TV, to look at it and he said he should have an X-ray and an anti-tetanus jab. He would not do anything and begged us not to say anything, as he would lose his job. I couldn't stop thinking of his dirty bandage. Serge was sweet and said we would go next morning with our first aid box. But I said tonight and off we went. It was 10.30. Horrors! It was a woman who opened the door. She looked mystified. I said we had come with bandages for his hand. The woman looked suspicious.

'I thought he'd gone to your house to fix the lights?' she said. 'Did he complain of his hand?' 'Oh, non non,' said Serge, and we repeated it in unison, terrified that this was the patron, and he would lose his job. 'Oh, dearie dear! No, no. We thought maybe he'd like some clean bandages. Being so late and the chemist's being shut I have this Red Cross box for the children so I thought we'd drop it in with it.' I backpedalled like mad, trying to be offhand. 'I'll leave the box with you; that way you can use what you want if it's any use,' I spluttered.

Serge and I plodded off home; I said I thought she was his mother. I was very proud of Serge. He was so kind and had come with me even though he thought it was too late. He was concerned, too; he liked the man and had had a cider with him a few days ago. He said I was a kind girl. He's a false cynic – he is really so kind.

Took Kate and Charlotte to see Josselin, the château and the church. We saw the pretty stone couple. Kate wanted to know if they'd been buried in their clothes. Charlotte ate her chocolate and I gave her such a wallop (I'd told her not to touch it until after lunch). Then I realised we were in church and muffled her screams with my hands and whispered threats in her ear that if she didn't stop yelling she'd get another! Poor Charlotte, she is very forgiving!

There is the procession tonight of the virgin. I promised to take them both.

1 o'clock in the morning

The parade started at 9 o'clock.

A statue of the virgin was paraded in a white robe with gold jewels on a stretcher, two little pages and a clergyman and town crier, followed by the entire population moaning psalms. Hardly the parade of pomp and circumstance and jolliness that I had expected!

At a café opposite the church, I signed autographs on the bills and we swigged Coca-Cola and ate crepes and swigged good home-made cider whilst the ceremony went on in the church. I made the children stand to attention as the villagers marched past and we trailed after them. Everyone gathered inside the courtyard of the castle. Kate edged forward to the front row, aided by a kindly nun. And I held Charlotte who was very solemn. All of a sudden in the 'repenting of sins' bit, and 'casting away the temptations of cash and worldly goods', my tiny child hollered out 'argent' ('money'). I had reclaimed my 2 francs from the café for returning the Coca-Cola bottles and stuffed her tiny hands with them so as to silence her and the service went on with dignity. Lots of wailing in French and casting out, but apart from that it had all been very pretty. Kate was struck by a religious blow and said she would say her prayers tonight. I said, 'Let's say one too for Serge and Papy.'

We went off to my Volkswagen and tootled off home. Serge's Irish stew was ready, and was very good. PE had a cider with the nice farmer and his mother. They were very touching, had never been to Paris. We said they should go together for a weekend. Serge gave them a bottle of Saint Émilion and they were very moved. His hand is much less swollen. No wonder he's drunk all the time, poor man. What can you hope for in life in his little cottage with his mother and no wife and no children at his old age? Who will look after him?

16 August

The bloody dog woke us up, scratching at the door, and that got me awake in a bad mood! Off to do the shopping with Serge. After lunch we decided to take the children to see the castle. PE came too as he loves the castle and wanted to help me book my plane ticket to London. Went with PE to the post office where a telegram was waiting for me saying I had to dub my film* from 24 to 28 August. So I phoned Olga,† who said to ring the director. The trouble is the unions don't work Saturdays and Sundays. I said it was quite impossible for me to stay the weekend, so he said he would try to persuade the unions to work and find Jean-Luc Bideau who I will dub with.

In the meantime, the children were playing havoc in the post office, which had become like a saloon bar, Kate swinging on cabin doors and Charlotte howling! Kate wanted to go to the loo, the kind post office lady took her. Chaos. I couldn't wait to get out (nor could PE). We decided to go to the 'syndicat d'initiative de Josselin' ('tourist information office') about my ticket. And there I was, fixing my ticket, when Charlotte began howling. She wanted to go to the loo. Kate took her, and I got pamphlets about ferries and aeroplanes. I

---

* *Projection Privée* by François Leterrier.
† My agent.

am a wee bit scared of aeroplanes, especially this unknown company which flies from Dinard with 'flash' written on it did not inspire my confidence. I looked up ferries from Roscoff and saw *Poseidon* was the name, hardly a name summoning up safety and well-being, so I let it drop. Charlotte was yelling because she didn't want to let the lady in the loo. We all had to go back to the post office for me to ring 'Flash' aviation. I left Charlotte and Kate with PE in the car this time and told them to be good.

A piercing scream, followed by bloodcurdling yells, filled the air, even into my cabin in the post office. I rushed out to see PE trying to hide his shame, cowering in the front of the car, with a red-faced brute of a child stamping her feet and yelling blue murder in the back. Kate was bashing her and trying to silence the fiend in kiddies' clothing. It was a sight to be seen! I bounded down the steps of the post office like a mountain goat and issued a series of whacks and threats! All faces were out of the windows, convinced that PE was the criminal uncle of the poor mites, and now a fiendish, red-faced, sweaty mother was spitting fire and pressing down on the accelerator to get the hell out of it.

Off to the castle. 4 francs each and children don't pay. I said they were mad and didn't know my children, who should be made to pay double! Never has a truer word been said. Charlotte refused to walk, I threatened to leave her and she spat and yelled and tapped her tiny feet. In the end I had to carry her because of all the onlookers tutting. But once out of sight of witnesses I gave her such a wallop I MADE her walk. I was sorely tempted to cast her into the twelfth-century well or over the historic battlements. Maternal instincts had diminished and I would have handed her over to the first buyer! PE, I think, has never been so embarrassed and walked two yards behind us to avoid any association and disowned us forthright! Charlotte won; I had to carry her and then discovered she'd peed in her knickers (after refusing to pee at the syndicat d'initiative), thus rendering me not only fuming and sweaty but also smelly!

I carried my wet bundle round the guided tour until she dropped asleep. Meantime, Kate was playing with barriers and poking precious objects. I happened to mutter my dislike for the unpleasant expressions on the faces of the old ancestors' portraits. 'Quelle horreur' was the way I expressed myself in a hushed voice, but of course good old Kate, ears flapping, repeated loudly, 'Laquelle tu trouves une horreur?' ('Which do you find a horror?') I collapsed into giggles, made all the worse by the reverent hush and churchlike surroundings. PE was in hysterics and shaking like a road drill. He tried to hide his face, trying to have a reason to turn away and look at an object or painting, but his pursed lips were aquiver. I don't think I have wept with laughter like that since Andrew dropped the hymn sheet at Aunt Madge's cremation service. Kate was trying out all the old State chairs and playing hopscotch on the 'façade' so we returned to the teashop where the children had ice creams and looked like angels. When I said, 'What a nightmare,' PE said, 'Oh no,' only to follow it up with, 'a series of nightmares!'

Sunday

The day has come. I am very sad to leave Sergio. I know he doesn't need me any more and that he's well but I really hate to go away from him. Packing, passports . . . that's horrid.

Serge asleep and so must I. Up at 7.15 tomorrow, poor Papy is to be operated at 6 o'clock. Will kiss sweet old Serge goodnight.

Monday night, *London*

Well, here I am, on Papy's bed at 65 Deodar Road.* So lovely to have been able to be with Ma and Linda, had such a cosy afternoon and dinner at home.

---

* Cheyne Gardens had been sold. My father wanted a barge on the Thames; my mother wanted a swimming pool. So they found this house with the unpleasant name, *doo-dah*. Pa never bought the boat but Ma did have a swimming pool dug, where only she and Linda used to swim, and soon they were to return to Chelsea.

Arrived after a two-hour drive with PE, me being sick as a dog, then catching aeroplane, sitting next to a man who was terrified of take offs and landings. I said I was terrified of the bit in the middle, so our flight was full of promise. It wasn't a jet, so very bumpy, and I got very sweaty and sick, am prepared to aim into the *News of the World*! What a dreadful flight. I was all wobbly when I got out. Got a taxi to Putney. Found Linda at home. Ma already with Pa at the hospital. Sat with Linda in the garden, which was sunny and lovely, for an hour. Ma arrived looking lovely. She's grown her hair and looked very soft. The doctor saw Pa for an hour and half and said he would do his best! But only on his bad eye, and he could always use specs for reading with his head between his knees!

Went with Ma and Linda to the clinic, saw Pa who was so funny about his anaesthetist who had been in and probed him that afternoon, knowing nothing about his lung or anything. Pa said his face meant something to him but he couldn't quite place it. Maybe a Nazi on the Brittany coast! I was so glad to be around; I gave Pa Munkey to give him luck and he made us all laugh so much. He really is brave as I think he was dreading it. The anaesthetist has been in and given him a coffee and biscuits, which is a bit odd, as he was not even allowed breakfast! We went to the teashop for tea and buns whilst we waited. I sent Serge a telegram to say all was well so far, and love.

Tried to see Pa afterwards but he was asleep and the nurse said we couldn't see him till tomorrow. But whatever, he's safe, that's the only important thing.

Had lovely bangers and bacon and eggs with Ma and Linda and told them about 'le petit négro'. They thought it was so sad. Then we talked about *Madam Kitty* and Andrew and the trip to Berlin* and the Wall which sounds extraordinary – two hours to get past with visas and passports and special permissions, etc. And then, oh

---

* I think that Andrew was writing a script about Albert Speer and for that he had to cross the Berlin Wall.

dear, police see Andrew's telephone receiver in his car which hasn't worked for months, but no persuading them of that! He had to find a screwdriver and undo it all before they let him through. They found the hotel too, where Ma stayed before the war with her pa. It was Hitler's favourite hotel and Mme Kitty's real brothel site!

Off to sleep now. I'm so happy that all is well with Papy and I so hope all is well with Sergio as well. I really miss and need him. I do worry that he's being good. Not drinking too much or eating too much or got a packet of ciggies hidden away, but PE is there to take care of him, I know. I will write again tomorrow.

So cosy being with Ma and Linda again; I feel quite young again!

Tuesday

Andrew telephoned to know how Pa was. He sent a sweet telegram from Germany. He was very funny and his good self. It said, '*Heil mein brat!*' We all had a good giggle in funny German. I hope there was no eavesdropping on the telephone. Maybe he'll come through Paris in September. Anyway, it was lovely to talk to him and he was very relieved about Pa; he's a good boy.

Wednesday

A bad day for Papy. Very sore and depressed and tired, so I stayed with him until 10 o'clock at night. Read him P.G. Wodehouse and we wept with laughter.

Friday morning, *Paris*

Caught the night ferry so was in Paris at 9.15, an hour late. Luckily left a message to have a production car so Roland was waiting and I was at Billancourt for 25 to 10 – worked all day non-stop and then went to buy Scotch for PE's wife Ginette as I know she likes it, found a bottle and off I went to Avenue Marceau. It was a heaven to a lost soul! Ginette was so divine, everything in hand: drink, hot bath, comfort. She tried to ring what's-his-name, Pierre Barrière, and to my relief he never replied and we had what I'd hoped – a divine evening out together. We went off to that outdoor restaurant onto the Champs-Elysées – oh the beauty of real Paris, and sweet Ginette. What laugh, what fun. She insisted that I must have all the drink and food that was the richest and most sticky and sweet! So a sort of salmon fresh-and-smoked paté and a saucy beef thing with a bottle of wine, oh bliss! How we giggled about our boys together! What a hoot! She couldn't believe it! Then the owner of the restaurant invited us to Castel's. I asked if we were being kidnapped and off we went with a chum of his and Ginette and I staggered back at about 2 o'clock.

Next day, oh dear! I up at nine with terrible hangover, eyes wouldn't roll round, great thirst – not a pretty sight. I went off to work at ten, had a very hard day. Jean-Luc Bidot was his usual adorable self but oh dear, what a perfectionist: 'Que je peux faire mieux, que mon caractère dirait ça un peu plus sec, non?' ('Maybe I could do better, maybe my character would say this a little more drily, no?')

François Leterrier took me home and I asked if he was sure he was keeping my voice for Hélène (the character) and he said he was having me dubbed by a French girl as well and he would choose at the very last minute, i.e., maybe all the work was in vain.

Rang the lady at Coin du Bois to say I'd be at Vannes at 2 o'clock. I got a darling telegram from Serge, said, '17 kisses – Serge'. So sweet. I was so proud, I left it on Ginnette's table, and now it's still there!

31 August

The last day of the month. The holidays are over, and my last week home with Serge, PE and the children just flew by and since I'd got back it felt as if it was all over. Suddenly it got colder, Serge was very fed up of the Morbihan, PE was feeling homesick. London and Paris had broken the last week.

5 September, *in the airplane*

Here I am; off to England again to do the Russell Harty talk show. We are just about to take off. Said goodbye to Sergio and Kate in her nightdress this morning. They looked very sweet.

Serge's not too bad. Probably won't work as hard again. He's doing the music for my special TV show, plus his book. I had lunch yesterday with Michel Deville (*L'Ours et la Poupée*) who asked me to do his next film with Trintignant. I'm so excited and the script is so well written. I am a tart who falls in love with JLT and he with me. I help him to become a super stud and then I marry a very rich man I met Chez Prunier, but of course in the end I marry JLT (in a little straw hat). The last lines are 'Maybe we'll go and watch the trains' because that's how the film begins. But it's so pretty, so sweet. A sort of funny Shirley MacLaine part at last.

We left Brittany last Thursday much to Serge's relief. He really was fed up with the country. We stopped on the way to look at a very posh hotel where we signed the last page of the 'livre d'or' ('guest book') just under President Pompidou! Not bad!

Serge wanted to revisit his old farm, where he stayed just in the beginning the war, in the Sarthe; off we went. In this town. We found the village (rather pretty pinkish stone, unlike Brittany) without much trouble. Was so touching, he was so excited as we approached. 'In a minute we'll see the church spire!' he squealed – and we did! A little church in a village square with a café. Serge recognised the houses. 'This is where I bought my sweets . . . ' He led us to his farm; it was so tiny, he was amazed to find it so small. I saw from outside the room, which was la petite Thérèse's room, where Serge saw her let her hair down when he was twelve and she was nineteen. But no one was in. Serge spoke to the next-door neighbour who said the old man was dead, the eldest daughter paralyzed in hospital and the second daughter's husband died two months ago. They'd sold the house a couple of years ago. Serge said, 'D'you remember me, Lulu? I came here every year for five years.' Yes, she remembered. But all the family Serge knew were gone.

There was a man who was cutting the hedge. It turned out to be his farm now. Serge said timidly, 'I was here when I had . . . when X had the house'. 'Ca se peut,' ('Could be') the man said coldly. 'Peut-être, peut-être pas.' ('Maybe, maybe not.') He didn't recognise him and he didn't ask us in to see the house. So we just peeped through the windows and Serge said it had changed.

We went to the square and PE and I went into the church where Serge had painted cardboard angels one Christmas and the vicar had hung them on each side of the church, not knowing it was a little Jewish boy who would soon be hunted down.

Serge recognised the dreadful plaster Catholic statues of St Theresa and Mary and was happy. But no vicar any more. The iron-monger lady didn't remember him. She said she was there fifty years but children remember old faces and old faces forget children. Mme X is dead; everyone was in the cemetery except for Thérèse's brother, now the mayor.

We went to visit him. Serge said how sad it was that everyone is dead and gone. But, Jean said, they'd be 100 years old by now, of course dead – and he was right. Poor Serge. I think he regret-ted having gone back. We had a drink with Jean who tutored Serge and who'd kept his drawing of him ploughing with the horses. They remembered the old horse's name, Mouton, and laughed. I took their photo with my Pola. I thought that Serge's friend would like that and Serge wrote, 'To my friend Jean in memory of the old days', and I took one of Serge and him for Serge. He asked us if we had lunch and we lied and said yes. There seemed no point in bothering him. He was very kind but very matter-of-fact and not at all sentimental. Maybe he's right, but Serge was sad, I think, and once again thought sadly of his father and dying. When we got home the children were all there and Raymonde

1973

179

had cleaned up the house and Serge and I were very happy to be home again.

* * *

His sisters, Liliane and Jacqueline, had been hidden away in a convent near Limoges. But the religious institutions for boys didn't want to keep Serge; it was too dangerous, so he had to go elsewhere as a boarder near Oradour. He even spent a few days and nights in the trees. The other children came by bringing him things to eat like in a fairy tale, Little Red Riding Hood. Jacqueline told me afterwards that this episode only lasted a couple of days, while their parents who had been denounced were stopped and interrogated. But Serge made me believe it was much longer. He said wearing the yellow star was like being a sheriff. Jacqueline said that they were all conscious of the danger but Serge spoke about it as if it had been a game, an adventure. But much later when he found himself attacked as a Jew at the time of *Aux Armes, Et Cætera*, he became vindictive because, after all, their survival had been a miracle. Michel Droit of the Academy Française wrote in 1979 that Serge's presence and works were like being forced to breathe in exhaust pipe fumes – in other words, a sort of poison, after which Droit was accused of racism. Serge found himself for the first time on the political page of the paper and he made out that he was delighted.

* * *

Now the airplane is landing, will write again tonight. I wish Serge had come with me but he couldn't because of work.

Oh, what pride! In this month's *Union* I am given as an example of a small bosom! It made my day! As I was flipping through the letter section I saw it loud and clear. How lovely, now no more complexes – much!

13 September

Got back from the UK. Very puffy and hung-over.

The Russell Harty show was sheer hell owing to my nerves, and the seating arrangement. I was so drunk, so absolutely pissed, that when my parents were due to arrive, to be in the audience, I asked the girl who does the arranging to say to them, 'Jane is so frightened, so nervous, I think it is better that you stay away from her, in here, for example' (indicating a projection room). She added that for me to see them beforehand would put me in a worse state. But I believe they were placed in the audience in any case. When I saw my mother looking edgy and angry, I wondered what I had done wrong. I thought it must have been the show, but I'd said such nice things about them.

'Were they the shockable, upper-middle-class parents?'

'Oh no,' I said.

And told them about Papy saying, 'It's not too late to turn back,' on the way to my wedding. And Ma saying, 'When's the next?' after Charlotte, and being so pleased. I'd been drunk and that was my problem, but at least I was a bit funny because of it, and I'd got through my song as well.

Ma and Pa had been put in the 'régie' where Serge always sits on my programmes. A little box with a TV in it. Papy was divine and said he would rather have been in the box and that it was all lovely, but Ma was terribly hurt and we had a row at 235 King's Road. She said that she's got the impression I was ashamed of her and her being an actress. I hadn't even been asked what my mother was! I told them at the production lunch that my mother was an actress and she'd helped me get my first job because she took me to a party with Binkie Beaumont. And that her name was Judy Campbell. But then, in the few minutes' interview, I wasn't asked anything about her, or my films for that matter, or anything! Except 'Je T'Aime', and that was a bit outrageous.

At the dinner it was sheer hell because I saw Ma hurt and

bitter and sad, and it was all so she wouldn't be hurt. When she had asked if she could come to see it, I'd said it will be lovely to know that you are both in the audience. So why on earth would I deliberately put them in a box? I couldn't understand why it was all such drama when it was so clear that it was a misunderstanding. She said the song was lovely, leaving out anything about the interview, and said what a pity they didn't ask about my films, but I could tell, even the next day on the way to the airport, that she was still hurt. And I had an immense hangover. Papy took me to see his paintings at the 'Artists of Chelsea' so I bought the one of Serge.*

I was so sorry to have hurt Ma; I always seem to do it these days but not when Serge is there. I seem to bungle it on my own. I haven't had a row with Ma for ages, then, bang! these last two times, it's terrible, I had meant well, and had done, I thought, everything to please. So it was a very bug-eyed me who rolled into Orly Airport. I was so relieved to be with Serge and in a country that likes me.

Since then, silence, but two divine letters from Papy. I wrote one back today. He really keeps me going, he is so funny. Got a film offer because of the programme, which went out on Sunday, apparently it was very 'ME', whatever that is!

Kate's first day at school. The grown-up school. She was very excited and has come back full of it. Never have I seen a child so pleased to go to school. Others were howling but not Kate, she was in the door so fast! She came back from JP Cassel's with 'aoûtats', a sort of harvest mite, I think, like a ringworm. Charming! But she looked very happy after spending a weekend with a boy so there we are.

I'm trying to fit in Mocky's film with Pierre Clementi in the four-week gap in between the Trintignant film. I don't know whether it will be possible, almost too good to be true! It always happens that

* My father was a wonderful painter. I think that's what will last from the Birkin family, his paintings and my sister's sculptures, more than my singing or my films.

way. The day I signed the last film (*Projection Privée*), Mocky asked me to be in his.

The children are watching TV. Serge is working on the title song for *Projection Privée* which Françoise Hardy will sing. It sounds very pretty.

Saw the doctor with Serge yesterday, who said he must never smoke again and that his coronary artery is still blocked. And ciggy smoke will be terrible. (I had rung Mme Hazan to get her to ring Bensaid before we arrived and warn him that Serge was hoping he'd say yes to cigarettes so he was very firm.)

October, *Venice*

I am sitting in the most divine drawing room looking over the Grand Canal. The motorboats are chugging by, it's 11 o'clock and the winter sun is blinding my eyes. I've had to draw the curtains to go on writing. Serge is having a bath, miracles do happen! And I am sitting here alone in this vast blue rococo room and feeling very very happy. Serge and I are at last on our honeymoon, and all the nightmare of his accident seems so far away. La Salute hasn't changed and so many memories from five and a half years ago are coming back. Serge and I will try to find our hotel (where we were the first time) this afternoon.

We arrived at 7 o'clock this morning and poor Serge had hardly slept at all, and me barely. Only enough for a ghastly dream where Andrew had shown us a terribly haunted house on an island, which was condemned, and I knew it was going to fall down and kill the children Andrew was playing with in the ruins. It was so high and towering and I was always running to save the children – it was terrifying.

It was freezing when we stepped off the train but sunny. I spent a moment in the sun, waiting for the boat to take us to the Gritti. Venice looked so beautiful and all the colours were waking up with the workmen.

We wondered what our suite would be like. Well, it was all pastel and pink and pretty but somehow not what we had hoped for. Serge was disappointed and asked if we could see another. They said yes, but not before ten so we had breakfast in a little dining room looking out onto the canal. On termination we got another room and I thought it was going to be just the blue version of the first. But no! A divine, eccentric, very Venetian sitting room; high ceiling and grand pale apricot bedroom with a big bed and romantic nude painting in a golden frame – in other words, sexy! A marble bathroom ... really, it couldn't have been more beautiful and I was secretly so happy to have one big bed. (Two little ones joined so Serge can jog!) It's so much more romantic so I am happy. Serge is such a perfectionist and I could see he had been disappointed but now he's happy as a lark. The proof, he's had a bath!! Now he's in his new trousers and looks very sweet. Now he's taken them off again and is back in jeans. He says they were too smart.

Saturday

Woke up very late. Serge and I had lunch in a lovely fish restaurant by the Rialto Bridge. Tiny little crabs and green beans, etc. Of course Serge had all the things that were not allowed but, as he says, it's a holiday.

After lunch we went off in the gondola to the Ghetto in the old part of Venice. The synagogue was shut (of course, it was Saturday). We saw the Main Square, full of tiny high houses; they could only build up.

A little gift shop with an old man making jewels. I bought a Star of David for Serge's ma, in a pink cotton and plastic box, so touching. I think Serge got a sort of affinity with the little children playing. It wasn't sad – the sun was shining – but it was a very different sort of Venice, very poor; even I felt nostalgic. It was a beautiful afternoon, blue, blue sky and we were very happy. Serge was in good spirits. I am just back from the hairdresser's, all very curly!

Monday

Woke up last, Serge brought me breakfast in bed at 11 o'clock. We
went off to Harry's Bar for lunch. We went in a motorboat as it was
half an hour away and we had lunch in the sun. On the way back we
went to an island with a monastery on it, where all the monks were
having a siesta so we couldn't go in.

Such a beautiful winter sun! Venice was sparkling and gay. We
put off at the Danieli and asked if our room of three years ago had
been modernised like Mme Hazan had said. It happened, apparently. It was room 10, green and dark, only spent two days in it on
the way back from Sarajevo, it was very erotic and baroque. They
didn't make the champagne and peach cocktail in winter, like the
one Serge sent me when I was miserable in the Danieli, five years
ago during *Slogan*.

We walked to St Mark's Square and I saw the sign for the aquar-
ium that Serge had wanted to see. Not very jolly fish and piped
music, and then it all had to go wrong. I had the stupidity to look
at a poster with George Segal on it. I think he's a good actor but he
is not my cup of tea at all, and I say, 'Oh, what a good actor, and
Glenda Jackson, they were in *A Touch of Class*.'

I thought Serge would be interested as he'd been asked to write
the lyrics, which he had completely forgotten. I don't know why he
was so furious but he turned against me. He said I'd mentioned that
actor too many times and he was a rotten actor anyway. He thought
he should be an extra. No personality. All actors bore him, etc., etc. I
walked off in a huff and then said far too much, which I didn't mean
as nastily as I said it, but I remembered that he'd been an actor, and
he had not said no. Anyway, I wish I could have the afternoon back
again and never mention that stupid film again but it all became
such a thing. I was grumpy. We went back to our old hotel the Feni-
cia (from *Slogan* days) in silence, now I'm back at our current hotel
still in silence watching the water from my beautiful room, waiting
for a telephone call to Paris. What a stupid end to a lovely day . . . I

wish I knew how to make it better again.

All is OK. We said sorry together, five hours later, just before dinner.

Serge said the 'par'.

And I said the 'don'.

Wednesday

We are leaving today. What an amazing night we had, a real honeymoon, just like the old days. So I'm writing this in the divine sitting room and bedroom feeling sad at leaving it all, it's been so lovely, even better than I expected, and I'm a bit dismal at the thought of going, but of course, Serge has had an idea, a very strange one. We stopped for a drink at the Danieli last night and Serge asked them if room 10 was free for this afternoon? So instead of being kicked out of here at midday we will have an extra afternoon at the Danieli in our old room. What a way to go! Night train tonight at 9.30 so just one more afternoon, we must make the most of it . . .

Tuesday

Mood over! Now in Évian with Serge and the children in a lovely apartment. Everyone has got bronchitis now, thanks to good self's generosity!

Did 'Sport en Fête' as guest star. Bought lots of books about Tim Birkin and showed photo of Ma. She would've been pleased had she seen the show.

* * *

A cousin of my father's and a well-known racing driver, he'd won the 24 Hours at Le Mans in an Alfa Romeo and died several years later of septicaemia. He had a green Bentley, a moustache and a spotted scarf. Very chic. In England when I say my name, people ask, 'Any relation to Tim Birkin?'

* * *

Serge saw his two children. I wish his wife would come with them Monday so they'd know Charlotte. I know I'd love his son who has slanty eyes like Serge. Ma and Pa are in Spain with Angie* and Ma comes to Paris for Easter, which will be lovely.

* * *

The two children Serge had had with his second wife Béatrice Pancrazzi, Natacha and Paul. Serge had paid an enormous alimony after his divorce but he still didn't have the right to see his children without their mother present.

---

* Pempie's sister, Angela Laycock.

1974

March, *Rue de Verneuil*

Here I am, in my little room, which is a dream. I've got my sofa back, so it's really cosy. We're off to dinner with the very red moustached Comte d'Anvers (who I first cottoned onto apropos of anti-death penalty stuff, which I hoped he'd fix for me, prison visiting, etc., but no, just cocktail parties). Serge doesn't want to go but is being gallant. I am now a member of the French anti-death penalty committee. I did it on my tod. Plus letter to Mr Pompidou. Very grand and full of morality, ending, 'Je vous prie, Monsieur le President, vous qui avez leurs vies entre vos mains, d'avoir pour eux de la compassion chrétienne.' ('I beg of you, Monsieur le President, you who have their lives in your hands, to have some Christian compassion for them.') Not a word he can say against that! I was aided by good old Serge, despite his disbelief in the cause. He did correct my spelling and the 'compassion chrétienne' bit was his. I was proud of him.

Le Mouton Enragé comes out Wednesday. Was very proud to have Trintignant's name on my photo and my name on his! Romy Schneider must be hopping mad!

Serge did his analysis this morning. His diet is murder for him. All he loves he can't have but all he can bores him stiff.

Serge has now read me *Adolph* (not the one you think about) and *Madame Bovary* – we were both in tears, Serge could barely go on. We finished *Le Désert des Tartares* last night. Sad to think we had dinner with Buzzati the year before he died in Milan.

Kate and Charlotte are being lovely, a good 'époque'. They now play together, which is wonderful, and Kate is teaching Charlotte to write so she 'won't be backward like me', Kate proclaimed. It was so sweet and shows she has no malice to Charlotte, who is far more cunning and lies like mad! She is irresistibly funny.

Gilbert C of A will from now on be known as Basil Brush (well-known TV puppet of foxy character), a very 'right-wing gent'! I said 'dégueulasse' ('disgusting', not knowing all the right-wing chaps were chums of his). And I said I thought it was very impolite of Pompidou not to read my letter. 'Oh, how sweet!' Tapping of kneecaps, kissing of hand, dear, dear, every good course is like this, even the Panda Club! The PDG ('The Count') started to say he'd something important to discuss with my good self so he drove me home and on the way he said, 'Annule ton rendezvous pour 3 heures, j'aime les femmes qui savent ce qu'elles veulent,' ('Put off your rendezvous for 3 o' clock, I love women who know what they want') and then he touched my arm at the traffic lights and he added, 'On pourrait faire tant de choses pour le WWF.' (petits animaux). ('We could do so much for the wildlife fund.' (little animals))

13 March, *Saint-Tropez*

In the night train, a rather sweet sleeper. I am on the sort of first floor looking down on Serge on the sofa below. He is reading a book about mountains for the Sport en Fête on Sunday. We're off to Saint-Tropez for two days for TV.

Read the children stories before leaving, *Cinderella* to Kate and *Miss Moppet* for Charlotte.

Arrived Saint-Tropez this morning, I hardly slept and Serge was very tired too. Beautiful sky. (I'm now in bed with a burning sun-blistered face after one hour in the sun!) We went from Saint-Raphaël to Saint-Trop in the car with a group who turned out to be rather sweet. We pushed off to the Tahiti plage but the whole place was shut up. Workmen banging and no one 'au courant' ('aware') of our reservation. A sort of zombie told us in a very unfriendly way that he had not heard of our booking and that the patron was in Marseille for the day and that the patronne was in the bath! So we went off in a huff, straight to the Byblos. Memories, memories . . . the receptionist remembered our favourite room number from six years ago, so voilà.

Rang home to find out if all was OK and poor Charlotte has my cough and cold and a very high temperature. I rang the doctor and implored her to go and visit (she didn't want to and suggested that Charlotte came to her). I've phoned twice since and all is well. Kate asked after Serge on the phone and sent him kisses for the first time; I was so pleased.

Claude François (that rather horrid satiny teenybopper singer of 35 and still jumping) who is unfortunately very popular was there. Anyway, Serge and I wanted him for our *Top* because he'd been surprisingly nice to me when I met him at *Taratata*.* He said I was his cup of tea! So he said he would do it, but give and take. Will Jane do something in my magazine which is a sort of sexy magazine that I'm starting? But Guy Bourdin takes all the photos so, la classe. It's called *Absolu*. I said OK and an interview was given by good self to an ex-girlfriend of Serge who I was very against, as he slapped her face once, and knocked it off with her sister, by the by! She turned out to be very nice and I did a long interview. Two hours of chat, rather intimate stuff about my adolescence complexes and theories, etc. This girl had a rather butch chum who wanted to take my photograph to illustrate the article. I said fine but not sexy, maybe as a bloke? In a very strict tie something for contrast. So it was vaguely fixed and I went off. A week later, Claude François' secretary rang to talk about the photos. So I said, 'Oh, not nudies though.' And she said, 'There must be some mistake, Claude said it was OK, Jane said yes.'

I said not at all, let him ring me and I will explain. So he rang as well! He said Guy Bourdin wants to take some beautiful pictures

---

* They are TV shows.

of me, but going further than anything I've done before. I said 'not nude'. He said, 'Guy Bourdin is a genius, we've got a fantastic studio, with real light and a fresh-air look and everything.'

I said that if he'd read my article he'd understand. I hate complete nudity, I think it's a bore. I don't find it one jot sexy. I do photos that are sexy, not nude. Denim in a raincoat, etc.

He said that his magazine was not perverted.

I said I was!

He said he wasn't surprised. So I said I do photos that were nude, saw nothing (like in this week's Spectacle Page in *Elle* where I'm nude but crouching so nothing is seen, pure).

He began to be rather unpleasant and said, 'Oh that's nothing new.'

I said it was especially for *Elle* magazine, a double page in the cinema pages with close-ups of my knee, hand, foot and eye, like a beauty photo in *Vogue*. I've never seen that done on an actress before.

And I said, 'So you want me to go further than I've ever gone? Not pubic hair by any chance?'

'Why not?' he said. 'Why not legs open?'

I was aghast, yes that's what he wanted. What was more beautiful than woman's . . .? I was like a ripe fruit ready to be plucked. What horror. And I said never never that I would show between my legs. It was mine and I wanted left mine and he said, 'Tu trompes ton public, alors.' ('You're lying to your public, then.')

I nearly fainted. I said no actress opens her legs for a magazine. He said that in America they did and that France was three or four years behind and his magazine *Absolu* was absolu, etc. Jargon about a member of the House of Commons' interview, a psychiatrist and me. I said who else? Well, I said models may do it but I would not, even for Guy Bourdin who I like very much. Clo Clo the Maniac Megalomaniac continued, 'Do the séance, you never know, between Bourdin and you there could be an atmosphere.'

I said I would do a sexy photo as long as it was understood that

I was NOT going to be 'nu intégral' ('fully nude'). He said I could choose the photos and say no to the ones I regretted doing.

'Serge will come too,' I said, 'he makes me more at ease.'

'Oh yes, maybe you can be persuaded to go as far as you can,' he replied.

The conversation of a madman. I knew I should say no after what he said about pussy. What a nerve.

Today I rang Guy from Saint-Trop. I asked him what his idea was and he said to make me naked asleep and legs open on the sofa with a wedding dress tossed on the back of the sofa. QUELLE HOR-REUR. He said his original idea was too naughty to say. I insisted he did say, so he said, well, me naked, legs apart with TV in between my legs and a great big open fanny on the screen or God knows what. I died.

'The woman automat.'

I said I couldn't do it. I telephoned Clo Clo afterwards and said I couldn't. Or as a man (Guy had liked the idea). He said the idea of me as a man or in a dress was of no interest.

I change from 'tu' to 'vous' in an instant and he said, 'À bientot,' cool as a cucumber. Vexed, was the word. The man was a loon. Of course he won't do our *Top* now, so Serge phoned the Carpentiers to say to ring him and find out. We couldn't care less. Blackmail on my pussy, we were flabbergasted.

* * *

In the end he did do our show with the Carpentiers. He arrived at the set in a Rolls-Royce and I danced with the Claudettes, an extraordinarily difficult dance, but he'd been gentlemanly, clad in silver satin.

* * *

Friday night

Am very tired as my bronchitis was worse today. I nearly collapsed on the beach, coughing, so we got a doctor who said I had 'bronchite chronique' ('chronic bronchitis') and gave me an injection in my bottom. The fever has gone and he's coming to give me another tomorrow. We finished the TV stuff anyway, in a bed in the square in Saint-Tropez. Singing 'C'est La Vie Qui Veut Ça' with Serge behind a newspaper.

Got a super review in *France-Soir* for *Mouton*: 'Merveilleuse JB'! and the *Figaro*. Serge said he was proud of me, it made my day. Bumped into Charlotte Rampling for the second time this week in a very good fish restaurant.

Memories again, lovely sun. What a pity to be sick. Serge very divine and loving.

Saturday

Serge and I on the bar balcony looking onto the pool. Lovely sun. Had temperature, but better.

Lunch in the old port. Saw *France-Soir*, which had an even better critic. I shall stick them in my diary in case I never ever get such kind ones again! Warm sun warm hair, Saturday in the sun with Serge, I am happy.

A journalist asked me my formula for happiness. I said it was 'un état d'âme' ('a state of mind'). I don't know the formula, but whatever it is, I am in it. I know it's not work, it may be having children? I know it's love for me!

Got a phone call to see Otto Preminger Wednesday; not very excited, as I know that sort of test is never the one I get. America frightens me, England has been cold to me, I wanted France, because France has wanted me. Maybe I feel happy and secure, as if I've been adopted. I'm not jealous in France, as my position is unreasonable. If the French girl gets a part I think, 'Of course that's fair' as most of the things I did would've been better done by others. Except *Mouton*. I knew that was mine, a small part, loving, losing, funny and sad, not pretentious and with better actors and actresses than me. I had to be good, everyone was on my side and helping me.

Tuesday, *return from Saint-Tropez*

'Tu es nourrie et logée,' ('You're fed and housed') said Serge tonight. I said I haven't got anything. Because my room is private he has to go poking his nose into my papers and saying it was a mess.

A., it isn't a mess, and B., even if it was I don't know why it is any of his business. In most houses there is the sitting room, which is cosy. In this house there is a beautiful museum and even if I put my basket on the piano he says I scratch it. The fact that I found the tapestries and gave them to him and the rats and as many monkeys as I can find has no importance.

It's all his and I have no right to say anything. And perched on a chair, scared to break it if he's in the room and I never go in alone. I stay in the kitchen or in my room, which I thought was mine and where I bought the curtains, so why does he blow me up? It's my patchwork that I bought, so why has he got the right to say it's torn? I paid for it. All the details are mine and I like it that way. It's only cuttings, papers and bills etc., in a heap, so why does he have the right to say it's dirty? It certainly isn't. He is the one who's filthy. No bath in four months at least and filthy black feet. He's got papers in his library, so why can't I? He says he's my secretary; why doesn't he teach me how to fill in the BNP cheques? I have no idea about money. He says he's got the goodness to house and feed me and my children but, good God, one of the children is his, and when he took me on, he took on Kate too, so why does he turn round now against me?

Probably he has rooted around in my drawers for secret letters. He has already steam-opened one I left on the table to send to Andrew and he opens most of my letters anyway. But it's true; I don't really belong anywhere in the house. He's got to live with an untidy girl and I've got to live with an object maniac, which is tough for me too.

He's popped in to say 'oh là là là là', but I'm being grumpy. I'm going to get a cottage of my own so when he comes to stay in my house my rules go. But I've got no cash and the lease is soon to run out for Cheyne Row. John has never paid anything for Kate so I'm hardly in a position for land investments. When will I have enough cash to buy a house of my own? Super weekends, and, even humble, at last be able to decorate it and have a real place I've done myself.

I'm full of self-pity. Six years with a man who throws 'tu es logée' ('you're fed and housed'). I think that's a bit much; some people would have married the woman. I have the impression that after ten years he'll say the same thing and I'll realise I don't count at all for him.

Wednesday, *Deauville*

Oh, what a laugh! Took the children to the stables for a ride on one of the horses. An old guy said in a very offhand and unfriendly way that Kate was too small for the horses and the only horse she could ride was Castor and he had twisted his hoof, so we couldn't stay on him long. We had to go and Kate got two rounds, falling off the saddle which no one could tighten up. I got Charlotte on too, but she just sat right off to the right so I put her on after Kate and it was so uncomfortable she begged to get off. I thought I'd give a tip and they socked me for 20 francs! For five minutes on the lame and nasty pony. The snow is an hour or so away, so no chance of la piscine, as it's outdoors and freezing. Serge said you bet the golf course only had one hole and that it was blocked up by a mole looking for the telephone!

So Kate, Charlotte and I went off on two bikes I'd hired, Charlotte pillion on mine, and Kate, poor thing, pushing as the chain was slack and it didn't work on anything but the tarmac, i.e., main roads and it had no brakes. There was no way of stopping. Oh yes, one, and she did it, breaking my fingernail with a great loss of parental blood! We did some roly-poly sliding downhill with some village kids and then home to the doctor. He says Kate must stay in tomorrow and Charlotte must get back on her pills. I still have asthmatic bronchitis and I'm back on cortisone and an X-ray on Saturday if it doesn't clear up.

Dinner in our apartment, which was very nice. Kate was sick all over the supper table just as a horrid sausage advertisement was on television. Serge thought it was because of the sausage advertisement and was very cross that the poor thing has caught Charlotte's bug. 'On dirait que le pâté va tomber sur la table,' screamed Serge. And Kate vomited all over the chicken cutlets.

Friday

Oh, what fun! Serge, kiddies and I arrived here at Clos de Sadex after an hour's car drive (Charlotte was sick all over my arm). Oh dear, oh dear, what a laugh! Two vast blank rooms like in Yugoslavia, entirely Spanish staff that serves breakfast at 7 till 10, lunch 12–2 and dinner 7–9! Terrible cold dining room with a pansy Spanish waiter who, far from recognising Serge, offered him regional wine and water for kiddies. Serge shut the weighty green shutters and one fell off – thank God we were on the ground floor. Serge and I nearly died giggling, getting it on again. Him in the flowerbed, like Romeo, with a shutter on his head and me, Juliet, lugging it up onto the pins with two howling children collapsing with mirth at their stupid, aged parents! When Serge had said, 'Merde, j'ai fait tomber un volet' ('Shit, I broke the shutter'), I hadn't believed him. True, true.

Monday, 1 April, *Lausanne*

Here we all are, bathing in luxury! Sweet Serge, fed up with country life, has paid for the most enormous splendid suite in Lausanne at the hotel Le Beau-Rivage. Our suite takes up all the first-floor corner. The children have a double bedroom and bathroom. There is an enormous sitting room, a little boudoir and another bedroom and bathroom. There is a big balcony and a terrace leading from our room. Serge looked in the rococo hall and he was in paradise. Forgotten the rustic hell of the country, the miserable lakeside hotel. He is now moving around the chic bars of the biggest palace in Lausanne.

We went off in a motorboat with Serge driving this afternoon. You don't need a licence, as it doesn't go very fast. It was great fun. Good old Serge! He always finds something super to finish off the holidays. (I wrote to stop the killing of baby seals, there was a demand on Swiss TV.) Tomorrow is Serge's birthday.

2 April

Just came back from jolly dinner with the children: birthday cake, candles and presents. Switched on the television to see a newsflash. Georges Pompidou is dead. At 9 o'clock, he died in his Paris home. Kate collapsed in rather melodramatic tears and Serge and I were absolutely flabbergasted. What a surprise. Poor old Pompidou! I think everyone was laughing about his piles – 'Many a bad thing is hidden behind a pile' and 'Don't let the pile be like the tree, stop you from seeing the forest'. On the news it said he was completely lucid about his illness but didn't believe he was going to die. Whilst poor Pompidou was dying, Serge, Kate, Charlotte and I were eating

birthday cake. Serge is very happy with his presents, Charlotte gave
him a white rose and a pair of socks and Kate gave him a boot made
of metal to put watches on, rather like a soft leather child's boot by
Dali, with studs on the sole that we found in the Rue de l'Université.
I gave him an ivory lady with a baby clinging onto her, Japanese,
that I had found before we left. I fell in love with her and I hope
he will too. She is so perfect and her baby has a tutu. Kate made a
birthday card that is so like him. I'll put it in my diary. All the radio
programmes are full of the news 'mort de Pompidou' ('Pompidou's
death') on Serge's birthday.

We did boiled eggs, painted blue, pink; salami, viande des grisons,
chocs, donuts. The children were very gay and so was Serge. Lovely
day in the sun. Charlotte's face was as red as a tomato. I'm afraid for
her health, a little temperature.

Serge thinks it's dangerous for France, Pompidou being dead. It's
rather sad that we were all giggling about his fatness, saying he had
been eating too much when he was really dying, poor thing.

Friday, 12 April, *Paris*

It is 5.30 in the morning. I am alone again. B made poor Serge go to the American hospital. We had been out to dinner and to see the *The Night Porter*, a rather boring film but great reviews. Serge had taken one of his pink pills in the cinema and when we got home at about 00.30, he said his chest hurt around his heart. We talked about it over a herbal tea. It went on hurting and he took another pill, which did no good. And at about 1 o'clock, he rang Paul-Émile who rang B. It all took ages. In the meantime, Serge was in a very good mood and wondering if it was all worth it. B rang, and said he should come over to us, as a pain that had lasted one and a half hours was not to be treated lightly. Serge rushed around, washing his feet in the bidet, so they wouldn't pong. I dried them and he covered himself in scent. He said I'd better open the door so that when B came, Serge wouldn't look too sprightly in the circumstances and B wouldn't be cross at being called out so late. B arrived and he said it was sensible to go to the hospital in case something should happen in the night. Serge protested, B insisted. I thought we would never forgive ourselves if something did happen. Another attack would be so awful and that would be two months in hospital. So at last Serge said yes. I collected his toothbrush, pyjamas and Munkey in a little case and B called for an ambulance (B went off in a taxi). Serge was furious.

Serge had an electrocardiogram done at once. The English doctor could see nothing different from the ones he had had before and said there was no sign of any attack, but for security he must stay and have all the tests done tomorrow. Serge was so depressed and furious as he thinks it was melodramatic, but he doesn't panic easily.

I have just rung the hospital. S hasn't slept. He has even taken a Mandrax. I can't bear being without him. The panic of all those weeks in the American hospital. I do hope he can come back for Easter Sunday. He keeps promising to give up smoking. He's gone right back to three packets a day, whatever he says. Why risk it for a puff or drink? But poor Serge just says, 'Maintenant je suis bon à rien' ('Now I'm good for nothing') in a sad voice.

I hadn't been very nice at dinner. I was in a bad mood. I'm feeling neglected and it always happens after that. I felt rotten afterwards.

* * *

June, *Aix-en-Provence*

We were in Provence for the shoot of *Lucky Pierre (La Moutarde Me Monte Au Nez):* my parents, the children, the nanny, Serge and me. When I met Claude Zidi for the part of the starlet with a sort of Kissinger love story, I said, 'You should have Brigitte Bardot, it's much funnier if it's a real star,' and Claude replied, 'After this film, you will be a real star,' and he was right – the film beat every record, which made Pierre Richard and me an extraordinarily famous couple even in Russia. The shoot was lovely and all the photos of me and Serge and the children in the hammock were taken in that little hotel in the garden, where we lived.

During an improvised scene with Ava, my friend and hairdresser, the caravan door came down on my face. They'd been using that same door for gags all morning. Some actor hadn't turned up so they thought, 'We'll just do the scene with Jane and Ava.' The car-avan door was made of mahogany and it opened up my entire eyebrow. Pierre Richard told me that I'd given him more than any other actress, because in France, when you have an accident, it's better not to be the one that's the victim. The shoot had to stop, but the other actors were on overtime and were paid a fortune. Pierre was able to buy himself a sports car! After a week of coughing up, they begged me to come back, sticking my fringe down over my stitches with glue for the press conference.

* * *

Here I am in bed, stitches out of my eyebrow but still unable to frown. Exactly a week since that stupid caravan door fell on my head. What panic! I never knew that blood has a smell and a special way of trickling and a terrible way of being warm. Even with my eyes tight shut, I knew it was blood, not tears, running down my nose. I could hear myself screaming as if I was a witness, pushing the lady away as she slammed on the ice. The self-pity and fright of being ugly. People kept saying 'Oh là là', and 'Oh la vache' ('Oh damn'), so I know it wasn't pretty. Someone said it was deep and 'get an ambulance' and undid my shirt and took off my sheriff's boots. Claude (Zidi) was so kind and held my hand in the ambulance all the way and he stayed with me while they X-rayed my head and decided on the surgeon. I asked Ava to find Serge, as they were not going to operate until 2.30. I was terrified of being scarred for life. Claude was wonderful. Claude Berri rang and said I was in the hands of the best doctor, otherwise he would've flown in his surgeon from Paris.

Serge came at last. I asked him to have a look under the bandage. He said it was deep but short and gave me a kiss. A sweet man came in from the next room with some flowers. It was a lift to the morale, 'de la part d'un fan' ('on behalf of a fan')! I asked Serge to tell Papy where I was. Just before the operation, they were going to give me a general anaesthetic. I wanted to speak to Papy before I went. He came and I was wheeled off into a bright room, leaving Serge and Papy in my hospital room. I went home that night, very balmy, with Pa and Serge, and a bag of truffles from Serge in my hand, a patch on my eye and blood all over my sheriff's costume.

Now I know what Papy feels like with one eye. It's awful! Three days of being a Cyclops was quite enough for me. Had my stitches out and the insurance doctor says eight days more, so back to the film on Monday.

Undated

The Pierre Richard has come out and Chazal has been practically sweet to me in his critic. I must send him some candy! It's already number one in the first two days (beating the *The Sting*) which is a record breaker.

Charlotte is happy playing all day with popping beads. She will have to be very rich or an actress later on! Raymonde said she leapt from her pushchair into the road to pick up a 10-centime piece that someone had dropped.

Serge is so proud! It's become a running joke and I don't know how much of it she's doing on purpose, but it's very funny and she's playing along.

Thursday

Serge is far happier now he's back in Paris. A veritably changed man. He is writing his book about the man who poops and a film script.

By Monday, I hope Serge and I will go camping in my little grey mouse house. I can't believe I got it for 15,000, my tiny rectory at Cresseveuille. It makes me so happy. I will paint it pale pink and paper every room in Liberty print; it will be a dream. When I think back on that funny Sunday afternoon at Deauville and the man in the agency who said, 'Yes I've got this little rectory that came on the market yesterday', I thought it might be sinister and bound to be too expensive, as I wanted to buy it myself, with no help from Serge. We drove up the road past a tiny church and graveyard in the valley and there it was! Tiny and grey, not a fake beam in sight. Tiny shutters and minuscule little rooms, a little staircase and about four tiny rooms upstairs. There was a bird's nest behind the shutter. It was all magical and it was love at first sight. I said ALL one is NOT supposed to say to the house agent! Serge said that resources could be found and not to let it go. During the week we rang up saying 'counting on you' and on Saturday evening, from Aix-en-Provence, I rang up and it was mine! I sent the cheque off immediately, thus ruined at the BNP until the money from this film goes in. I want all the flowers pink and white, a girl's dream. If only I could be in by Christmas, what heaven!

* * *

Before I bought my little house in Cresseveuille in Normandy, I was looking for a cottage in the Morvan. So off we went, Serge and I and the children in a chauffeured car to the Hotel de la Poste.

In Avallon, we all had rather coy room names like 'Héloïse et Abélard'. We put the children to bed and Serge and I went on to dinner in a very luxurious restaurant. Albert, the sommelier, was very gracious, with his suit and tails, pouring the wine solemnly. We thought he was fun, which is why, when he suggested that we have a last glass in the bar over the road from the hotel, Serge immediately said yes, so we met at the bar. Albert was no longer dressed as before, suddenly saucy, with a fitted roll-neck jersey. He'd become a chum, and we all took it in turns to pay for rounds. 'Oh, this time it's on me.' 'No, no, it's on me.'

Albert suggested that we went for a last glass 'round at his place', so there we were in his little Citroën, me in front, Serge behind, lost in the formidable Morvan fog. I whispered to Serge, 'Serge, Albert is touching me up!' He replied desperately, 'Let it go, Jeannette, we're lost!' We entered Albert's house, donning felt slippers, going, 'Shush', so as not to wake his wife. We were quite hungry so Albert took us up to the top of his house, showing the way with his torch that he sometimes shone on our faces, opening bedroom doors and waking people up, saying, 'Look who's at my place, Gainsbourg and Birkin!'

At the top of the house he unhooked a ham that was suspended in a cage, and I understood that it was Albert's winter reserve. When he came down, with us and the ham, he picked up a few plates, served the ham and while we were drinking local digestifs, suddenly he grabbed a hunting rifle that had been hooked on the wall. He pointed it at Serge and said, 'Now get up on the chair and sing "L'Ami Caouette"'.* Poor Serge started to obey then, thank God, Albert's wife came storming in, furious to have been woken up; to see her reserve of ham on our plates; and to discover her husband, gun in hand, with two guests climbing onto their chairs. The owner of the hotel luckily showed up at the house and we were saved. The following morning we left before breakfast, not out of fear but ashamed of the situation we'd found ourselves in the night before. Off we went in the vast limousine. The children didn't understand what was going on. And I searched for a house far from the mists and eccentricities of the Morvan.

* * *

June

I have bought Serge a 'poupée gonflable' ('inflatable doll')!! Very generous on my part because I could have bought handcuffs or the complete erotica kit for ladies for the same price. I only had 100 francs, as an old 'gitane' ('gypsy') got 250 francs off me. 150 for taking my hand and giving me good luck in WORK, and then said 'et maintenant pour le coeur' ('and now for the heart'). I couldn't give less for that, given Serge's condition, so I was a sucker for another 100 francs.

I was with Ava; we had lunch and then went off to Rue Saint-Denis to buy a straw hat (which we didn't find). It was next door to a sex shop. After a lot of giggling we went in. Ava had been spotted by a big black tart who was 'doing' the door next to the sex shop and I was introduced. So Ava and I went in. The man in the shop

---

* 'My Friend the Peanut'.

thought it was a 'caméra invisible' ('private eye') joke and treated me rather sheepishly. Then I saw, displayed in a vitrine, God's gift to women, a sort of leather pair of knickers with studs on them and a big pink tutu sticking out of a hole. I nearly died and got Ava to ask the manager how much. He said the prices hadn't come in yet but very expensive, real leather and I said his price was mine. I said 100 francs, he said OK and opened up the window, took out the jewel and showed it to me. 'Very nice,' I said, 'would you wrap it up?' I could just see me with it poking out of my basket.

A bit intrigued the big black tart asked Ava what I wanted it for; lot of giggling, then oh, disappointment; the manager pulled the tutu out of the leather knickers and presented me them with a hole in them. 'Mais qu'est-ce que je vais mettre dedans?' ('But what am I going to put in it?') I asked all dismayed, to the uproar of dirty old raincoated blokes peeking the porn books. It was for a man to put on! and the tutu was only made of hollow rubber. 'Très triste,' ('Very sad') I said and Ava nearly died in confusion and hysteria.

Not to look too amateur, we had a look round the handcuffs window and chain counter, all 100 francs but hopeless: no hooks to hook them onto a wall or bed or anything and very serious locks and padlocks and keys. I thought Serge might lock me up and leave me like it. Nothing for rubber maniacs, only some blow-up dollies, so we got out, said bye-bye to the salesman who thought the whole thing was a put-up job and said he liked my films. Said good afternoon to the big black 'pute' ('broad') who was talking to an enormous blonde and we strode off. But regrets ... I still had my 100 francs and nothing to show for it so Ava and I popped into another sex shop after much reflection and this time I rushed for the 'poupée gonflable' shelf and, after a moment of hesitation between that or the erotic kit for ladies, I decided to be generous, think of Serge. So I handed over my 100 francs to a Chinese man – or rather, Japanese fellow – who said they were made in Japan and we rushed, packet in hand, to a taxi.

It was very difficult to keep silent at home, knowing I had 'Je dis oui quand tu le veux' ('I say yes when you want') in a bag in my chest of drawers all through the tennis match. I kept my silence and the film that Serge watched on TV closed down. I said, 'Go to the bedroom, I've got a present for you.'

She looked awful, all pink with painted hair. I hoped she'd look better blown up, so I began to puff and it made such a noise. It didn't take long but I had to pause a bit and was laughing so much. She was ghastly. A rubber duck was more attractive. She was about 5 feet tall and terrible and very, very decent, less bosom than me, a ghastly flat bottom, and dressed and with a terrifying expression. She smelt of plastic. When I brought her to see Serge he was terrified. We did laugh – nothing more unattractive could exist, not a hole or anything. What a cheat! I said I couldn't very well ask for my money back!! Serge implored me to unbung her and let her down. An enormous corpse on our bed with a dreadful willing-to-please Japanese expression. So we let her down. What a laugh when I think of the advertising on the packet. Once again taken for a twit! And I can't be the only one!! I wonder if only old men go to sleep with her . . .

Tonight, 1.30 a.m.

Serge at work. He's only got two months to finish his book so he writes like mad about a man who becomes a famous artist doing electrocardio poems like a heart thing. And he dies whilst being operated on because oxygen, gas and electricity going 'bang'!

15 July

Last night Serge took the children and I to 14 July celebrations. He had a very good idea to take us to a dinner spectacle at the Eiffel Tower. It was spectacular – the man who did the Chinese shadows with his hands and a woman who was blindfolded and guessed what you were holding. Charlotte was holding cash, as usual. We had just come back from tea with Serge's ma. We didn't even have time to get coats or change when Serge said he had managed to get a table. He was in a smart suit and tie, which made up for Kate, Charlotte and me, in jeans. At 10 o'clock, the best marvellous firework display, and we were right in front of it. When we got out, there was not a taxi in sight and we had to walk.

Serge is writing his book, *L'Homme à Reaction*. He is closeted in his room, so I shall be writing more often! I'm hoping to go to Normandy this weekend, for Charlotte's birthday, and sign all the papers for my house; I must take pictures so I can dream about it better.

Buying clothes for the Benayoun picture* tomorrow. I start filming in a month. I think at last Serge will let me go to England on 1 August. I went to the passport office to get one for Charlotte today. Only a week, good old British Embassy! When I think it's taken six years to get a residence permit for Paris! I see the doctor tomorrow and will be given a card for five years.

22 July

Charlotte was three yesterday. We were in Deauville and had a picnic on my lawn in front of my mouse house. We went to Deauville Saturday morning, or nearly didn't. I felt a sore throat, headache but Jean-François B. from *Jours de France*† came to fetch us to take us to the station and I felt I couldn't let them down, so we went off, Serge (who had a cough), Kate, Nana, Jean-François and Luc (photographer). Rain all the way and then sun. We had lunch on the beach restaurant, pressed by autograph hunters (Kate had already signed one before I'd got the chance to stop!). Léon Zitrone, who was very touched that I wrote to thank him for his article, took us for lunch and then swooped on an intensive snap shooter saying it was an advertising plot as he was holding a packet of cigars! He

---

* *Sérieux Comme le Plaisir.*
† A magazine.

tore out the film from the miserable admirer's pathetic little camera (the same make as mine, hardly the material for a 'bon publicité' ('a good advertisement') spotter), reminding me of Bardot in Almeria. Continued conversation of plotting and intriguing of the lowest order involving his good self. I really think he has a Kafka-inspired persecution complex. The poor snap shooter looked no more like a bandit than me and persisted in saying, 'Je voulais seulement photographier la dame!' ('I only wanted to photograph the lady!') Me!

July, *Paris*

What a ghastly day. When I came back tonight, Noelle* told me that Kate had been naughty in the park and I thought no more about it until I saw Serge, who said that apparently Kate and Charlotte were with Noelle in the Luxembourg Gardens and Kate started to chat to some children. The next thing Noelle heard was, 'Ma maman est Jane Birkin. Je vis avec Serge Gainsbourg mais il n'est pas mon vrai papa. Mon vrai papa s'appelle John Barry, maman est divorcée et on vit au 5 bis Rue de Verneuil.' ('My mum is Jane Birkin. I live with Serge Gainsbourg but he's not my real papa. My real papa is called John Barry. My mum is divorced and we live at 5 bis Rue de Verneuil.')

After this monologue, recited in front of complete strangers, grown-ups included and a few nasty old men, Noelle got hold of her senses and told Kate to shut up and to come to her, whereupon Kate didn't budge and went on with her one-sided conversation, giving away her address to anyone who asked. A few children said, 'Well we'll come and knock on the door, etc., etc.' Only then did Noelle give Kate a shout, and took her and Charlotte home. On the way back Kate was astounded and said, 'Well, it's the truth. I only said the truth,' and she seemed quite unconscious of the danger (of kidnappers).

---

* The nanny.

Pain for Serge, who has always treated Kate as his own, to learn she had described him as 'not her real father, only we live in his house' as if he was a hotel.

I could've been someone who had been on the TV – it made no difference to the people in the street – so to be my daughter was nothing to be proud of, like being a doctor's daughter. She must prove herself, not boast about her mother. Then I started about kidnappers and how many children are killed by madmen let alone by giving away your address in the park. Then I hit at the father thing. To be a father is easy, you only have to sleep with the mother. The real father is the one who stays, comforts, gets cross, loves you, brings you up, buys you food and is there, week after week, year after year. In the end I was in tears, Kate not so. Her coldness. Not a word on her part, not 'sorry' or 'I didn't mean it'. She didn't know why she started on about John Barry, or anything. She was just silent. I told her to go away and the only thing I would never forgive her for was hurting Serge. He was always so sweet to her. He never said, 'Kate isn't my daughter.' A few minutes later she was playing downstairs as if nothing had happened and this has gone on for two days. I made her do her tables. Serge was very cross about the kidnappers, but mostly hurt about her coldness. She could have said anything, or kissed him, but no, so he is left with a thought that the little girl he fostered boasts of her non-existent father after six years.

I pick her up from school; I signed autographs outside. 'There is Jane B and her little girl' and 'Doesn't she look like her mother?' I think I was very hard on her. I brought out a lot of my own spite against John, saying he doesn't take care of her, or ring her, or ask about her. So why does she boast about him when Serge does all the fathering? And a lot of my own sadness at her is her hurting Serge. It's almost worse than being hurt yourself. After all, she did nothing against me. But I so want them to love each other. Why does this happen? I hope it will blow over.

August, *London*

The last few days have been stuffed full of children. Chessington Zoo was so funny. We started off at 11 o'clock in the morning in the rain in Gabrielle's car. We had Emma, Lucy, Kate and Charlotte all on the backseat. As soon as we arrived we went straight to the monkey cage and saw an enormous orangutan picking his nose very slowly and eating it. Charlotte said, 'Oh, il fait comme moi!' ('Oh, he does it like me!') The second orangutan had a great big shiny pink bottom pressed up against the window. It was obviously fast asleep. I thought it was rather endearing. It started to pour with rain so we bolted for the restaurant, which was full of screaming kiddies. After sandwiches and sausage rolls we saw a monkey was playing with himself. That's all he did, much to the amusement of the kiddies. It was quite extraordinary: it grows and shrinks in seconds. Gabrielle took its photo.

And then to the circus! An hour's entertainment of trained dogs and all the same people in all the acts. Then to the funfair. I went on the big wheel with Emma and Kate. We were in a horrid basket. I was so scared, I cried and howled with anguish. Kate and Emma tried to comfort me but my nerves had gone and my legs wouldn't stop jumping up and down. Emma held my legs down and Kate tried to wipe my tears. I nearly upset the basket. We were stuck for ten minutes in the air and were very shaken when we got out. Kate was hysteric at seeing me frightened and clung to me like a crab. It was rather sweet of her. A fine sight, two kiddies comforting a snivelling mummy! Gabrielle took Charlotte and Lucy on the train ride, a pathetic ghost train. And the afternoon ended at five on the trampoline. Poor Gabrielle tried to drive while Kate and Emma ragged non-stop in the back of the car. She slammed her hand down on Emma's at a traffic light but of course, nippy Emma had moved her hand the second before Gabrielle had walloped her hand down. So Gabrielle's hand hit the back of the seat and it hurt her a lot. Kate and Emma collapsed in mirth.

Friday

Took Emma, Lucy, Kate and Charlotte to Battersea, it was lovely. Emma and Lucy had stayed the night. Ma came by at 11 o'clock and we all went back to her house where the children dressed up and did a terrible ballet. Kate was a queen and Charlotte a very self-contained nymph, very happy sitting alone being a nymph. Emma and Lucy were the bad and good fairies. Ma had provided jewels galore, petticoats and all her old clothes. They looked marvellous. It was raining outside but they still went into the small pool at the end of garden, which was freezing. Ma went in too . . .

Sunday

Today is Sunday; we went down to Dunk's Green to see Gabrielle's parents. Kate was sick everywhere four times in Gabrielle's car. I had a bag but no warning. Anyway, despite a bad start, it was lovely. Serge, who was in a bad mood to start with, was ecstatic at seeing Daisy, Gabrielle's parents' bull terrier. He was marvellous and played with the children all afternoon. After a lovely lunch and too many beers he broke the swing! Kate was hysterical, and so was I. When I saw Serge, he was motionless, prostrated on the lawn, but he was OK. It was his head which is, luckily, solid. Gabrielle's parents are so nice. They haven't changed in years. Gabrielle's pa, who is a doctor, has talked Serge into seeing a heart specialist.

1 September, *France*

A little dirty weekend with Serge! I set off from Rambouillet Castle after filming and Serge set off from Paris at the same time! Like James Bond. So here we are in a ye olde teashop stuffing cakes and China tea like two old English ladies!

13 November

Dear Munkey,

The silence is so awful I have to write to someone. If I had done something, at least I would have a thing to be ashamed of, but I have nothing because I love someone; I love Serge more than any living thing, I would not lose him or his love for me for anything but sometimes I feel that he could write me off as a 'bad lot' and think no more of me. I don't think he cares about me, except that I am his, but if I was even TEMPTED to be all that is bad, he would never have to think of me again and he would lie to the next girl. He would say, 'La petite Birkin is my fabrication; I can make any number of them and better and younger but they're nothing without me.'

He said last night that I drank only because he let me drink, that I lived only because he let me live. I'm his 'poupée' ('doll') with my 'qualités' as a poupée but completely re-makable with better material than me. All this is maybe just self-protective for my feelings, but I'm sure if I put one foot astray, he would be incapable of taking me back for me. I would have made my 'erreur' and that would be an end to it.

My erreur tonight was being one hour late for dinner because I was honest and told him I was having a drink with C and we'd join him at the restaurant. It was 8 o'clock and I turned up at 9.30. He said he would be there at 9, so I was chronometrically half an hour or so late.

The reason was C. I wanted to talk to him. I'm twenty-seven, nearly twenty-eight. I'm afraid I have put him in a mess in spite of myself. I don't know what he expects of me. I told him I love Serge, that no one can take away that love, it's important. I care for C, I like him, I wanted him to be my friend. It's unimportant except I have a right to have a friend. He's never tried to make love to me. He's interested in me as a person. Why I do certain things, why I am embarrassed about certain things, what makes me not a cardboard poster, because that's what most people associate me with. I wanted

Serge to like him, I wanted him to like Serge the way I do – I've gone on and on about him. If only I'd kept my big mouth shut. It's almost like Bobby* telling cousin Freda about his love life and expecting her to say 'Poor Bobby'. I know that. I can't say that he's like a girlfriend. But people are doing far worse things, sneaking and not getting caught. Everyone has been unfaithful but I haven't. So why should I suffer for what I haven't done? I don't want to have a sneaky 'amant' ('lover') like the bourgeois people do. I didn't knock it off with Trintignant. Why? Serge. I didn't want to spoil my thing with Serge.

Serge is sleeping peacefully and maybe he's had affairs but is far too clever to tell me about then. And the strange thing is that I now know I wouldn't mind as much as I thought. I would still love him, maybe hurt, certainly furious, but not to breaking-up point. I love him too much for that. I can't imagine having a holiday, having a memory, having my life end with anyone but Sergio. So what does the rest matter? I wouldn't like to look like a fool over the other girl, but if she was a pute or a thing of the moment, would I really die? I don't think so. I feel happy. I love Serge, I've come into my own, I'm standing on my own feet. I had a drink; maybe I wanted a drink. I wanted to talk; I talked. In ten years I'm finished, no one will love me any more, I'll be old and 'moche' ('ugly'). My problems won't interest anyone, I will no longer be à la mode. I won't be twenty-seven, I will be thirty-seven and it's over. I don't want to get old. I won't get old. Well, Serge will be looking at girls of seventeen and if I get jealous he will go 'Allez-y ma vieille' ('Go ahead, old girl') and it will be too late, even to have a drink, even to have a friend, and I will realise that life has gone and I'd be bitter of all the things I could've done if only I'd known.

But Serge has been twenty-seven, he's had fun with what he wanted, with who he wanted, in Paris. I'm not asking that, a weekend to screw all Paris. I don't like screwing. I just want to be wanted

---

* Bobby Casa Maury, Freda Dudley Ward's husband, was my father's first cousin. He couldn't sleep without telling his wife Freda about all his amorous adventures, after which Freda couldn't sleep and she had to comfort him by saying, 'Poor Bobby'!

and not feel ashamed and old and responsible. And if after six years being with someone you turn up late – and each to his own, and considering everything I have done – and with a child in tow . . . well, I thought Serge loved me more than that, but sometimes he makes me think because of what he says or doesn't say that six years is nothing, I'm only an episode in his numerous adventures. He's allowed to be proud of it, to shout about it, and I'm nothing more than Dalida, or Gréco, or Bardot and I'm certainly much less than his precious wife, because he married *her*.

Any mistake I make, I'm out and he starts again. Really, I thought love was forever and that I, Jane, was more important as a person with all my faults than anyone else in the world, but I'm not. At least that illusion is gone. 'Do you love me?' He says, 'Of course, otherwise I would have chucked you out.' After six years and all we've been through, that's all I am to him.

Christmas

The nanny says that Kate screams in the Metro, 'I live in Serge Gainsbourg's beautiful house and Jane B. is my mother.' She says that I want to marry Serge for his money, which, with a sense of profound horror, I can't believe. I will never marry Serge because he doesn't want to. We'd rather be lovers. After ten years I cannot imagine being anywhere but by his side. I am unhappy if separated from him for a day. I love him more than anything. I would live anywhere he wanted to live because I am incapable of living without him. I have my needs in life too. I have no friends (except Gabrielle) and Mme Hazan, but she is not intimate.

* * *

Serge had wanted us to get married so that we could have a grande fête in a beautiful restaurant in the Gare de Lyon station. We would take the train and leave for our honeymoon. It was to be fancy dress ball, 1900s. We had dinner there to have a look around with my brother Andrew, who unfortunately became outraged on learning that, in France, you had to have a blood test before a civil marriage. Serge said that if I couldn't spill a tiny bit of blood for him, he wasn't worth much. I'd begun to get nervous about this enormous fête which was taking on the proportions of the Cannes festival. Georges Cravenne, the famous press officer, was going to orchestrate this vast affair that had begun to resemble a publicity stunt more and more. So due to my lack of enthusiasm we got cold feet, and decided to stay lovers.

* * *

My whole life is Serge, Kate, Charlotte, Papy, Andrew, Ma and Linda. And that's all. I don't want any more loves than that. I know one could never replace them, ever. I would do anything for them. Out of superstition and fear, I will not let Serge even make a will. I don't want his money, I just want him to live forever. When people make wills it means that the dying has been considered. I have my job, which makes me falsely independent, because I hate being 'kept'. And my house in Normandy is for Kate and Charlotte if anything like a plane crash kills me. I am emotionally completely tied to Serge.

1975

'FICTION'

I'm thirty, married with three children. We have a house, money. My husband is kind, clever, fifty and absent. The house is big and empty. I am sociable but have no friends. All runs smoothly with or without me. I'm an addition to a beautifully organised unoriginal setting. Sometimes I feel as if I was the only unessential object here, less tidy than the maid, less loved by the children than the nanny, less useful than the telephone automatic-replier, less beautiful than the wallpaper, less perfect than the statue in the hall. I'm lucky I have everything. I'm not happy, I should be, I must be wrong. People say I'm lucky, I've heard them. If I'm not, then I'm ungrateful and spoiled. I wish I was ill but I went to the best specialists, I've done the best X-rays and I'm not ill. Nothing is wrong with me. If I'm tired, there's no reason. If I'm depressed I would go on holiday but where to? with who? Holiday is for people who work, who deserve it, who are tired for a reason, I have none.

I have been married for ten years. I married him because he asked me. He was the first, he was brilliant, I was flattered. I think I was pretty but nothing more than that. He was the first man I slept with. I'd loved other men before but hadn't dared to go to bed with them because I didn't want to be easy. I stayed the virgin, probably the oldest in Chelsea, till I was twenty. I remember being rather drunk and he carried me into his bedroom after the marriage proposal. I put up a very little fight, not very resistant but scared. I knew the shoes kicked off, the fumbling with my zip on the others occasions, the rushing to the phone and the minicab, and off! This time it was eyes wide open in the dark. I let myself be his with a few tears and surprising pain. He kept his promise that we would marry in September. I remember being happy and giggling a lot in a white crochet dress with too much eye make-up. I felt he'd done it before (he had twice). It was well-organised and I walked home with my sister, tripping along the embankment.*

9 January, *Venice*

Serge has brought me to Venice. We are in a beautiful suite in the Danieli Palace: golden walls and curly furniture, mouldy mirrors with dirty golden frames, so beautiful. A cold Venetian sun is pouring in the two windows looking over the Grand Canal. We have a whole corner of the Danieli, very dark and I think it might be sexy.

I thought we would never ever get here. Paris to Milan at 10 a.m. And then another plane to Venice, which didn't go from Milan but from Rome. No flying to Milan as there was fog. There was an hour of air traffic over Rome, so we were told to catch the 3 o'clock to Trieste. Whilst contemplating this horror over a nasty steak in the airport restaurant, Serge came up with a terrific plan. We shall go to Venice by car and if all goes well we we'll be there by 6. So we set off.

I was sick, a good start! The most awful fog – we couldn't see an inch in front of us. Ghastly! We were very pleased that the taxi was a diesel because he didn't try any Mercedes stunts. We followed the guiding lights of ambulances and other more daring cars and finally, at 8.30, we were here in Venice. The hotel porter nearly fainted at seeing us because there had been no flights all day and he had never thought of us arriving in this fog. Venice was in a pea soup that Sher-

---

* Strange little story mixing up my life with John Barry and maybe also my life with Serge in the Rue de Verneuil, where I wasn't allowed to touch anything, but it seems to me that it has more of the seduction of the first night with John. He too had an impeccable flat. He too was elegant, rich and talented. And it was with my sister Linda that I'd come back to my parents' house after the ceremony, skipping along the embankment with her whilst I prattled on about all the ways one could make love without having to have a baby.

lock Holmes would have stammered at. We couldn't even see the Salute on the Grand Canal. We trotted off to Harry's Bar in clouds of mist and it was a dream of beauty: meowing cats, figures looming up in the cotton wool, hatted and muffled, everyone breathing cigarette breath (everyone being the four people we saw!). A ghost town.

Super dinner at good old Harry's Bar. A few English and American men and pasta. And then early to bed, Serge out like a light in the wonderful hotel bed. So special when it isn't your sheets, so much better. Rather rough linen (like chez les Rothschild where I got a blister from their monogram on the pillowcases). We polished off the Venetian breakfast and now have been waiting an hour and a half for a call to Paris to see how Serge's record has been accepted by the good gents of the press. My film comes out on the 15th, quelle horreur!*

Mamma and Papy have sold the Isle of Wight. Andrew is downcast and I must say I feel pretty sad. But I can't say anything as I have Normandy now. But it was nice to think of Kate and Charlotte having the same summer holiday memories as Andrew, Linda and me. Still, Ma and Pa need the money for the house in Chelsea, so what can we do? Sadly it ended.

Serge sacked N. directly when we got back for being so uncaring to both children, the proof being that she couldn't give a hoot when she went and didn't even want to say goodbye to the children after three years. We had really had enough of Charlotte in the corner and Kate slapped for not eating fast enough, Charlotte crying nonstop, and the television morning, noon and night. They are so good with Serge and I, Kate beautifully behaved, good and sweet. Charlotte funny and no pipi in the bed and walking instead of screaming at each step with Noelle. The penny dropped that our children were not the terrible, untidy, naughty things Noelle made them out to be. They just didn't like her. Charlotte pipied in bed to prove it. Alberte is in charge and all is much happier.†

---

* Michel Deville's film, *Le Mouton Enragé.*
† Not according to later accounts by Charlotte.

1976

30 August

Dearest Munkey,

I'm back from London where I was with Papy for three weeks. It's been a so-called success but just before I left for Germany he got an infection so leaving was hard. He's been so incredibly brave and I must say so has Ma. It was a five-hour operation. Ma, Pempie, Linda and I waited in a café whilst they took him away. Five minutes before he had broken down and cried, and I had so wanted to be strong but I couldn't. To see him so alive and yet to know what they were going to do to him, and the suffering and the pain. I just couldn't bear to know they would cut into his sweet back and butcher him. And what if he should not make it? And what about his heart? Suppose he couldn't take it? And when I saw his tears and his hands clenching at nothing, I wanted to die for him, let them do it to me. He said, 'Look after Ma if anything happens' and I knew he was as frightened as hell and all I could do was promise everything and hide my face in case he saw me crying.

Pempie was so good and kind. Poor Mama was in a terrible state but with the great courage that she has in awful times she was a force and strength. Linda believed, maybe more than many of us, that he would be all right. And poor Andrew, who was in the hospital himself, ulcer, was by the telephone with Serge. It was all right. The surgeon was pleased, and then it was up to Papy. Tongue was so swollen he couldn't talk. Even in that special care unit he was an angel of no complaining and bravery. In two days he was out and in his room and there the pain began.

Munga* and I take relay. I read P.G. Wodehouse either afternoon or evening and then Ma did the opposite. He was so funny and we did laugh. I didn't know how he managed being beating up by the physiotherapist every day on his scar. In four days he had taken his first steps, which has never been done and in six he'd walked down the corridor.

Papy was out ten days after. Everything had gone so well but he caught an infection on the sixteenth day. I hope the antibiotics can control it. Papy said so on the phone yesterday. Anyway, I so loved being with him and reading and laughing.

Andrew and I took the children to Hyde Park and we went to a bit of the lake which was not allowed. It was like being on the Isle of Wight again. He was an angel, so funny, just the same. He saw we weren't allowed but didn't say. I only saw while I was rowing back: No boats beyond this point! And he said, 'I didn't think I'd mention it!' And out we clambered, his tennis shoes full of blackberries. So I have enough to make pie for eight people.

Serge was able to know Pempie and I'm so pleased; he had never had the chance before and they got on so well. And Freda (Serge took Ma, Freda, Andrew and Pempie to dinner) thought Serge was terribly attractive, and so he was! Poor Pempie looks so sad in her house in King's Road. Carol† is missing and you can tell. It looks and feels empty. And Pempie looks frightened and lost, all alone. She's been marvellous and had a smart boy of thirteen to stay for the holidays and took him everywhere, even to Wembley football stadium by Tube. I bought him Serge's recordings and it was all very nice for him.

Serge and Andrew had a quarrel the night before we left, all about a bad joke, of course! But Sergio was so hurt and pained. Poor Andrew cried as the last thing in the world he would have wanted to do was hurt Serge, who he loves. And Serge came downstairs

---

* Dear Mama didn't want to be called 'Granny' but 'Grandma'. Kate, dyslexic, called her 'Munga'.

† Carol Reed, her husband, had just died.

bleeding: he had cut an A in his wrist with a razor blade so that Andrew see how much he had wounded him. Poor Andrew, what could he do but cry? I was terrified he'd do the same. In the end we all cried and kissed one another better. Serge said he loved Andrew so much he couldn't understand why he had hurt him so much so he cut himself – to hurt Andrew, I supposed. But Serge said no, it was to show him how much he loved him.

Oh, the children when they saw the blood and the tears!

Had a long talk to Linda. Her man left her and she was broken up. Very Linda-ish, wouldn't say too much and defended him. Then another night she opened up a lot which was lovely and we chatted about her complexes and how we had the same ones. She's a dear girl, very honest and independent, hasn't changed at all. Nor had anyone, which made for a strange and nostalgic visit.

Then Serge and I went to Germany. I was worried about Pa but most of all I was sad about not being next door and losing roots again. We went for 'Je T'Aime'. I did four countries in three days and then home. We slept nearly two days and now the hibernation is over I'm rather missing the children. Hey ho it's always all or nothing, and for the moment it's nothing.

* * *

All the same, I had shot eight films in two years, amongst which were some of my best: *La Course à l'Échalote, Sept Morts sur Ordonnance* and Serge's *Je T'Aime Moi Non Plus*, with Joe Dallesandro (who was a treasure) that seemed to stand the test of time. We lived in an old castle that was made into a hotel for us; Serge and me, Andrew, Kate and Charlotte, Joe, Hugues, and the whole crew. Every Saturday night we had a party. Serge played the piano for everyone, and the children were with us most of the time because it was the holidays. I had short hair to play Johnny Jane – Serge didn't want me to cut my hair because he didn't want me to look the same in other films.

During the shooting of *Je T'Aime Moi Non Plus*, Andrew had found an abandoned house in Uzès and one night, with Kate, we'd crossed a park overgrown with brambles like in *Sleeping Beauty*. In an out-house, there were stagecoaches, and on the staircase walls there were slogans in German from the last war. Then, when we arrived under the attic I saw Andrew shoot up a ladder, as always. The excitement in his voice when he said, 'Jane, I've found the entire Dreyfus case!' He'd found an old chest full of newspapers, *La Libre Parole*, with the editorials by Drumont. None of them had been opened, so we took as many as we could and went back the follow-ing evening with Serge and our producer Jacques-Éric Strauss to take away more of these extraordinary newspapers. Andrew gave Serge the most magnificent one to put in a frame: '*Down with the traitors, down with the Jews*'. I remember panicking and saying to Andrew, 'But we're very well known in France, what happens if we get caught?' But inside I was proud that it was always he who found fascinating things. Even at Harrow he'd found a bronze Chinese dish which is now at the British Museum. In Germany he'd phone my mother from what was the rest of Hitler's bunker. Not very sur-prising, therefore, that Stanley Kubrick hired him as an assistant on *2001: A Space Odyssey* and then to do the recces for *Napoleon*. Not surprising either that he wrote about J. M. Barrie and Peter Pan; about Napoleon and Joan of Arc, working like an archaeologist, digging up other people's stories. That's why he got on so well and so happily with Serge.

Just before *Je T'Aime*, I'd done one of my favourite films, *Sept Morts sur Ordonnance*, because Michel Piccoli had insisted that I pass the screen test. Jacques Rouffio was the director and my partner was one of the most exciting actors of our times, Gérard Depardieu, then unknown. He did a few days filming on *Je T'Aime* for a case of champagne!

During the filming of *Sept Morts sur Ordonnance* we lost Nana, our bull terrier. Andrew, Gérard Depardieu, Serge and I had gone out to dinner and left her in the hotel room, in Madrid. When we returned to the room after dinner, Nana was no longer there. Later we learnt that she'd jumped into a taxi and the taxi man, astonished, had seen her strange face in his mirror when he finished his work. He took her to a refuge for lost dogs that belonged to an old English woman but that night, Depardieu, Serge and I were on all fours whispering 'Nana, Nana' under all the doors of the hotel bedrooms. An American suddenly opened the door and I was blubbing about my dog that was lost and he replied, 'I don't fucking care, I wouldn't care if your fucking dog was dead.' Depardieu decided to intervene, and I heard the American bark to his wife, 'Gladys, call the police!'

We were in Spain under Franco and we were all trembling in my room, waiting for the police to turn up. Two or three weeks later, after the end of the film, Serge and I went back to do a television show in Spain to show a photo of Nana. Serge was miserable because in the only one he had of her she was wearing a straw hat and he didn't find that dignified enough. People phoned all evening saying yes, they had our dog. But when Serge and I ran to the rendezvous, it was to find Labradors, St Bernards and Dalmatians. Finally, a woman said that she'd found a dog that resembled a pig and that she'd called her Palerma because she was all white, and it was Nana. She sulked in the train going back to Paris. Maybe she had loved her wild life and knew she was going to be shut up in the Rue de Verneuil. She escaped again and was found at the Deligny swimming pool on the Left Bank. A woman had phoned the radio station to say she'd found our dog, who was safe. After her performance in *Je T'Aime Moi Non Plus*, Nana lived a few more years before escaping forever.

I was filming one really bad film (amongst others), that was in Italian, a comedy by Giorgio Capitani called *L'Amour, C'est Quoi au Juste?* I was staying in a really rough hotel in the outskirts of Milan and I'd phoned Serge from the plastic telephone cabin that had a folding door to tell him that we were in a super hotel and that he'd be really happy to be with us. Ava and I drank a vast amount of sambuca, an Italian liqueur in which you put coffee beans that you light up. You drink it afterwards, being careful not to burn your lips. Serge did arrive in our hotel, lost in some dreadful no-man's land. He was quite furious. He took a room opposite mine. It was such a second-rate hotel that we had no individual bathrooms, just one at the end of the corridor where we used our shampoo bottle cap as a plug.

Serge was so fed up while I played a country girl on my bike, that he started to write *L'Homme à la Tête de Chou*, very much inspired by the circumstances and by the red fire extinguisher that was in the corridor. I'd no doubt given him some ideas on murder! He waited impatiently for me to arrive in the evening where he amused the crew playing drums with the saucepans like a one-man band. I found a photo where he and my brother were dressed up as ladies, so I presume we had quite a laugh together as soon as the day's filming was over.

1977

September, *Death on the Nile*

Serge and I caught the 7 o'clock flight, leaving the children with a new nanny, with a somewhat heavy heart. I was told that Egypt was terrifying for diseases and I had to have five injections against every living thing. I was told that Nile water was mortal and the river was swarming with poison and snakes, and that it was 120° in the shade.

First-class tickets too. I gave Serge his, as I couldn't have borne to go alone, and I gave one to Papy to join us when it was cooler. We stayed in a ghastly modern hotel in a clammy heat for a short night. The plane for Aswan was at five the following morning but I wanted to see the pyramids, so Serge and I took a taxi and went at nightfall. It was rather dreamlike with dusk and Arab voices and suddenly, bang outside, three great looming mountains. I had got jasmine wreaths around my neck, so heavy jasmine smell and the dusty pyramids, and the sphinx rising out of the sand. To be truthful, I thought they were a bit small (too used to skyscrapers). In retrospect, I can see they were magical.

Serge was scared because our Egyptian guide wanted to show us some special tombs and he didn't want to go into holes at night with a cigarette lighter for a torch. So I went alone. It was a bit creepy and Serge thought the man wanted to rape me! Anyway I just said 'um, how lovely' and got out again.

Next day we caught the plane to Aswan, sweltering heat; unbeliev-able, unbreathable heat. We were at a military airport so no photos

in case we were Israeli spies. Serge was a bit nervous as he is Jewish.*
A hair-raising journey – we drove at 100 miles an hour, not a camel
in sight, but sand, sand, sand. We get to the Nile and cross over by
ferryboat to the Oberoi Hotel. Very flash, run by Indians, and we
meet all the assistants for the film and Simon MacCorkindale and
Lois Chiles. We have a pretty room and I started to think how I
could have brought the children, everything was very civilised.

I did my first scene on the boat (finding the body and coming out
screaming). Ted Sturgis, the first assistant, was great, but Guillermin
screams a lot, 'Walk fucking faster, Jane!' I was trembling with heat
and fear. Anyway, that done, I did my 'running down the deck in a
frenzy' bit and he was quite pleased. The ambience seemed tense to
say the least. Camera crew and assistants terribly fraught with his
'fucking' all the time. He also gave instructions like 'north north-
east', instead of 'turn right', which having no compass and not being
very nautical was a bit obscure.

Serge was nicely installed at the bar, drinking Shabnam, a sort of
poison.

We wait and wait for the 'grosses têtes' to arrive, Bette Davis, Peter
Ustinov, Mia Farrow, etc. They arrived a week later. Guillermin had
his human side and I started to like him, in the bar, anyway. He
seemed nervous of the grosses têtes' arrival.

At last they came. We all craned our necks to see them. Ustinov
jovial and rather hot, Niven a gentleman as I hoped, and Miss Davis
still to come.

As I came up the staircase, D. Niven held out his arms. 'At last,
someone who will cheer us up. How are you, lovely?' I thought that
was extremely kind, given that he didn't know me.

Every day, what group was the question, on what table with who.
The tourist groups came and went – a lady had a haemorrhage
overnight, as they are all over eighty years old apparently. There

---

* He'd written a song for the six-day war, 'Le Sable et le Soldat' ('The Sand and the Soldier'). Serge felt more strongly than I'd imagined about Israel and its possible extinction.

was blood everywhere. The technicians were sweet, especially one called Chunky Hughes who said, 'Don't worry love', when I was nervous.

At last Mia Farrow arrived, complete with child Fletcher and child Soon-Yi (a Korean adoption), plus nanny. I regretted not having mine again and again. There was nothing to do all day but wait in the bar if you weren't filming, as too hot by the pool. Mia was not at all what I imagined, not sexy at all, like a child. As she loved Andrew she was nice to me. Her children were a bit 'sauvage'. She was a sort of girl with courage, the sort of girl who made me feel a coward. Full of fun and very Peter Pan.

* * *

One day John Guillermin screamed out, 'All those that are doing fucking nothing go to the other side of the boat!' Mia imitated him, saying, 'Do you think we could do fucking nothing on the other side of the boat?' Guillermin heard and said, 'Miss Farrow, when you're a director, you'll get up at four in the morning and that is your call for tomorrow.' Personally, I looked at my shoes.

* * *

Tourists kept asking if Serge was recording a concert in Aswan (they took him for André Previn).* Serge was not at all flattered!!

Then, a miracle, Maggie Smith arrived. Dizzy with travel and having lost her suitcase with her shoes and pills in it. 'Darling, no shoes. Bloody Italians have nicked my bag, a tempest from Toronto too, a nightmare, nothing to discuss.' (This was her favourite phrase.)

She was so fragile, so thin and delicate, very camp and funny. I was immediately terrified that she would be catty.

'Dancing shoes? Are you going to be doing some ballet?' she

---

* Mia Farrow's husband at the time.

asked me. 'No, I only wear them so people think I am a ballerina,' I muttered.

I think she thought I was at least honest. At dinner with her she said, 'I'm only doing this for the cash. I haven't even read the script, drifted through it. I haven't even found Miss Bowers yet,' she cried.

I took to her at once. Mia said she was doing the film for cash too, and really only wanted to act in the theatre. 'I'm doing it for the prestige,' I said and Maggie laughed.

From then on, life with Maggie and dear Anthony Powell, the costume designer, was all uphill and lovely with promenades on the Nile with Mia and her brood. It was like Kensington Gardens in the springtime, only 120° in the shade. Then Miss Davis arrived. Wig and small sailor cap, she scared me to death. When at last I said hello, she said, 'Hi, what are you doing in the film?' 'The maid, Miss Davis,' I replied.

'Oh, how nice,' she retorted and went on talking to her emaciated secretary Peggy.

After Telex and Telex, I heard that Papy was coming Sunday, what a joy! Race to the airport where Lord Brabourne's son was saying goodbye to Jerry, a member of the art department, who was in tears and hysterics because his wife had threatened to leave him, so was racing back to England on any plane. Papy's plane arrived and he came into the sun, chic in his navy jacket and fresh as a daisy. I ignored the official verboten and ran to him. What a divine surprise, after four weeks of no news, no letters, Papy at Aswan airport, it was like a dream. I quickly put in the picture that tearful Jerry was off in a drama, that sweet Ted Sturgis had left two days before with a nervous breakdown because of the way JG (the man with the pipe, as P. Ustinov nicknamed him) treated him.

The ambience was like *Mutiny on the Bounty*, quelled by Serge's piano playing at night. He played for four hours non-stop, all the old English war tunes plus 'Land of Hope and Glory', which made all the technicians cry. Everyone was laughing and crying and Serge was the hero of the day. Lord Snowdon also gave voice! He had been

fired by JG but made to stay by producers who wanted snaps. He
was sauntering around the bar, a little drunk and divine, clutching
arms and explaining his impossible position with the man with the
pipe. He was irresistible and so funny.

* * *

Tony Snowdon was our set photographer. He was terribly attractive,
telling us to meet him behind the pillars in the temple of Karnak
with directions like 'third pillar to the left in half an hour'. So we all
disappeared from the film set in our 1920s costumes, so flattered to
be photographed for the *Sunday Times* colour supplement where
Tony's photos were going to be shown. Guillermin naturally took
umbrage to see his cast disappear at the moment he wanted them
for a scene and fired Lord Snowdon, but Tony didn't want to leave
and hung about the hotel, making his own studio in which we all
posed in secret. Serge and he went off one day in search of the
sand dunes and Tony took a photo which became the cover of *Aux
Armes, Et Cætera*.

The nights in the bar were more memorable than the actual
film. One evening we were all grouped as usual, drinking the local
poison, when a terrible scream went up from by the piano, where
one of the other actresses was seated with little Soon-Yi. Mia immediately scooped up her daughter from the mysterious incident we
hadn't even witnessed, mumbling under her breath. Maggie Smith
murmured, 'There goes a woman far from well!' Mia's other child,
Fletcher, spent his evenings observing a rat under the bar, hoping
that the occupant would come out at last and amuse him a little. He
was a very pale child who resembled the naive illustrations of the
young Jesus in our Bibles.

* * *

Anyway, Papy was duly introduced to one and all. Instant friends with Albert, head grip, who was in Portsmouth in the war near Papy. And an instant success with Maggie and lovely Anthony Powell.* We were given a lovely duplex. Serge and I on top, and Papy in the sitting-room below. Stuck in Egypt for six weeks and never a complaint.

---

* A lovely man who had at least three Oscars, one for the costumes in *Mort sur le Nil* ('Death on the Nile'). He'd been Cecil Beaton's assistant at the beginning and he'd done the costumes for *Tess*. He worked with David Lean, Steven Spielberg, Roman Polanski and others.

1978

3 March, *Hotel Ittol, Austria*

Tomorrow is our last morning here. It has been such good fun, skiing every morning from ten till four with Kate and Charlotte who have taken to snow like ducks to water! Charlotte bobs up and down like a rubber ball, red too. And Kate, who knows no fear, jumps every jump like a day-old Bambi, all elbows and knees, stays upright while I go down, face first, skis over head. Kate waits and helps me up while Charlotte is already over the next hill. Our instructor says Charlotte is the best – not a surprise, she's always that, whereas Kate and I try everything, she with more grace than me.

I am red as a lobster. Serge and I did laugh. I said that in films, upon waking, the man says, 'You get lovelier each day,' and Serge says to me, 'Tu es rose comme un cochon Fräulein' ('You're as pink as a piggy, Fräulein') or 'Mets tes lunettes de soleil, tu as des cloques' ('Put on your sun specs, you've got blisters') or 'Ça va, porcelet?' or 'Ça va, Gretchen?' ('How are you, porky? How's it going, Gretchen?'). Insults, insults! It's true that I have got some-what 'grosse' ('fat'). Serge said everything had swelled to twice the volume except my bosoms. An enormous bottom like a Rubens painting. In fact, I got out of my bath and noted I looked very like a Rubens, plus blisters on lips. It has been a lovely, lovely ten days. We have all been little pigs and very sporty. Serge has written his script for *Black Out*, which is wonderful. I never dare tell him so. Some-thing holds me back and I say, 'Ça va', ('It's OK') when in fact it's terrifying and such a GOOD idea and the three people will be real and ghastly.

Tomorrow the train. Me doing the TV show for 'Ex-Fan des Sixties'.

* * *

For the recording of 'Ex-Fan des Sixties' in London, I made Serge mad because I wasn't able to sing the chorus of the song in rhythm; one had to wait a beat, then *bam*, then 'ex-fan des sixties'. He screamed at me, banging out time with the ruler until artistic director Philippe Lerichomme pleaded for it to stop; in his opinion I'd got a creative block and the recording was put off until September, I think. In the original versions the lyrics finish with 'and poor Janis Joplin,' but two months later, after the summer, Serge was able to add 'Janis Joplin, T-Rex, Elvis'. When Elvis Presley died Andrew and I were inconsolable on the lawn in Cresseveuille. My father said, 'Poor old thing!' and we called back, 'He wasn't old!'

* * *

Serge finishing his script. Sometimes I miss Maggie. I dreamed she was a squirrel in danger and that I held her, all fragile, in my big hands and guarded her against Los Angeles (silly of me, she's far funnier and stronger than me and will absolutely love Hollywood and will surely never think of me for a moment). What a strange and rare woman Maggie is, I wish she needed me, even to help her to her room.

I want to get back to Paris to see Mme Hazan. I think she needs me. I wanted to have big bosoms and to be able to put her head against them like in Bergman's *Cries and Whispers* film. I felt so incomplete, such a skeleton, whereas what she needed was a mass of maternity.

All this has been turning in my head this week. Men are so different. In spite of everything, it's really their ambition that counts above everything, where women are always looking for the thing that will make them whole, not an attribute to someone, not an accessory. Why is being 'normal' normal? Maybe it's all the others that are the empty ones, the incomplete ones, the ordinary ones. How lucky to be able to discover that you are not alone. My own panics, which I considered madness because the man I was with TOLD me so, are just uncomfortable for others, a waste of THEIR time. Thank God for my Kate, my Charlotte and my Serge. They don't understand but they are THERE and it stops me feeling strange.

I still haven't grown up. It must be quite rare to be with a man like Serge who lets you grow up, not with much interest but without squashing you, and I think he loves me and I love him. I can't do anything without his 'regard, pour ou contre' ('view, for or against'). I NEED his view. I NEED his regard, I need his 'force' ('strength'), even if it inspires me to go against his will. He MUST be there, always there, he keeps my great feet on the ground and sometimes helps me to fly.

Friday

Serge has finished *Black Out*. He found the twist he needed, rather a grim twist too! Paris seems so far away, just church bells, masses of 14–18 and 39–45 war graves in the cemetery. Forgot they must have them, the same as in Cresseveuille. Pretty onion domes on the churches here.

Put a mass of goodies under Kate's pillow last night as she has lost another tooth. Soon they'll all be gone . . . Nearly set fire to the hotel, burning an authentic-looking envelope to look as if mouse had nibbled it. An Austrian mouse with a message for 'mein Kinder'. It looked rather good!

The man who works on the train from Innsbruck has just popped his head with a fag in his mouth to say someone has pinched Charlie Chaplin's body from its tomb in Switzerland. He said it all nonchalant, like someone's bag had been stolen.

In bed. Children giggling next door. How lovely to be that young and how lucky I am to have them. Whilst my own childhood seems not so far away, already twenty years away, but sometimes it doesn't seem it. I wish I could explain to them not to lose a second.

16 March, *Vienna, Sacher Hotel*

A lovely two days. Left Friday night with Serge. Had a drink with Odile and Louis at the bar and then off to our regal suite. We only wanted a double room but when my Russian Prince saw the sitting room in red satin, we went for the 'complet'. All was very 'Visconti' and erotic, debauched and lovely. It had been so long since we had been alone together. Egypt, London, me on tour with record alone. So we made up for our lack of sensuality in the past six months.

Next day off with Odile to see Vienna. My leg in plaster thanks to the bastard who broke it Chez Castel. Saw Klimt galore, liked them better before he added gold. Then to see Mahler's tomb, just his name and dates, very plain, felt curiously moved. Saw a beautiful house built by Otto Wagner and lived in by rich painter Ernst Fuchs. Then to Sigmund Freud's house (two tiny rooms), reconstructed décor, and his hat and suitcase the colour of a mole. We went to join Serge and Louis who were at the hotel. Had a wonderful dinner with Nana Mouskouri in a little room with a zither player who played *The Third Man* theme; it makes me cry because of Carol.

Another lovely night with Serge. He had written more of his script and seemed happy. Odile came into our room because she couldn't sleep so we ordered pink champagne. I think the waiter thought it was debauchery night! I was in my pale pink satin nightdress and we were all lolling about on the sofa.

Next day, went to Odile and Louis. Nana came in without make-up and looked very childlike. Heard the news: Claude François was dead, electrocuted in his bath. We were all stunned: thirty-nine years old and so dynamic, he had touched a light bulb whilst sitting in his bath. We all reflected on how short his life was, and so little time for living. Always leaping about, not the sort of person you could imagine dead.

Saw Cranach. I loved the Velázquez because there was a little girl, Princess Margarita Teresa, who, for me, had something quite indefinable, quite unmistakable, of Kate – the sad eyes, the mouth. There was a painting of her at about four years old – Kate. Another about six years old – Kate. Another at about eleven – Kate. Not the same nose (Kate was none too pleased when I showed the photograph) but it WAS like her. And Velázquez loved her more than any other royal child. So delicate and precious. I looked at them for a very long time.

Lunch at the Sacher with Louis, Odile and Nana. After I had to rush to Zentralfriedhof to look at the 'carré des musiciens' graves. Brahms, Beethoven, Strauss and his strange statue, and especially the mad Hugo Wolf. Half happy, half delirious with madness. On way to airport I insisted on seeing Carol's great wheel in the funfair. Serge and I took photos. How strange life is! The great wheel there, and no more Carol. Will send pics to Pempie.

Nana dies, Serge's bull terrier

Poor sweet Nana died on Saturday. I would never have believed such sadness and such emptiness without that silly, eager face around. She's missing in every room, every corner. Her great white body was always there to be pushed aside or patted, always running away. And now she's run away for good, away from us. When I think of her now, I cry, and it's too late. Only five and a half years old. We didn't even help her to die, on that cold step alone. Why is it always too late when you know what loving is? Why does it always end up in death? Please come back again, please. Poor baby, what was wrong inside you? Why didn't I guess, why didn't I know?

20 May

Leaving Cheyne Row.

* * *

John Barry had only taken the end of a lease and, as he never paid
what he should have for Kate or me after our divorce, Cheyne Row
was the last chapter in that story. The judges had proved that I lived
in Paris with Serge and we had to leave the Cheyne Row house
quickly. If not, they were going to demand that the house was in
the same nick as at the beginning of the lease, which meant twenty
years before! I panicked; no one was able to give me any advice,
so I left.

* * *

I am packing up Cheyne Row, going through the children's nurs-
ery, throwing away half puzzles, legless dolls, broken toys. Suddenly
it looks like a bombed children's home after a raid. Old Christmas
trees, tinsel, silver balls ... and I have broken down. Of course I
have to leave, it's sensible and I have no choice but the pain was
sudden. A list of the miscellaneous articles I saw today, the last ten
years of Christmases, of fun and memories, all gone. I feel like a
miscellaneous article myself. Church bells are ringing but not for
me, people are wandering by in the sun and I am saying goodbye to
a life which will never be the same again. The house, the memories,
the sun, Andrew in the basement, Ma and Pa across the road – it
will never be the same. Linda got married yesterday, Andrew's got a
flat and I've got Paris. Ma and Pa will always give me room but it will
never be the same. I've hardly been back except for Christmas and
the holidays but it's always been here, just in case, just for love. And
now the line will be cut, no more FLA 6078, no more grumbling
at the children jumping over my head, no more coffee for Andrew,

no more popping over the road to Ma and Pa. Suddenly like losing
a bit of the past in one go, no time for memories that fade quietly,
just one week and gone. A leg amputated that was giving pain and
worry, but a good leg, so used to that there's no more reasoning to
be done or comfort to be had. Like when people die, it's the worst
thing in the world, it's just over and it can't get better as time goes
on. And it happens more and more. The roots are hacked up and it's
normal – but God, it hurts.

August, 2 p.m., *Deauville*

The day before yesterday, Kate showed a great display of courage.
We were on the beach, Kate, Charlotte and me, somewhere near
Villers-sur-Mer, near Cabourg. I had spotted a patch of beach far
away from the crowd and we marched along to the two old bunkers
which had fallen down the cliff. Shut my eyes and Kate says there's
some boys looking at Charlotte oddly and she told Charlotte to
come away. When I peeped over the rocks I saw two boys of about
twenty and two girls, uncomfortably close to us as they had all the
rest of the beach. I took them to be curious fans and told the children it was nothing. Then Kate asked if we could swim. It was a bit
perishing but the sun was in and out so I tried to get into a bikini
bottom whilst Kate held up a towel. It was then that I saw the young
group was very close indeed and I felt embarrassed. Off we went
to the sea which wasn't far. But I kept looking back because of my
basket and all our things and every time I looked at them, the two
boys and girls were looking back at me so I turned away and we
splashed into the sea.

I said to Kate, 'Look back if our things are OK', and Kate ran out
of the water screaming, 'Au voleur!' ('Stop, thief!') at the top of her
voice. I see the two boys rushing off at top speed with Kate haring
after them yelling, 'Au voleur!' Charlotte and I rushed to the spot.
I told Yotte to stay put and ran after the group that were hoofing
it up the beach. Kate was sprinting so fast I thought, 'She's got the

blond fellow.' I reached the car park exit and horror, not only wasn't the strong hand of the law slapping Kate on the back and giving her the Victoria Cross but there was no man of the law and worse, far worse, no Kate. Just as a crowd was gathering and I was crying – Kate's disappearance was far more worrying than my bag – someone said, 'Is that her?'

I turned and saw her cheerily waving her arms in the air; she was smiling. I could see she was OK. But no basket. Kate said, 'Charlotte's got it', so I was relieved like mad and bolted back with Kate to poor Charlotte, crying with confusion at being left alone behind the rock. Charlotte had found it there. They must have dragged it a bit on the way, but it was so heavy, and dumped it thanks to Kate screaming. Brave Kate, dashing off after the suspected criminals, but I hope she's never that brave again!

1 a.m.

I wrote my diary till 3 o'clock in the morning. I got everything ready for Andrew coming. And then at three he rang and said disaster had struck and he wouldn't be here till next Tuesday. He has to write his article about J. M. Barrie for the *Sunday Times*. Kate cried with disappointment. I felt like it too. We were longing to see the sweet boy. So not until Tuesday and we go back to Paris on Wednesday. A sad blow.

Had a drama with Charlotte two weeks ago. Gabrielle's Emma and Lucy were staying, plus Serge's ma, and my ma and pa and Linda, quite a house full. I took them to the Deauville swimming pool and when I picked them up after tea with Ma, Pa and Linda, they told me that Charlotte had fallen on her head on the edge of the pool. Then Charlotte began to feel sick. I went to a chemist with her and Emma. The moment the chemist saw Charlotte she thought she might have concussion; I'd better go to the hospital. I waited hours for an X-ray with Emma, who was a great help. I felt bad about Kate as she wanted to come as well but so had Lucy.

It all seemed so undramatic. Then Charlotte went very white and I told Emma to phone the restaurant and tell Serge what was happening as the doctors had mentioned keeping her overnight. Serge turned up, very green and worried, with Kate and Lucy. Just as the X-rays were coming through, the poor thing was so sick all over the floor that the intern said that they must keep her overnight at the hospital. I said I wanted to stay with her. Serge and the children kissed me goodnight and then we were alone. Charlotte, by that time, was right as rain and wanted to watch TV, but there only was a 1-franc slot machine and I only had 1 franc. So we played bataille navale. Yotte beat me three times. She's a champion at cards and any intelligent game. It was rather good fun and we checked out in the morning, just like out of the Hilton Hotel.

3 a.m.

Last day and night here. I always feel so frightfully sad, like leaving a piece of me behind. It's been so lovely for me, in my house, with Kate and Charlotte and all my family. Max came. Serge and he got on so well at Club 13: in the swimming pool naked at 3 a.m., with the children, and singing while Serge played the piano, and he and Serge playing chess, in cafés, with me, talking about Max's parents, Pempie and Carol. I am so happy to have been able to know him better. Andrew rang this afternoon from Paris and will come to dinner at L'Aigle d'Or. It's so good to see the old boy, even if it's for two hours. He showed me the copy of his book in print, the first manuscript. So exciting as they haven't cut any pages. And lovely to think his name will be in print in December or January. And very flash to have the *Sunday Times* colour supplement written by him on his J. M. Barrie series. I do love to spoil him, even in a rush.

1979

Friday, 13 March

Nearly a year after Nana died. She still makes me cry when I see her on a home movie or a photograph. She's always there. Five years of film and she's on every one. Charlotte burst into tears drawing Nana's nipple on a picture for Serge. What a strange, secret child. Kate is more . . . She believes in an afterlife, quite the opposite from me, thinks it's unthinkable otherwise. How strange to see children thinking for themselves. I wonder what will become of my girls. Sometimes I have the most certain feeling that I will not be here to see, in which case I would like to describe them as they are now.

Kate is my Kate. I torment myself with fears that she will leave me for her father John. Now he looms ahead an electric light for my sweet moth. Promises of cowboy boots, ranches, wild ponies – what child can resist that?

Enough of John Barry! Kate is the interesting one, she is the life. She will be twelve in April and I'm taking her to Raspoutine's at midnight, where we will break the glasses to celebrate. She dances like a crazy woman and it is her great talent, rhythm, such as I have never seen. The American Church's dance teacher says the same. She is moody and sulky and has tantrums, just the way I did, and is easily hurt. And very wilful! A bit bossy but so was I with Linda. People will think these are faults, but I don't consider them as such. She is all these things because she is insecure and doesn't believe in herself. Romantic but childlike, and has difficulty in expressing herself. This makes her frantic and incoherent, all these symptoms were my own. She is loving to a degree that warms me on the most miserable day. She forgives like a saint, she is admiring about things, and I'm jealous – these qualities were certainly not mine! She is the best company one could wish for in catastrophe, a sweet, dear friend, and I admire her as I watch her climb through childhood.

Kate is a child who judges acts. She despises weakness and she did not like me killing the redfish in Normandy but she was proud of me taking that child to hospital in Africa. There she is for me. She has no faults, only symptoms of proud character, but without roots. The French are not her people. I'm sure that's why, somewhere in her subconscious, she doesn't care about the French. She tries outwardly because I did and she longs to please. Oh, my darling Kate, how you please me in simply being you. I scream at you too much, and I'm a sulky person. Understand, if you can, my temper – I sometimes care too much – and forgive my weaknesses! I hope you will do whatever you want to do, never compromise. Work has to be passionate. Try everything that you feel you must try. Don't be frustrated. Sleep with whom you wish but stay proud.

I think, and I may be old-fashioned and wrong, but for us it is of great importance. A man has to merit (by your great love or passion) the gift of your possibilities, of your mind and your brain. When one realises that one hapless night you were taken for a 'hole', it is so painful to the heart and to the pride. I don't wish that ever as an experience for you. Magazines give you complexes. 'I touched her nipple and she came like a volcano.' Well, my angel, good luck to all who sail in her, but it's not always true! Articles are written by men to turn them on and give their morale a boost. But never forget that man is fragile, he has to show his virility and if it doesn't happen, he's teased, mocked and treated as 'impuissant' ('impotent'). It is unfair, too. Sometimes it just doesn't happen, he's not automatic. And we, as women, can cause much wrong in that game. Dead bodies are precious too. Exterior, therefore vulnerable, no mystery, so banal. There are men who will love you one day, Serge already does.

If you can have passionate love, it's the best.

So, my darling, enough of 'doctor's diary'. I would've liked to have talked about it more to my mother but one is always embarrassed and that, too, is normal and right. Anyway, parents always do something wrong, have pity!

Darling Charlotte, tomorrow I will write to you. A night's work, not a half hour resumé. One cannot resumé you of all people.

Tuesday night

Charlotte is seven years old. She has that strange fascination which makes people in the room turn around and ask her who she is and she will reply, quite poised, 'I am Charlotte Gainsbourg.' And so she is, individualist to a degree, happy with older people. A best friend in Normandy, Didier, who is fifteen, treats her like his queen! She has to know every detail, everything, if not she will cry, until you answer her question completely. She is a perfectionist like Serge. She will not stand a drawing or a piece of writing that is not her idea of the best that she can do. Her writing is simply beautiful, small and spidery, full of character, italic and perfect to the last detail. She draws incredibly precise sketches, objects she can see: Serge's rats on his table, lamps, the injection syringes.

I asked her to draw the elements. First water: she drew a straight line encased in a square. 'What's that?' I asked. 'Water,' she replied, 'in a bath.' Second, I asked for fire. She does lots of little things in the square again. 'Fire, dans la cheminée' ('in the chimney'). 'Terre?' ('Earth?') Another square with a tunnel wiggling through it, and a line. 'A mole under the earth,' she explained to her silly mother who looked boggle-eyed. Air? A fat cherub blowing air out from his fat cheeks.

'What is acupuncture?' asked Charlotte as they were watching a TV programme using dogs as acupuncture patients. 'It was to help people, like to give up smoking,' explained Serge. 'These dogs don't smoke!' protested Charlotte. Such adult logic, sometimes I am in awe.

Charlotte is so totally sincere. She doesn't do things to be falsely kind or even tactfully kind; in fact, my great enlightenment came about Nana, when the whole house was mourning because Nana had died, Serge crying, Kate screaming, me puffy and exhausted with despair. Serge slept on the sofa in Nana's place. Charlotte played ball in the kitchen.

'Nana is dead, don't you think it's sad?' I asked.

'Yes, it's sad,' she replied logically which I took to be a coldness of the heart.

'Why is Papa crying?'

'Because Nana is dead. Charlotte you know that.'

'Oh yes.'

And that was Charlotte's reaction. Two months later, Nana was buried in my garden in Normandy. Life went on.

A scream from far up the hill made me run to the door. Charlotte uncontrollably crying and Kate frantically trying to comfort her. 'What is it?' Kate said Charlotte suddenly went white on the hill and started to cry for Nana. Poor Charlotte had scraped at the earth of her grave with her nails. 'I can't touch her,' she wailed, 'I can't touch her!'

It was like when she drew a dog for Serge in a restaurant – of course it was Nana.

'Do you think it will make him sad?' she asked me.

'No,' I said, so she gave it to Serge.

'But you've forgotten her nipples,' he remarked.

And Charlotte dutifully started to dot them in carefully. Suddenly a great tear plopped onto the page – it was the memory of her pink buttons. That is the sort of private and secret, faithful long-memory mind that she has.

I am sure she is unconsciously jealous of Kate's childhood. She has often said how lucky Kate was because she was alone and didn't have to share or be 'two' at everything. I had never thought of that before. I had always been so worried that Kate's nose would be out of joint by having a sister. Never that Charlotte would con-template Kate's first few years as being unique, with that strange envy. I do understand. I often take her out to learn to do special things, just her. She never forgets a gesture or a word. She is so secret.

How often do I hurt her by mistake? Petite Yotte, little dark jewel. What a lovely and unique little soul you are. Such a personality that sometimes I think you have been here before. So wise you look at me sometimes and I feel stupid. So 'pudique' ('chaste') that I feel vulgar. What talents you have, that are all your own.

Charlotte has a sense of humour that I find very rare in a child. She makes people laugh; a clown, but a fragile clown. I, like Kate, think she knows who she is and has no worry about feeling secure. She is lazy, she wants to be the best and is cross when she lets herself down. Sometimes she is helpful to Kate and at seven she can be sarcastic, like Serge. She has an attitude of being the best or smartest or brightest, and has no fear of Serge – she answers him back! It's because, inside herself, she knows with him she can't go wrong. Whereas Kate is careful.

Well, Charlotte, how we'll laugh one day; you were always so worried about memories.

When I talk about years ago or look at an old movie film . . . 'Was I born or only Kate?' 'Was I there?'

How happy you made Papa and me, from your first delicate day to this one. I kiss you and I love you and always will.

* * *

It was that summer that Claude Berri's wife, Anne-Marie Rassam, both great friends of ours, suggested that I play the lead role alongside Michel Piccoli for *La Fille Prodigue* by a certain Jacques Doillon. I'd imagined him, because of his name, Doillon, to be an old Protestant gentleman with white hair, a bit like Alain Resnais, so to my surprise, when he rang the doorbell at 5 bis and I found myself face to face with an incredibly beautiful boy. I said, 'What do you want?' and he said he was Jacques Doillon and he'd come to meet me to talk about his scenario, a very personal, intimate story about a father and daughter.

I let him in and it seems to me that I took him straight up into my little boudoir that contained my things, my mementos from childhood, photos, diaries, my letters, so that he would understand me and wouldn't think I was just Serge's doll. Serge was downstairs in his salon asking for the best table in the best restaurant. He'd take care of everything, as he used to say. Maybe I even kissed Jacques, to his surprise, I so wanted him to find me interesting just for me, and much like the character of desperate girl in his magnificent script.

* * *

September

My depression is momentarily pausing. I'm on my way back to Paris by train.

The Lugano* film is coming out and the rotten distributors are so gloomy. I can't believe it's as bad as that. I said, 'No reviews yet?' on the phone yesterday. They said, 'It's better they come out as late as possible, to give the film a chance.' Very funny! Enough to make the sole star long to give interviews and show her face on TV. Still, what can happen? Everyone's had a disaster.

Have got the script where I have to climb the Eiffel Tower for an American TV show! I would just like to know how they intend to do it, even if they pay me 2 million! Olga will have to do a bit of mountaineering to get her 10 per cent.

Serge is depressed about his film. Moshe Dayan's son has been with us for a week to try working on the script, but even he feels that Serge's film has to be Serge's film and not a compromise. So

---

* *Melancoly Baby* by Clarisse Gabus.

what will happen now, I don't know. Find another producer? Every day things change and now I've given up interfering as Sergio and Arnon* are like a married couple. You criticise A and Serge agrees, then you get a phone call and Serge yells at me for having made him doubt A, and says what a great fellow he is, and how he can get the biggest stars. Serge is flattered, and so it has gone on for a month.

Saturday, 22 September

I feel so cold today, it's sunny outside but all I can do is shiver and sit about, changing from chair to chair. I try to think about my life but I am so worried and confused all I want to do is to sleep, the coward's way out.

Serge, who was so terrifying in his ways in Normandy, so systematically drunk, has changed and is now happy. Surely all his hopes are coming true, his film, his book, his record,† which is such a wonderful success. He is being very thoughtful and kind about my life and my growing up in a different way. I feel so strange – I don't know what I want except I've always wanted everything.

I also know that whatever I do I'll never be happy without Serge. If I go away, I will always regret my exceptional life with that exceptional man. Is it even remotely possible to live as three? I don't know and in a way I feel Serge would never be able to share me, even mentally, no more than I could share him. We talked about it all last night. We all had dinner together and I was so happy with Jacques and Serge. It seemed to me, if only it was possible, this would be my happiest moment. And if Serge could love Jacques, even if they went away, I wouldn't be sad as they will be together, and I know they would be happy. I don't want a 5 o'clock lover, I don't want to lose a friend, but I do so want to LIVE. When in August, I so desperately wanted to die.

---

* The producer of the film.
† *Aux Armes, Et Cætera.*

I am so amazed to be loved at all, that the sweet boy actually finds me interesting. I feel as if it's in a dream. I just like sitting with him, or walking, holding his hand, and seeing Serge and him laughing. I am so proud of Serge, making this sad boy laugh. So here I am, feeling a little afraid but such a new feeling. I touch my mouth and think: it is this wound that smiles?

Thursday

It's 12 o'clock, home alone; I let Serge go to the Élysée-Matignon without me as I've got bronchitis. The days go by; Jacques wants to see me every day. He doesn't seem too tired of watching this indecisive creature wrestle over mind and matter and conscience, and I feel at a loss when he's not there. Maybe it's only vanity and he's my mirror, and he makes me believe I'm beautiful. I'm just watching my rather ugly hands writing this UNinteresting page. I know that I'm infinitely forgettable. When Serge tells a story, he'll always say, 'I was in India' or 'I was in Yugoslavia'. I was there too, but there was no point in saying it.

* * *

October, *Austria*

Concert in this little restaurant. Ava is in hospital with a viral hepatitis. She was all yellow today and I said to the production manager 'Maybe she had jaundice', and in a flash she was off to a local doctor. Half an hour later I was yanked out of the make-up place, no question of filming, bunged into a car, and Ava and I were carted back to Vienna like lepers. Poor Ava! That's why she had been so poorly for the last three days, sick and weak and yellow, whilst I showed her Klimt and Schiele, then carted her to teashops where I scoffed and she looked rather sad. We went to three hospitals before she got a bed (one with nuns, I'm glad to say, didn't work out – there is a law that you have to come by ambulance and we came by car, it was very austere and religious). At last, along to welcoming hospital which has a view of the cemetery and 1000 crows perching heavily in the trees. Ava was diagnosed as being very yellow (which we knew!) and suddenly there was no question of her leaving. The doctors said two to three months in hospital. Months, good Lord! I know hospitals, once they have you they never let you go. I insisted she must go back to Paris. They promised that Monday, after the day of diagnostics of the blood tests, at my risk, she could take the plane with dark glasses as suggested. Then she was put into a room with a very old English lady who had only one lung and a very weak heart but a sense of humour. (When she heard that Ava had an infectious disease, she said, 'Oh, that's all I need!')

The doctor said I must be injected, ugh! If Ava has hepatitis A, we will only know after the test on Monday and he can't give me an injection before. If she has B, he can plug me in 'tout de suite'. And if on Monday she has C, there is nothing to be done. He said it was very painful and I said, 'Let's not talk about it. Just jam it in', and he did. It takes ten minutes to do, very slowly. He did it nicely and said I was a 'brave Fräulein'! The poor nurse had my fingernails implanted in her thumb for a week!

Serge and Mme H. arrive tomorrow. I will go to the airport with my kind chauffeur, then Charlotte and Isabelle* come on Wednesday for five days, and poor Ava will be back in Paris. I feel a bit odd tonight, but maybe it's only in my mind and being alone again. And how short this life is of the ones you love. My own life matters less and less, I never clung much to the idea ongoing. Except for my girls, they're fine and maybe they have a better idea of me now than when I will be older and sadder and won't be much fun. If my humour goes, I have nothing. I love to make them laugh. Me at forty, what will that be? I was so sick at thirty. The idea of going on,

---

* Serge's niece Jacqueline's daughter.

oh là là là! Sometimes I'm so tired of me the only thing that wakes me up is the 'regard' of others. Suddenly I think I only live for that regard, I suddenly feel alive, I see myself as if I was a witness. I watch the most uninteresting specimen, the colour red, breathing again, as if I was in a rather bad film.

Undated, *Vienna*

In bed watching a film very cosy under an eiderdown. I had dinner in bed so my jeans didn't make a mark on the body beautiful!* I feel such an old body with all those lovely young things floating about, full bosomed and new. I make up my tired legs and scratch out the stretch marks and so to work. It's 7 o'clock and we film to midnight.

Charlotte and Kate arrived this morning and Charlotte has her tooth in a box waiting for the Austrian mice! The decorator has written a marvellous note in German, to have faith in the mouse dream! Should be very inspired tomorrow, plus the goodies that Serge found, like tiny dolls. I can't wait for tomorrow morning when she announces the arrival of Austrian mice.

It's a holiday tomorrow so I'll take them to the cemetery for a bit of culture. It's 1 November tomorrow. The day of the dead here, so should be impressive. Mme H. has gone back to Paris and Serge is taking the children to dinner in the Sacher restaurant with the zither. Yesterday we had a jolly evening with Chabrol and his jolly girlfriend (exactly like his wife as always!). We drank till 2 a.m., laughing about this and that. Serge said, 'Do you want a Helmut burger for dinner?' and Chabrol said, 'God help me no, the film is quite enough!'

Yesterday we had such a good day. Took Isabelle, Kate and Charlotte to the big Viennese cemetery, the one with the 'carré des musiciens'. They were all really impressed by the names, Beethoven, etc., but even more by the red squirrels which were hopping from

---

* I was playing the girl who'd inspired Egon Schiele. I was naked throughout.

grave to grave. We tried to touch them but we had no nuts. And then we went to the Jewish cemetery where the graves are so romantic and wild. We walked further and further into the overgrown alleys. Charlotte nicked a wreath and I caught her putting it onto an old tomb. Then, just as crows were crowing in the grey afternoon, I saw a ghastly rusty body coming out from the grave making a sort of gurgling sound.

God, I screamed so loud, and Kate and Charlotte gave wild yells of fear. Isabelle stood rooted to the spot as great fat pheasants flapped into the air. We had yelled so loud that the deserted alleys were filled with anxious faces looking in our direction, and a policeman with a dog came striding up to us. Seeing that we weren't murdered, stated that it just wasn't done to scream in cemeteries! I imitated a pheasant as best I could, flapping my arms and saying, 'nervous, nervous', and he said, 'go and have a drink'! Hiding our faces in shame, we left to have lunch in the restaurant where Serge had been waiting. Then back to the hotel to find out that all the museums were shut, as it was All Saints' Day. So off we went (without Serge) to the funfair and the big wheel. It was a bit high and we felt sick and nostalgic. Charlotte wailed with fear and I shut my eyes but Kate loved it. And then, out of motherly love, I went on a horrifying turning torture ring which seemed to never end, then the bumper cars which hurt, then we shot at targets, which was very good fun.

Back to the Hotel Sacher. Dinner in the very stuffy but beautiful red bar with Mathieu Carrière,* who has joined us but has had to put on a tie. Charlotte and I played pick a stick with the toothpicks. Isabelle and Kate were a wee bit drunk and went off to bed. Charlotte made her dream house out of toothpicks and wrote 'maman chérie' ('darling mum') in toothpicks. I was very touched. Serge muddled it all up as she hadn't written papa! And then Serge went off with Mathieu and his girlfriend to the nightlife of Vienna and I took Charlotte to bed.

---

* Who played Egon Schiele.

Couldn't sleep, 2 o'clock in the morning and no Serge. Took one and a half Noctran 10 mg and still not a sheep in sight! I was miserable, as I had to get up at 7 o'clock in the morning. Serge got in at 2.15 and told me about the nightlife, then four hours later the alarm clock went off. Scoffed scrambled eggs and off to work.

Ava still in hospital, poor thing. Serge is off on Sunday, and Kate and Charlotte on Monday, so I'll be alone again. Jacques sends me letters every day, he's lonely and depressed as I don't know what to do and it's because of me. I've had at least eight now and all very sad. I hope he and Serge will have a dinner in Paris to cheer him up. Serge is drinking quite a bit. I do so hope he takes care in Paris when I am not there. Mme H. will keep an eye but there's nothing to do when it's four in the morning in the Pigalle. Hey ho, I wish I knew what to do.

December, *Ava has died*

I wake up in sweat, late. I slept from after work yesterday till this morning. No dinner, no breakfast. I feel so cold and so tired. I am obsessed by Ava. When I wake up I think of her and the slightest thing in the daytime reminds me of her. Yesterday a lot of soldiers were by surprise in the café. Ava used to like soldiers, lots of extras in the location. The make-up man grumbles, I cry. Today I thought I smelt the smell of Ava when she was ill and it was me. I ripped off my nightshirt – it *was* the same smell, and at the same time as being terrified, I wanted to go back, to smell her, the breath, the sticky tongue and the eyes, her face all yellow, like a great moon on a foggy night. That she was alive. The hope was not a hope, it was certain. You can't die, did she know she would? Did she know? Was she scared? I will never know.

* * *

Ava Monneret was in fact called Mauricette. She'd worked for Monsieur Alexandre, barefoot; with her red hair, she was a character no one could forget. Her mother had told me that when she was a little girl, Ava, who lived in Chalon-sur-Saône, used to get onto the bus with a little cardboard suitcase, and she'd stick close to women in fur coats, saying she wanted to come up to Paris. I pinched her from the actress Françoise Fabian, when I was making the movie *Projection Privée*, and from then on she was the creator of all my hairstyles; she made the little wig for *Je T'Aime Moi Non Plus*. She was the champion of France for curling tongs, as were her brother and her parents who had their hairdressing salon in Chalon. She was on every film I did from that moment on and when we left for Vienna, usually we'd knock back a vodka and a little tin of caviar, but this time I found her a bit bizarre. A few days later her eyes became yellow. She died in Vienna very shortly after. She'd been my friend and confidante on all my films.

1980

8 January, *accident, London*

I think I know what is the worst thing in the world. On 24 December I was in London with the children (Serge was doing his concert at Le Palace). We'd flown in on the afternoon plane and were staying at Ma's. Andrew rang and asked if the children would like to go to midnight mass at St Paul's Cathedral. I said good idea, as I wanted to fill their stockings and thought St Paul's would be beautiful. At 11 o'clock Andrew came around and picked them up; Kate didn't really want to go as she was tired, but off they went with Barnaby* and his sister.

I had a long talk with Pa and watched *Singin' in the Rain*, then Max called and I was taken away over the road for a drink. It was gay as Tracy was sorting out her stocking presents for her children too. I was feeling very tired and curiously sad as I have felt ever since Vienna. It must have been midnight and there was a ring on the door. Pa. I could see by his face that something was wrong. Serge or the children, I immediately knew.

'They've had an accident in the car.'

'Have they been hurt? Are they all right? Where are they? What's happened to them?'

In hospital, my poor babies in hospital. Pa said Westminster Children's Hospital. I must get there. I've never been so frightened, so

---

* Andrew had met Bee while working on the film he had written for the BBC, *The Lost Boys*. Ian Holm, who played J. M. Barrie, and Bee had had a son together, Barnaby, and a daughter, Melissa. Andrew fell in love with Bee and the children around her. They lived together for about twenty years and had two sons, Anno and Ned.

terrified. My poor Kate and Charlotte, there seemed no way out of the hell. The policeman had said it wasn't too serious. Could he promise? Could he promise? All I wanted was to see them and be with them. We didn't know the way very well; some drunk Scotsman told us the last bit, it all seems so long. Then that rush to the door, their ghastly hospital doors with drawings of sick children looking sadly on. I was screaming inside and out. When we went past the river I thought if they are lying and anything has happened to my children I will die, want to die, could do nothing but die. Ma was comforting and practical and the angel of force. We got to the casualty and I saw my poor Charlotte on a stretcher, terrified and covered in bloodstained clothes crying out 'Maman, Maman', her darling face all spoilt but alive, a great swollen black eye, stitches in her forehead and trembling with shock. Poor little Charlotte, poor little white face. 'Ce n'était pas la faute d'Andrew!' ('It wasn't Andrew's fault!') she cried. The nurses said they must do an X-ray on her head. My God, her head maybe damaged, and concussion.

I heard 'Maman' from the cubicle next door. Kate. I explained to shaking Charlotte that I must see Kate and she understood, and Papy took her hand and didn't leave her during the X-ray. Kate, my beautiful Kate, panicked and white with blood running from her mouth. My beloved Kate, her poor lips swollen, had a great gash. She was so worried about Charlotte; they were so worried about each other. They had to stitch up Kate's mouth. I had to hold cotton wool over her eyes and promise it wouldn't hurt. My God, the sight of that beautiful face with scared eyes. They gave her a little injection, not strong but the worry of them hurting her . . . They covered her face with the piece of white paper, cutting a hole for her little mouth. She was so brave. She hadn't let them touch her before I came. Then she was done and was taken up to the ward. I asked her if I could go and see Charlotte, if she could be brave. All those papers, name, religion, what will happen? Ma stayed with Kate and I rushed to the X-ray department, demented for news about Charlotte's head. I promise to stay to sleep beside her so that all will be all right. She was panicking because her eye was completely closed and blue. She kept touching it with shaking fingers. The X-rays were all right, nothing is broken, but then she was sick, sick, sick.

We were wheeled back and put in beds against the wall. Then I think the most touching scene I've ever seen happened. Charlotte saw Kate being wheeled up to the ward. She sat up in her white hospital gown, arms outstretched in fear and love, and she cried, 'Kate, oh Kate!' They flung themselves in each other's arms, structure to structure. I have never seen such beautiful sisters, always one caring about the other, even when in pain. Kate scrambling to Charlotte who was agitating her little arms in the air, 'Kate, Kate', and Kate comforted Charlotte and Charlotte caressed Kate's bruised face, and I thought I must be the luckiest mother alive to have my children safe and in each other's arms. Charlotte wanted everything explained, what they were doing, where the stitches were going, and she tried to understand and even replied in English.

Kate was only concerned about Charlotte, her eye and the horror of this accident. Having seen poor Charlotte in Andrew's arms, screaming and covered in blood, what a nightmare! It had been 11.30, headlights straight at them. Andrew groaned in a voice Kate said she'd never forget, 'Oh no', and they all thought they were going to die and then bang! The Jamaican who hit them didn't move. Four hysterical, blood-strewn children. Poor Andrew, the horror must come back and back.

I was allowed to sleep in between Kate and Charlotte. Kate slept, thank God, her face like an Egyptian king's statue I had seen once, deformed but beautiful. Charlotte didn't stop crying, stomach ache, headache – poor angel, everything hurt. And she pleaded for water, but the nurses said 'no' in case she has to be taken to the operating theatre, no liquid allowed. I talked and talked and she cried for hours but she talked sense, which was important. Every detail of that crash. The nursing sister told me to leave her alone, but how could I? They told me to sleep, otherwise I'd be no good for my children tomorrow.

Andrew and Bee came into the clinic around 5.30 in the morning and brought stockings for the children, as it was Christmas morning. Poor Andrew, shaken and white, with a cut on his forehead, told me how he wished he had been the one with the stitches and not them. Bee's children were across the ward. Barnaby was asleep but Melissa had stayed awake all night; she had had stitches in her lip too. We all slept in the ward, the nurses so kind and patient to me who had to go and be sick in the loo. I was afraid that they would hear me and think I was an hysterical mother and not let me stay.

In the morning, troops of people in dressing gowns came in at about six. Relatives. A lovely hospital where mothers and brothers and families can have rooms upstairs to be close to their children. At seven the nurses changed over and it was Christmas Day. Charlotte woke as gay as anything, a bandage on her head and one mauve eye shut. So happy, she opened her stocking and the nurses brought more presents. Then Kate woke up; she had slept all night but was feeling terrible and started to be very, very sick. The nurses said it was shock, but it went on all day, poor little angel. Then Charlotte started to be sick as well, she trembled and moaned and vomited.

10 a.m.

Bee could take her children away as they were better. The doctor said mine could not go home as they were still in shock. I must ring Ma, who doesn't know what to say if Serge rings from Paris, no reply all night at Old Church Street* and on Christmas Day nothing. I said I would try to call Jacqueline, who would know what to do, as I didn't want to frighten him. So I fixed that she would call him. I said there has been a slight accident, nothing grave, and gave the extension number in the hall of the hospital so he could call immediately and talk to the children. That way he would believe all was all right. So that's what he did, and Kate and Charlotte told him they were

_____
* My parents' new address.

fine. Thank God, he couldn't see them being sick on the way to the phone, he couldn't see their faces.

Ma and Pa came at about twelve and were kind and proud of the children. The nurses said how wonderful they were. Linda and Mike came and played games with Charlotte and I carried poor Kate to the loo to be sick again. By six they were feeling better and they tapped a white balloon from bed to bed.

I talked to Andrew, who was miserable and looked so ill himself. All of his bones hurt, and his poor head, and his brain. He thinks the ambulance and police had come in three minutes. I rang Ma and Pa and Serge to say all was OK and all was quiet. I must've nodded off for a bit. The man with the boy in the next-door bed gave me a gin and tonic and I took a tranquilliser as my children were sound asleep each side of me.

In the morning we were told we could go. I rang Ma, told her to put the turkey on, Boxing Day would be our Christmas Day. I rang Serge to say we were home and then say it was a bit more than 'stitches' but that they wouldn't show. The children were very merry with all their presents. It was a lovely and miraculous Christmas.

That is how I know the terror of being a mother.

January, *Cannes with Serge*

Am in Cannes, with Serge. He has five awards. Europe No. 1, Best Song, Best LP, Best Personality, Best Everything.* We are going off tonight in a private plane with Daniel Filipacchi and his wife to Geneva instead of catching the night train. Serge seems to care more. Whether it's because of the pursuit by Jacques Doillon or what I don't know; anyway, a sort of kindness I had forgotten is being rubbed over me.

I will write to Ava who I sometimes believe to be still with me. I talked to a boy at work who knew her well on the Zidi films; he said

---

* For the album *Aux Armes, Et Cætera.*

the news of her death was so incredible he thought of her as if she'd gone away for a while, that she will be back. I wish I could think like that.

Serge has made friends with Jean-Michel Jarre who is married to Charlotte Rampling. They talked until six this morning. I went to bed at four and was very sick (too much drink plus pills for the stomach which has been so bad ever since Vienna). This morning we went off with incredible hangovers on to Daniel F's boat. We had dinner on an island, the boat rocked a lot but it was fun and now I am drinking TEA in the bar, no more Black Russians for me! Naughty Delabey taught me that poison! Delicious, but to be avoided.

We are waiting for the national hero to come back and drink his orange juice. Serge sang his 'Marseillaise', the true version, with his arm up and fist clenched all alone in front of the paratroopers who had threatened to bash him. He was such a fragile sight, so brave. Because of a few individuals from the extreme right we can't do our concert tonight. 'You'll get your money back, but I have the balls and I don't have to show them, I want you to stand up and sing with me "La Marseillaise"'. The audience (and paras standing, saluting) joined in. A standing ovation. Serge ran back and made a 'bras d'honneur aux paras' ('an Italian salute to the paratroopers') – this insulting gesture is also known as an Iberian slap – and off we went to Brussels. All this in the newspapers and on the TV. Everyone applauded Serge's courage. With the bomb alerts and police everywhere. His Rastas let him down and wouldn't come to the concert hall (except Sticky).* It all looks so dangerous and I was terrified that a maniac would have go at Serge, a madman, and there could be any number in that vast hall. Anyway, 'Gainsbourg face aux paras' ('Gainsbourg versus the paratroopers') was a very frightening and moving thing to see.

Idiots. People are frightened too much by other people. Black-

---

* Serge told his Rastas to stay in the bus, that they had enough problems in their lives and that he would go alone. Lerichomme and I followed him and were witness to that historic moment.

mail: you sing that and we'll kill you. It's an attempt to censor the individual. One can't step down to threats, especially racist, rightist threats. But they are worrying. Brassens rang to felicitate Serge, and when we were in Strasbourg he rang the children in Paris to find out how we were. He'd heard about the hotel bomb on the radio.

Will try and ring home to talk to the children in case the plane has a prang.

11 February

We're all at the bar, waiting for dinner, in a chic restaurant. We're at Cortina in Italy, in the Hotel Cristallo. We thought it would be like the name, but it is full of Americans, rather cold in comparison to the little Austrian chateaux and Serge has not put one foot outside and has written in our room. Kate, Yotte and I have been skiing every day, I'm so scared, I yelled and moaned all morning. The children are champions of courage and don't seem to be afraid of anything.

I cried all night as I remembered how Ava and I had our affairs at the same time, and then went on thinking of going to the loo in the Evian bottle on Serge's film, all the things nobody will never know or understand. Went on crying on the ski lift and was so depressed and could not explain, just wanted to cry and stop and go home; afternoon better, and went on skiing with kiddos. Kate was sweet and waited for me, then she and Charlotte got the giggles and at least had some fun. The monitor got a snowball from Kate.

14 February

We've just been thrown out of the hotel, charming! No room at the inn. Actually, I'm delighted. We'll leave tomorrow morning and ski all day, ski all the following day and then get to Venice; if we have enough cash, we'll have a night in Venice and so the children won't have missed out on skiing.

15 February

Dreamt of Ava last night. She was in a hospital in England, she looked a bit better, her cheeks looked pale pink in spite of the tinted glass. I went into her room and she said, 'Oh it's you.'

'Yes, you're in England.'

And she replied, 'Oh, that's why I'm no longer in Vienna. But how did I get here? I don't remember. I've been sleeping for days and days.' And in my dream I thought, 'How can I break it to her? That she got here with a cargo of oranges? That she was in a wooden box?' So I said to her, 'You came by helicopter,' and I brought in her mother who was waiting outside with her father and Bijou,* and I said, 'She's better,' but to myself I thought, 'Maybe that's a bad sign, she was like that before she died.' So it was a dream where one had a second chance, and on waking I knew that she was no longer there, but I was pleased to have seen and heard her last night. A curious feeling. I hope that I'll see her often like that, gay as she was before.

Today we moved to the Europa Hotel, they've been very kind here. Not like back there. And tomorrow we leave for Venice. Serge and I have been to the bank and we'll have enough money thanks to my bank card for which I'd been so mocked! I went skiing with Kate and Yotte without the monitor – we'd paid him 3000 francs but we did perfectly without him, the children jumping over the bumps like fleas. Had a quarrel with Kate who went off looking for a bumpy slope, climbing up the hill in the way of all the skiers coming down the hill in the opposite direction at such speed. I was furious. She's always breaking the rules. Anyhow, all was forgiven and we had a good laugh going over the bumps, and Charlotte was like a little red devil with her low voice, screaming, Kate and I were doubled up laughing, looking at her.

---

* Ava's brother.

13 March, *John B./Kate*

Couldn't sleep last night, worried about Kate. J. Barry apparently has intentions to ring Kate up soon and invite her to California. That's what Gabrielle has heard from Michael, who is going to stay with John and take Emma and Lucy. Gabrielle can't say no and, as for John Barry, he makes me ill. I know he's got a rotten plan to swarm in after thirteen years of silence and steal my Kate away. What's he got to lose? A beautiful daughter, teenager, whom really he couldn't be bothered to send a Christmas card to for twelve years. I sometimes wish Beverly Hills would collapse in a landslide. But what can I do if Kate wants to see him? I can't stop her. I mustn't think of me but of her. Oh dear, oh dear, divorce is a ghastly thing. All the gaiety about having a baby and being able to bring her up, and then they turn up. I'll worry about it all my life, and if I die, HE has the right to take her away from Serge and Charlotte. Gabrielle was very gloomy about wills.

8 April, 1 a.m.

My little Kate is thirteen today. My baby Kate, my sweet and loved Kate. And here she is crying, my poor Kate. For fear of leaving being twelve behind. I went to her room to kiss her and to say goodnight and she clung onto me as if in a panic. I thought that it was because of the earrings she'd lost, but she said, 'Maman, I don't want to be thirteen, I want to stay your baby.' Her little face was full of tears and I explained that she would always be my baby, at thirty years old, at sixty, always my baby. I tried to comfort her, to kiss her forehead that was covered in sweat from fear. She'd heard from a friend at school that when you're thirteen you drift away from your mother. She was afraid of responsibilities. She said, 'But films are forbidden for children under thirteen – that's the proof that something's going to change.'

My poor little girl that I love. I hope that I've found things to say that were reassuring, that no one drifts away if they don't want to; not to trouble herself with responsibilities; to look at Isabel, who's twenty and gay and young, and still doesn't have to take on responsibilities; that no one changes in the night. Tomorrow won't be different from today. Each age is a beautiful age and new, not to be afraid. To forgive me if sometimes I haven't been the perfect mother, but for me too, it was a first. And that she could hold onto me whenever she wanted, that I love her. I rocked her in my arms like a baby, she who'd thrown herself against me like a frightened bird, and my sweet Kate fell asleep softly like when she was one year old.

Nothing ever changes. Poor children don't change. Maybe out of shyness, we change as parents, we draw back for fear of shocking them, out of the respect for the child who's become a young woman, and maybe we get it wrong. They need us as much as before, but they too, out of modesty, hold back from falling into our arms, and yet that's all we long for.

My little Kate, if one day your daughter is twelve years old, read this. You, who have given me so much pleasure, so much joy. I hope that your daughter will be as sweet as you have been for me. And don't forget, even at sixty years old, even at a hundred, you're my baby and I'll take you back in my arms whenever you need me, and even if I'm not there any more, and you are a hundred, and you need me, think of this night and my arms will be around you, forever. And I'll rock you and I'll kiss you, if you're in pain. It makes me cry to see you unhappy. Whilst you sleep, my tears wet your hair. I don't want to see you sad, dear Kate, not sad, life is going to be such fun with you . . . my God, how I love you.

10 p.m.

I am at the hotel Intercontinental where Catherine Deneuve is singing Serge's song. It's all very long and I'm in the bar, as I would rather write my diary than be flirted with by the idiot bodyguards talking in loud voices about their respective princesses. How lonely it all is, how lonely. I seem to do it all wrong. I'm in a mess and it's all my fault. I so wanted to believe I was not alone.

May, Saturday night

At home in England with Ma and Pa and Serge. Had a jolly dinner. Read Pa two P. G. Wodehouse before he fell asleep and then had a two-hour talk with Ma. It was so quiet, so strangely peaceful to be able to talk to her alone about her worries and mine. Papy and Serge resemble each other a lot. How I love my own mama, my own mummy. I like to sleep with her, she's so warm and childlike in my bed. And like two lovers we retain respectability when I'd like to fling my arms round her and for her to be just that, a mother. She is my only mother and sometimes I need so much to be able to get back into her again and be quite safe.

May, Wednesday

Melancholy has set in, maybe because I talked of Ava last night, I don't know. You can feel it coming on, starting to cry, not being able to sleep for this darkness in your head, such sadness, not even fear, just loneliness, something awful and quiet. Full of regrets and I can't get out of it. I can't change a thing that has happened. I can't see her again. Wishing I had sent her home, would it have been different? Dying is maybe not the end but it's the end for those who stay. Maybe for the one who dies there is something else I hope. But for mothers and fathers, brothers and friends, there is no hope.

I saw Vienna yesterday, a little film I did of the children in the cemetery with the squirrels, and I remember that Sunday four months ago, when there was hope that she was alive, that the nightmare hadn't begun. And the optimism you have. I don't think I will ever have that the same again.

Friday, 9 May, *Baryshnikov*

Have been dragging myself about all day due to alcoholic ravage and no sleep. Went out last night for Armel Issartel's* birthday where the company was very flash. Misha (aaah) Baryshnikov was in Paris and very gay. Bearded and drinking like a fish! (What lovely eyes, most unlike a fish.) Polanski was shrewlike and in a very jolly mood. He was with a girl (or nymph!) who had exactly the same profile as himself, most uncanny, same tip-tilted nose, only prettier! The Baron was also there and Reichenbach, who was giving the party for Armel, which we had understood too late when we were in the nicest place and he (Reichen) was in the corner practically behind the curtain! Sergio wasn't sorry because he doesn't like him!

I thought an ambulance had drawn up outside the food house, flashing lights, etc. Stupid me hadn't noticed that across the room facing us was Christina Onassis, so brown and jolly and twinkling that I hadn't recognised her. It was Misha who told me who she was, and we were soon to be joined by Mick Jagger. I am goggle-eyed and couldn't stop staring like Kate. Anyway, there were no ambulances outside, just a grizzly group of gentlemen of the press who had hounded Miss O. all evening and were waiting to pounce, noshless and cold on her as she sauntered out. Serge had got a séance with a pop group so I was handed over to Roman and Misha for the night. Roman never stopped the Polish jokes and strode about, expressing himself in gestures, up and down the restaurant. I had never seen him so extravagant, maybe he's happy?

Then he, Misha, Nymph and I went to the Paradis Latin, rather rude as we had hardly finished the 'pièce de boeuf'. But Roman absolutely insisted that Misha should see it as he's going back to America today. So off we went at 100 miles an hour in Roman's flash Mercedes, crossing red lights and blocks, going the wrong way up streets, very frivolous. I was rather frightened, especially as time

---

* The owner of the Elysée-Matignon.

was not important, we weren't in a bomb raid!

Seven minutes from L'ami Louis to the Paradis Latin. In we went. Jean-Marie Rivière* spotted us. How couldn't he? We were spot-lighted. And Roman and Baryshnikov were named. Then I won a rabbit in the most unorthodox way. So re-spotlighted. Rabbit was yanked away. The 'toreador' in the spectacle threw me a bull's ear which was also recuperated two seconds later by an assistant. Then a fast birthday cake, candles and 'happy birthday to you'. The enor-mous cake was made of cardboard and he made us blow the candles out for photos. All this was a publicity gang-up. It wasn't our birth-day but everyone thought it was!

Roman beamed with delight; I think he'd promised Jean-Marie the prize of Misha, world-famous ballet dancer, at the table by 11 o'clock at night! That's why we had all risked death to get there. I couldn't think why it was so important to go to the Paradis in the middle of Armel's birthday party and be in such a rush. Aah, all was clear! It was quite jolly. Roman and Misha were very happy. And then we went to the Élysee-Matignon for a drink. Re-Mick Jagger, who teased good self without pity as per usual about my accent (in English, not in French).

I danced with Misha who was rather tender. I was so afraid to walk on one of his priceless feet, to be clumsy by comparison to the elfin prima donna. I whispered this to him as I bumped his knees for the third time, and he was very tactful and said he wished they were all like me. I think he was drunk! Anyway a bit of Rus-sian-vodka compliment isn't a bad thing and I was rather flushed. Then we left the others and had a bit of a man-to-man conversation upstairs. Sergio, rather early I thought, arrived just as the thoughts of kidnapping this sweet boy to the Bains Douches† were forming in my mind . . . grrr! So we all went off to La Calvados for a nosh and champagne. Poor Misha was most fatigued as it was 5 a.m. and he

---

* The owner of the Paradis Latin.
† A nightclub.

does rehearsal at the bar (not the same bar as Serge!), so we didn't stay long and I saw the children wake up at seven when I got back before I went to bed.

* * *

This was our way of life, and Serge said that it was like listening to little birds in a nest waking in the morning. After breakfast the children went off and we went back to sleep to wake up at 3.30 when I got going to pick them up from school.

The filming of *La Fille Prodigue* started I don't know how long after, in Trouville. For once I was dressed in a man's shirt, buttoned up to the neck with my hair pulled back and jeans that were twice too big and new, a wonderful study by Mic Cheminal, the costume designer and Jacques' first assistant.

Michel Piccoli was a magnificent father, he wore a moustache and a sunhat like my father, and Jacques made him paint paintings of skyscrapers on fire like my father's. It was an extraordinarily intense shoot; never in my life had I had so much text to say and Jacques was surprised. He thought I spoke French badly on purpose, making so many mistakes. At the end of the film, which is probably one of my best films, we said goodbye, tearing ourselves apart in an underground car park.

Jacques said, 'If you go back to Serge, I want you to be happy. I don't want to hear about you being drunk at four in the morning in a night club, the way I found you.' And I went back to the Rue de Verneuil to Serge.

One evening when Serge was at the Elysée-Matignon nightclub as usual, I watched the television alone in the kitchen and I remember clearly that it was *César et Rosalie,* and I said, 'That's me, that's me!' Serge knew very well that something had happened,

---

* *César et Rosalie* by Claude Sautet is a film with Sami Frey, Yves Montand, Romy Schneider. Rosalie is torn between between César (Yves Montand) and David (Sami Frey).

but he didn't know that we would separate forever. He went off for a drunken evening at the Elysée-Matignon until three or four in the morning. It seems to me that he'd become Gainsbarre with the phenomenal success of *Aux Armes, Et Cætera*, with TV programmes where the viewing figures shot up as soon as his face appeared, with everyone wondering what he was going to do this time. Now I find all that delicious and charming, but at the time it wasn't the Gainsbourg that I'd known, and that I'd loved. When he came home that night, he left me alone in the big bed, and went off to sleep in my little boudoir, saying that he had nothing to reproach himself for.

* * *

Undated, midnight

I don't know what to do, I seem to bring out what's worst in Serge. I try to stop his drinking, then I give up. I now go home alone, more and more; he stays out till the morning with anyone he manages to take with him. After a certain point he doesn't remember and when he does, he says it is his life and I am a bore to go on at him. Two nights ago, we had a terrible argument.

May, 10 p.m.

God, what a night yesterday! Had dinner with Diane Dufresne and smoked a little thin ciggie (plus alcohol in abundance). Then, whoops! A ghastly feeling of being very far away and I watched my knees swell before my very eyes, and when I tried to speak once, it didn't come. But we went to the Élysee-Matignon for Rostropovich's birthday party. I could only sit with my head going round and a feeling of the furniture drawing away. So in spite of Rostro's arm around my shoulder (as I was watching my knees), I didn't even realise the maestro was close. Then, as I was feeling very, very sick, I rushed for the door and out. Diane was very kind and tried to make me 'prendre l'air' ('take some fresh air') but to no avail. So home I went and sick, sick, sick. At about five o'clock in the morning, I made myself a corned beef hash!! Still no sign of Serge, so I popped into bed. He must've turned up at eight as per usual and told me I'd been rude to Rostro (my hero) and that I shouldn't have refused to be photographed and then rush off into the night. Hey ho, I can't keep up with Serge.

May

Had a service for Ava two days ago in Saint Germain's church, no one came from the film business, in spite of all the posters I put up in all the studios, even in Epinay, no one bothered to waste one hour on someone who kept them happy for months. Yann Le Masson and Monsieur Alexandre came because they have both loved her and appreciated her talent for years. Monsieur Alexandre was very unexpected and kind, Ava's parents were pleased. The priest was an actor, nice, practically too sentimental as he'd never met her so it all seemed too much, but Ava's ma and pa have talked about her for an hour, so maybe he was sincere. Anyway no matter. It was all so far from Vienna, and when he talked of the mercy of God, I remembered the mauve face and the still eyes and the morgue and the horror, the lavatory walls and the tubes running cold water under her body on a slab, and the men like butchers and the frightful knowing that it was all over, no hope.

Box and worms, what does it matter, when the soft sweet eyes are gone and the hope of a smile. In a second, it is all gone and a waxen face which works like a reproach is all that's left. So what a preacher says? No matter, if he helps Ava's ma and pa, and I think he did, then that's good for as long as it lasts, before the great longing comes back, to touch, to hold, to see, all that's forbidden, all that was life, death is a wall that shuts you out, a dark great wall where the doors disappear when the person enters, and no window, no light and no hope of a message, it is all over.

Bijou's wife fainted and was sick and we took her home and called
SOS doctor. Yves came, that was so kind of him, so kind, and Ava's
ma and pa were drunk with bewilderment and tiredness; Serge took
us over the road to dinner and then to bed, then hotel, they were in
limbo. Bijou was ill and took it bad, poor thing, and Evelyne was very
white and so was he. Strangely I did not think that Ava would mind
if she'd see me unmoved. I tried but I could not get the coldness out
of my mind; the church, the priest, it was all so wrong. Even in trying
to do right, I'd cried so much the day before with rage at Polanski and
so much bottled up when I ran round Paris with my posters, writing
them in the taxi, bordering them in black, then writing her name in
those familiar places I knew I'd never see her again. And that was
pain. It made a part of me twist with trying to control the despair of
not seeing her face, then to *France-Soir*, *Figaro*, *Le Monde*, *Le Matin*,
running so to get the advertisement in time. Certainly in that panic I
had a use again, then that running, that spelling her name, rammed
it all back again. *That* was missing her; missing her . . . that's the only
pain that does not go away. I envy you to be free sometimes, Ava,
and I'm very rarely glad to have survived. Just Kate and Yotte, yes,
for them. But now I know what they can do to you. Ma? Pa? Serge?
Whose turn will it be, when will the telephone ring? I now know it
will ring. And it's all just a question of time.

28 May, *Doillon*

Going back to Paris in the train, I'm in a different car than the
children. It's raining outside. I have just had Pentecost with Kate
plus friends, and Charlotte plus friend Sunita (who looks like a myxomatosis rabbit, poor thing, as she is allergic to horses; and what did
I take them to do this afternoon? Ride horses!)

Riguidel* stayed for dinner last night before he goes off to the

---

* This was the sailor who went round the world solo. I was asked to be the godmother for

races around the world. I was in fact rather down and bored and should have brought a friend myself, as Serge was in the recording studios for Deneuve and Depardieu. I talked to him this afternoon. He was feeling very bad as after four days without alcohol he has withdrawal symptoms. Will Serge ever be able to get over it? Alcohol is my nightmare. He turns into someone so different and frightening. And sometimes he says he's had glory, money, fame and now the only sensation he doesn't know is to kill. He never used to talk like that but when he's drunk . . .' I wonder how it will all end.

And when I'm depressed I sometimes want to die very much and by his hand. Why not? I'm so tired of the complication of living. I always seem to do it wrong. And I'm aware that I am sidelined and have to start from scratch with someone else. I don't want to start again. I'd rather die. Serge loves me in his way and it's been my way for twelve years. I don't think I know another way. It's too late and it must be some strange instinct that wants to be hurt. That's the only way to punish my life which I've lived in spasms, against rules. I must pay for that one day and I really want it to be done.

How can I explain that to anyone on earth? If only I had no moral judge in my heart! But I do and it hurts. And then I think I'm thirty-three and I'll soon be old and here is someone so in love with me that I can hardly resist knowing what it is like to be loved that much. I know I'll never change. I know for sure that I can't love anyone as much as I love Serge, in spite of the heart, in spite of the disdain and pride and the indifference; or maybe it's because of it? Two days ago he said, 'You are the person of my life.' He's never said that to anyone before. 'You're mine and I'll kill anyone that tries to take you away from me. I'll defend all your mistakes, for better or worse.

---

his boat for the Route du Rhum, which I'll never do again because he got into a ferry and never got out of the port. Serge and I heard it on the radio. So when people ask me to be godmother to their boat, I say 'Remember Riguidel . . .'

* Serge told me he had bought a gun, but I never saw it. I think he was afraid, in his despair, of shooting himself, so he hid the bullets . . . I must stress that I was absolutely not a battered woman, and Serge was living with the pain of a separation. In fact, he was not at all a violent man.

I am your unconditional lover. I am "un unconditionnel" de Jane.' ('I am "unconditional" for Jane.') And whilst I was afraid, I was also moved and I knew it was true. He teases about Jacques, answers that maybe I'm in a time of life that I have to sleep with people where it becomes 'la passion'. I said 'no' so it didn't go on. Apart from saying if he ever found out, I better be careful. It is so complex because you fall into trap of thinking BECAUSE you are loved all is forgiven but it isn't. And it's dangerous to think it will be. It's also too much to ask anyone, especially Serge. What will happen? Something will happen. Jacques is willing to marry and he is always pushing. And I say, 'I can't promise' or 'We will see what will happen tomorrow'. I don't know but it's not easy and I can't leave Serge, and will probably never be able to, unless I get afraid. He's too necessary! Too essential, he is my life for so long. And then I wish for a pill, so I don't have to go on. I'll end up by disappointing Serge, I'll disappoint the children and myself, I was lost a long time ago.

Undated, probably July

I hate this film. I hate being far from Serge and the children. I can't stop thinking that I've made a terrible mess of my life and Serge's. I don't know how much I can tell him, he's my confidant. If I was to die now, would he be indifferent? What will he think of me tomorrow or in a year? I want to tell him everything but in telling him everything I'll lose him. My children won't understand and they'll judge me and I won't be capable of explaining. I can't imagine what it'll be like in ten years. One day I'll try to hang onto Kate and Charlotte. I can already see them growing up and leaving home in how long, five years? And one day Serge will leave me too, and Papy. And I won't have the will to survive. I don't have the will to survive today. How can I explain that, in a moment of distress, I met a boy who I could talk to and I no longer felt alone, days went past and it was like being twelve again, a summer of laughing and feeling so free, a boy who takes you on his bike and you don't want to let him go.

Then the film *La Fille Prodigue* ends and reality sets in. All those we loved are once again around us, nostalgia becomes a sad routine. And yet, at the same time, you feel disloyal, everything that felt simple now seems a mistake. Guilt and panic and the devil that screams in the night, saying, 'It's your life, what on earth have you done!' and my conscience that replies, 'What you've done was wrong, pleasure isn't everything. Repent and you'll be forgiven.' My God, but they don't know my man Serge, he'll not forgive me. He'll leave and to lose him will be the end of my life. Between all this torment and misery, is that not just as bad? What's the use of telling him about my fears? Suppose he can't stand the pain. Can he? I'm so tired of my life and its complications, so weary. If God does exist, will he show me the way? Or take me with him. That way I won't have to make the decisions. I've always been afraid of that. I can't stop thinking. I want to cry. Everything I've done is wrong.

26 July, *Cresseveuille*

What advice would you give me? Today I've gone from coldness to pride to this solitude, this misery. I have the impression that I'm doing harm and I'll always be frozen by fear. Serge says he's going to have a nervous breakdown. Of course it'll be my fault, that's for sure. I don't say that he did it on purpose, I just say that it's worked. And I still feel that it's because of me that such serious things have happened – Papa, Serge – I live in fear of their illnesses, I fear for their lives. I must explain what happened, what caused all this today.

Exactly a year ago the holidays here were steeped in drama. Serge was always drunk, there were scenes in front of the children. Every day there'd be an issue about alcohol, because he didn't like being in the country; anyhow, always one excuse or another and I felt myself further and further away. The drunken binges with Rassam, with anybody, actually, and if I wanted to go home, anger, a fight. I couldn't get out of it, and then, as always, he became the adorable Serge the day after.

Then the nightmare started again, in front of my parents, the children, drunk with the Paris taxi man, being six hours late, everything revolved around him, his films, his records, his life, the rest mustn't change, neither the children nor me, orders at table, hard words, and unfair on Kate, this masculine superiority that dominates everything, that arranges everything, the house must be just so and no other way, the children are growing but they mustn't change. He's like that. And if there's a revolt, I'm the one who's sick or changed, or good for nothing.*

Then one day I meet somebody who thinks that I'm interesting, that I exist, and, better than that, I make him laugh, I'm funny, and I really become a person. More than that, he falls in love with me. I push him away being very flattered, then I don't push him away so much, and little by little he becomes indispensable, the only proof that I have that I'm alive. We go out as a threesome. I was gay, Serge could drink if that was what he wanted, and I too had a companion, a friend just for me. I leave nightclubs instead of falling asleep on the banquette with Serge's nocturnal friends; I get fonder and fonder of my friend. Before it was just him for me, but now it's me, too. I long to see him again, more and more. And everything is permitted, because I'm going to make a film with him.

Serge pushes me into going home early with the boy in his car. In his car, everything is allowed with Serge's permission. Then I go off to Vienna; the boy writes to me more and more, and I ask him to stop before everything becomes too much. I beg him to give me time to think, and he pushes me to be a part of his life and I'm afraid, I don't know what to do any more. I go to Vienna, and he dines in Paris with Serge. Serge phones me, sick. He says, 'Are you having an affair with that boy?' and I say no, then I don't write to him any more, and I don't phone either.

Then Ava falls sick and I only think of her. I only want her and life

---

* Reading this back, it seems obvious to me that he was panicking about the idea of us separating.

becomes a nightmare. I stop phoning and so does he. Ava's my only concern. And then she dies. Jacques knows, through Serge. I have a short phone call to say how sorry he is. That's all.

Serge comes to Vienna. Everything is so sad, so terrible. Death everywhere, in everything, and I become sick with everything I've seen. The terrible sadness, missing her, her parents in such distress, life suddenly became dead with her. Then Yugoslavia,* ghastly, solitude, the smell of death, the smell of mortuaries, and I'm so afraid that I would invite anyone into my room to push away the horror of being alone. I think of all my errors; could her death have been avoided? Is it my fault that she died in that clinic in Vienna?

I come back to Paris, Serge is playing at the Palace, it's a triumph, and Jacques comes too. Serge had invited him so that I'd be happier. And there's still the question of the film that we are to do together.

I go to London. Kate and Charlotte have an accident. I can't get out of the darkness, and coming back from London, the darkness continues. Depressed, I can only see Serge, who's still drinking, talking about himself. He didn't come to London; even an hour would have sufficed. He didn't come to Vienna, I hold that against him, but in secret I've become so solitary, and I have another secret, 'J.' We meet up again, the film starts, then scene after scene, I can see Jacques. I *want* to see him, it's my right to be alive, whereas for such a long time I've been being dragged along behind Serge.

I said to myself six months ago that I was hardly alive and here's a boy who's loved me for six months without ever taking advantage of me. I'm ashamed of being a cheat. What can I give him to hope for? Have I already made him dream too much? It's all my fault. And I've taken him along on my indecisive path. And he's suffering too: dramas in front of everyone at the Elysée-Matignon, but this time it's worse because I've slept with him, and the panic, the fear, the shame, I didn't want to cheat any more; he waited for me for such a long time and I wasn't able to resist. Then I see that I can't go back,

---

* Egon Schiele's film was shot in Yugoslavia.

that he wants me more and more, and I give him so little, but I don't want to lose Serge.

I go to see Jacques and tell him my fears, he's in pain, and worse. We go out at the Elysée-Matignon with Serge after the Césars. I dance with Nastassja Kinski, and Jacques becomes jealous. I don't phone him, he's unhappy; another week, I go and see him and he says that he can't go on. I don't say anything. The film will be a nightmare, so I turn it down. I leave and it's over.

Two ghastly months. Serge nagging constantly, I've given up Jacques and all I get is insults and fights in front of the girls, being dragged around on the ground. And everything is black again and I can't sleep, and I want to sleep to stop thinking and then Jacques has gone to South America. Then we go out again, Serge starts to drink again and so do I. I've never been so scared or as lonely in my life. I haven't gained anything, not even the right to be happy. Then three months later, Jacques calls me in Normandy, or rather my agent, and he says, 'Think before replying. Jacques wants to know if you will do the film professionally.'

I ask Serge and I say yes. And I see Jacques again in the Hotel Normandy; what a joy to see him, and everything starts again, this time with a film to do that will take two months. I try to be good, and look what's happened. I've been filming for the last month. Serge gets phone calls at night, people that say, 'Do you know about Jane and Jacques?'

I come back to Paris. We have a fight but without any violence. Serge is dignified and sad and at last I understand that he cares about me, too late, now he's hardly talking to me, depressed, with his eyes full of reproach, I want to go, I don't want to be ashamed, I'm fed up of being ashamed. I despair at his sadness, I'm afraid for his health, if he did love me, I know that now. Jacques is depressed too, he wanted to marry me, take me away. And that was true too. I'm navigating dishonestly, not knowing what to do.

Six hours ago I said to myself, 'Shit, I want a house full of sunlight, children playing in the garden, nothing forbidden, no more orders; I'd live alone, I'd do what I want. I'm thirty-three and I want to live as I want, without being dominated, without fear, without shame, but with Serge he'll never let me be like that. I'll go back to his house with him in command, and he'll squash me because he doesn't know how to be otherwise. He'll blow up at the children at table, he'll lay down his law and, what's more, I'll be blamed. He'll start drinking and blame me and everything will be like before. Oh, what can I do? I've hurt him so. And the children notice how tired he looks, and they love him. Why can't one do what one wants to do without hurting anyone? I've never been free so I don't know what it's like.'

* * *

During a recording session with Julien Clerc, Serge ordered champagne for everybody, as always. Bertrand de Labbey, his agent, was there, and I picked up my basket and left the studio. I hailed a taxi and asked him to take me to the Hotel Pont-Royal. There I was told that the hotel was full because of the leather trade show, and they suggested a room in the Hotel Normandy on the other side of the Seine. There, alone in my hotel bedroom, I called de Labbey to reassure Serge, so that he didn't think that I'd had an accident, and I started looking in the phone book, for Doillons living in Paris. On my first try a lady answered the phone. I asked if she knew Jacques Doillon and she said it was her son. I asked where I could find him and she said that he was sleeping beside her.

That was the end, or the beginning, however one wants to see it. I think that my children were in Ireland with my sister, Linda, during the recording with Julien Clerc. When I picked them up from the airport, I took them to the Hilton Hotel for the first time. Serge hadn't wanted the children and I to be in a second-rate hotel pursued by photographers so he'd reserved a room at the Hilton and the children and I hid in our room except when I dropped them off at the École Bilingue in the Porsche Serge had given me a few months before. I'd imagined when he gave it to me that he'd wanted me to kill myself. He used that theme for *Charlotte For Ever*, his film. He came to visit us at the Hilton Hotel, completely distraught. Catherine Deneuve had been filming *Je Vous Aime* with Trintignant, Depardieu and Souchon. She took care of Serge with great tenderness and a sensitivity that is all her own. She kept him safe, and in the misery of our separation they sang together, 'Dieu Est un Fumeur de Havanes'. I'll always have infinite gratitude for the person she is.

* * *

15 September, *choices*

Dearest Munkey,

I am at the Hilton with my girls. It is the first time I write to you without any idea of what is happening or what will happen. Charlotte lies next to Kate, in a big bed. I am in a camp bed, as Kate kicks so much, and Serge has just left to go home. The feeling of loneliness is not insupportable because I'm not alone, the children are here. For Serge, it's a nightmare. I watch him like someone who's maimed a precious being, and because it's their fault, they watch, don't move and you don't touch them. Poor Serge, after twelve years he doesn't bite, just kicks out as best he can with words. Was indifferent and now I know it's not so, but it's too late. Leaving home but to prove what? That I'm alive too? I turn away first but I don't blame him for that. I can't blame him as all his pride has been so hurt by me. I don't think he is able to love me the same again. I'm not the same. I refuse his powerful love, his orders, his superiority. I want to know what life is like with me. I have to know.

There, Munkey, you have it. All my self-righteous remarks, how life has been unbearable with Serge, his drunkenness, his selfishness, and I his puppet. So now here I am, I have wounded Serge so deeply I don't think life will ever be what it was, and Jacques, who is

so sad and who wants my life too. And me, loved by both of them,
like complementary book stands. Let go one and you slide, let go
the other and you slide, let go both and you fall. So there I am, stub-
bornly living my life as best I can without either, God help me. But
why should He help me? Help me to lose my guilt and curiously not
to lose Serge's love forever? And help J not to suffer? What a lot of
rubbish, they're all miserable and it's my fault.

Thank God for sleep, to dream like Richard II the coward King,
now I know why I felt for him, all the arrogance and loneliness of
the lost King.

1981

8 April, *Dakar*

Kate's birthday! We went off in the red open bus, Jacques driving, until we came to a river. A boatman ferried us across to the game reserve, to the crocodile stand shelter (observatory): not one! Buffalo observatory (not one) but a lovely looking Tarzan forest with monkeys swinging from tree to tree. A five-hour drive to the Club Méditerranée to get the fringed T-shirt for Kate and silver belt and bikini plus cream for my legs that are mauve and I can't move. The first day was fatal, and now I can't go into the sun for a week.

Kate's birthday night. Got African singers to sing to her, gave 100 francs to the black feathered dancers to carry Kate off into hut but she didn't want to go! Charlotte played on the drums with feathered headdress, fire-eaters and jungle music, all very jolly. Kate is very pretty and made-up thanks to Charlotte's present of red lipstick and silver eyeshadow and 'Joy' from Jacques. Slept well but painfully!

9 April

A cloudy day and misty atmosphere, luckily, as we are all beetroot red and should be in hospital for burns. Tramped to Club Méditerranée to get postcards and green parrot, nude men on beach! Very exciting! Charlotte and Jacques are playing boules whilst I write this. I'm moody as I saw a photo of Serge looking so sweet in the newspaper. I wish I could smoke a cigarette, three days without.

Kate and Lola have gone for a swim, I can't, as my legs are too burnt and I can hardly stand up with the pain. Grey sky, must go for a walk to get cobwebs out of my heart. Will write again tomorrow.

The fact of seeing Serge in a photo makes me sad immediately; why couldn't we all have lived as three? Sweet Serge, and here is Jacques, looking for crabs with all the children. I need him too, but I never had a holiday in THIRTEEN YEARS without Serge. Of course it's strange. He is missing. Even if I'm doing what I always wanted to do – Africa, mud huts, the children, Jacques and his love, hand in hand on the shore. But where is Serge at the bar? Any bar, waiting for us, drinking the local cocktail. Well, he isn't there. There is no one at the bar and no one can ever, will ever, be able to take his place.

Jacques is walking against the sea, looks like an Indian, very dark and long. I'm waving to him and he's waving back. He will come towards me, I know he will. A sort of Apache who walks along the shore like a girl, wiggling a bit! I wish I was twelve and had met him for the first time or fourteen like Kate, and he'd been the first, maybe not the last but the first. I would've liked to be adolescent and in love with him, but I don't think he would've noticed me. I wonder if he'll leave me when I'm forty; I suppose so, he's too young and I'm a bit too old for him.

My ankles are like bolsters, all red and as wide as my feet. They couldn't be more swollen, not very attractive.

11 April

Had long day on the beach, covered myself in beach towels but kids are bathing like savages. Lots of photos, more artistic snaps from Kate.

15 April

I'm in the aeroplane on the way back to Paris with burnt Charlotte on my lap (so difficult for writing a diary).

Last day in Cap Skirling, met Jean-Pierre Sabard on the beach with his wife and daughter. Took them to lunch at our hotel and then we had dinner at their hotel an hour away on foot. A lovely walk, Charlotte, Lola* and Jacques (Kate, of course, had gone ahead with her new friend, JP Sabard's 13-year-old daughter!). Their hotel was very flash but not such nice waiters, swish, that's not the sordid home-from-home of our place. Still, good company!

16 April, *Rue de la Tour*

I have bought the house and I have sold my 'beau cadeau'.† I feel so low to have sold my pretty thing. To sell his present given with so much love, to pursue my happiness far from him. I sold it to buy a life without him. This idea is so horrible that it hadn't come into his kind head the day he gave it to me, my flash car. When he'd showed me the real red leather seats, convertible, because it had been my dream, and I'd thought that he'd wanted my death – that he'd suspected something. I even wanted to test destiny, to be judged. Then I sold my little jewel. I should have kept it, even if I didn't have the means. And here I am, reasonable and petty, and he, unreasonable and great.

9 May, Evil under the Sun

Here I am in Majorca, making *Evil under the Sun*.

So lovely to be amongst friends and I do believe that Richard Goodwin is the kindest producer living and that Lord Brabourne is a gentle, kind, brave man. Fun to find Maggie Smith again – it was so exciting. Anthony Powell, Barrie Melrose, everyone who had been so good to me in Egypt ... It was lovely to see them all again. Plus Peter Ustinov, his same old self, and new people. Roddy

---

* Lola, Jacques' daughter, was exactly four years younger than Charlotte, and she was quite gorgeous. My brother Andrew did a short movie with her as Lorelei, we were all so fascinated by her beauty. She is now a film director.

† The grey convertible Porsche Serge had given me.

McDowall, who told fascinating stories about Chaplin and about Mary Pickford and very touching about Buster Keaton. Such sad stories. James Mason arrives tomorrow.

I miss Serge dreadfully. The last few days no sleeping and not taking a sleeping pill in case I HAVE A BABY and I would hurt it. I'm so exhausted and it gets hotter and hotter. What's Serge feeling like? Is he well? I want to see him and talk to him. Is he able to go on living? He made me able to be free and happy. I asked Jacques if he realised that if ever anything happened to Serge I wouldn't be able to stay with him, that I would never get over it. The guilt would be unbearable just to know that he was sick. And Jacques said did I never think *he* thought about him? It had been the same. I hadn't ever thought about how he felt, I never think about how he feels enough, only Serge and me. As if nothing will ever change us. I really wonder what will happen. All I know is that I love him dearly and can't tell him without hurting Jacques who was surprised when I said I would rather die than go on. He said, 'What, even now?' And I said 'yes' and he said that he couldn't count much, then, or the children, and I said it was different, nothing against them or him. I think he was hurt. Anyway, this is just for me* and that way I won't hurt anyone any more than I already have.

What is strange is that when you leave someone because you can't go on having betrayed him or her in their mind, by having a love affair with someone else, they say that you'll be sorry and sad because that person will leave you and doesn't love you the way they did. And the person did love you and needed you very much and you live together. And it's like running away from home. Then a year later you start to miss the other's face, his way of talking, and you forgive the bad times and only remember the good times. You even wonder why you'd gone away. The real reasons float away and the emergency of the situation has practically become someone else's life and it's as if you can decide again. Yes, that was the point.

---

* Until today . . . so much for privacy!

I couldn't decide otherwise. I ran away in the night. I couldn't go on, frightened, ashamed, wanting someone else. I had to go away, I couldn't think about it at Serge's side. So it's mad now, at Jacques's side, to be thinking anything. I love them both. It does exist because *I* do and I wish it was possible for us to live together and, as it isn't, I miss Serge, and I should think he missed me terribly a year ago, and now he has got used to it, and in a way I hope so.

I must try and sleep now, 3 o'clock in the morning and a wake-up call at 8. The children coming tomorrow night at last!

15 June

I am in such a bad mood. I'm missing Serge so much. Am more and more impossible with Jacques. I saw Serge in Paris Saturday last and can't get him out of my mind. Here we are, a year after our separation. My willing, MY doing, and now it's his face that is so lacking in this place. I don't want to go anywhere where I've been before with Serge. I try and do things to please Jacques, and then when he doesn't react like Serge would have done, I'm sad.

So when I'm told what to do or what not to do about the children, and yesterday about me taking a pair of old plimsolls to find the same again, I did not want to be contradicted. It was my money, my flat, on my day off. I can't bear the slightest difference of opinion. It drives me crazy. I shriek that I'm fed up, that I'm fed up of being treated like a 9-year-old child. I'm thirty-four and I don't need to be told what to do. John, Serge, Jacques just can't stop organising things or criticising my way of living. If I decide to go to London and take the children I want them to bring the chums. And Jacques says, 'They should come to see you. You undersell yourself.'

It's not a mean thing to say, it just makes me fed up because I'm the mother and I want them to bring their friends; I want them to be happy. Well, Serge put up with my relations all speaking English. Jacques is far less patient; last night I cooked dinner in silence. I am miserable doing the same things as in Rue de Verneuil. Maybe I'm better on my own. I can't bear not getting my way, I always think I'm right. If I'm going to be bossed around I'd rather be bossed around by Serge than anyone else. I know what I do wrong – I ask people's opinion too much. I sometimes do it because I want it and some-times to please them so they feel important, and then they start to get used to it and give their opinion about everything!

I know what it is now that's magical about Serge. His faults. He's such an egoist, such a silly jealous thing, such a dominating char-acter, but he's funny. Deeply kind and original in every stupid step he takes. There's just no one like him. His naughty face, his wicked drinking, his sweet charm. The most humane, the most receptive, most open, most sentimental. Soppier and prettier. Oh, I don't know! Not many men are interested in a woman's mind. Serge is not interested in anyone's mind but his own, but at least he says it. He's honest; he doesn't pretend to be generous with his feelings. I wish I could just go back for one day to be with him as it was at the very best when I knew I'd always have him. What did it feel like?

31 August

Dearest,

It's 3 o'clock in the morning and I am so sick, sick, a dreadful heavy pain which must come from guilt, I suppose. I wonder if ever, in all these years, you have ever imagined nights like this one? The self-pitying activity that I know I had once. I can remember the feel-ing was that of being a martyr, in the end, and I think that agony, or rather that rare pleasure, was mine for years, until you effaced it by loving me. This pain is different, this is a pain of the offender, and no matter how much I tell myself I had reasons, reasons that weren't all bad or wrong, my conscience is my enemy. I want to be pardoned because I was happy today, really happy. It was all over. I got through a day of work and I was proud of myself. I was with Jacques and I was proud of him, and I was with Charlotte and I was happy and proud of her. I got home to MY house. I did without

you, I made love happily without you, read a book – but now you've
come back.

In my dreams, Serge, you never left. And I want to ring you and
write to you and to be held by you like a father. I want you to say,
'I'm your friend, I'll always love you, you don't hurt me any more
because I know you love me, go to sleep.' I know you love me. But
Serge, how can I tell you of that love? It is large and grand and strong
as it is for Papy, who you know I love, because his absence is NOT
possible, his end isn't possible. You can have girlfriends – wives,
even – I'm not jealous of that or them. I so want you to talk to me,
to be my confidant again. I talk to myself as though you could hear;
all the year I thought I'd talk to you because I had you in my heart. I
held you, rocked you, but you didn't know.

How could you know me so little as to think I could be rid of
you? You know my mind, you practically built it. But you didn't
know. And how could I tell you? You were so painful to see . . . I
felt so cruel and Mme H. said, 'More cruel in seeing you.' I did call,
not saying much, but how could I say, 'I love you. But.' There is no
but. It is a life of love towards you, my darling. It isn't the sleeping
together, the making love, it's something special that I have for you
that is yours. You have my love forever, however badly I express it.
And then, when I see you, it all goes wrong. I am only guilty and
arrogant and I can't hold you. You are no longer mine to hold. My
privileged position is no longer there. I have to knock to come in.
And into your heart.

Dearest, will time heal what I did to you in time for you to realise
that place in my heart, which is always there for you, that no one
can replace? Will you come one day for tea and laugh with me and
not regard me as your killer? You are a part of me, a part apart.
And you will always be. The agony is not to see you, talk to you. And
when I do, it crumbles into a sordid story of being 'tromped' and
the humiliation of that. I try to come back to you physically, but I've
been away too long; even one night, and I knew it would never be
the same for you again. But I am the same. I am asking you to have

SOMETHING for me that you didn't think possible, but it is. If you are over the pain can you hold my hand again and make me hold my head up high? Life is so short and sometimes I worry that I will die without you knowing the immensity of my love.

All this sounds ambiguous as I am with Jacques, and life is going on, but you . . . Will I ever be exceptional for you? Will you ever say, 'Yes, but Jane is different, we have something else. It's not the same as anything else.' Or any cliché. It's more than a cold phone call. When you are in pain at night would you come to me in the rain, banging on the door? I would run to open it, take away what I could of bitterness, that you would know that I would come. I am asking a lot and I can't hope for a reply. Not now. The last time the violence that I have in me made me say stupid things, untrue things, hoping somehow you would understand that they came from the misery of your looks at me. How many times, nights like this, I've cried to be home so that you'd forgive me; not to be taken back, but to love me on another level, *any* level, to take away the pain that exists between us. I ask you for this friendship. We that were never friends – but you are part of my life.

In letters from Majorca I tried to tell you. Mme H. said, 'But you don't know how he suffered, you can't imagine the "abandon", you didn't even ring.' But I knew my name was pain to you and my face. What good could I do for you? Not ring as if I was dead?

For you it was my making home immediately with Jacques. I had gone too far, so far. I tried to go back to that year and remember you were in hospital and I only thought of me. Then the remorse . . . You can crucify yourself with the pain you have given and perhaps that is what I'm trying to live, not in daylight hours, not on the radio or telling it to friends; how can I say that to friends? I say, 'I am miserable' and they say, 'So was he, but he's coming through.'

Come through it, Serge, so that one day you could have a different sort of love for me. Try, try to understand mine. Tonight sadness is shame. After leaving you before Corsica, I was bitter and arrogant and so were you. But you had the right to be, I had not. My nights are full of this dread that you don't respect me as a person, too much dirt, too much covering up. It happens when you don't believe you're being loved – you fall in love with the boy who says he loves you. Your face bores you, depression seems so self-indulgent and then a boy wants to talk about YOU.

I wanted to be discovered for that other me. Flattery at first, then indispensable affection, and patience and kindness. I'm not easy to live with, violent and insecure about my beauty that I only believe in the eyes of others. You looked no longer, I thought I was dead. Your profession, your house, your prizes ... I wanted something for me, and when I found it I tried to let go. But the four months were agony because you didn't even see what I had said no to. I had said no to me. I wanted so much to be me and I said no, and you had other things in mind, you treated my poor liaison with disdain. 'Poor thing, couldn't get any better, he'll leave you. You were only interested because of the film; of course a film means you. Use the you you were so frightened of losing.' You said, 'It's just an affair, a bit banal, it won't last. But it's broken for me; without me you won't be able to work or be popular. I made you.'

I know all that was said in the bitterness but when I said he wasn't the first it was because I wanted you to not think worse of Jacques, who is not a character 'banal' as you put it. How to say he waited six months before seducing me? I was seducible before that, that's what I wanted to say. I also have my pride, so I didn't. But I could have. So, bitterly, I lied. So that you would judge Jacques less severely. I hurt you again, trying to hurt less, so that the blame was on me, which it is.

Serge, this night is like so many others 'nuits blanches' ('sleepless nights'). I write, then don't send because I think somewhere in all I will wound you again and I can't bear it. If I see you, how you look, how you cried, I think, haven't I done enough wounding? I love you, I don't want to wound you, never, ever again. If only you could take me by the shoulder and say 'poopoopidou' and smile the way you did, I would feel that you are happy and could talk to me again, not to try and get back to you. Did I destroy you? Did I drive you to drink? Now you drink less, you love your house, and I love mine, but I can never be happy until you say 'poopoopidou' and that I am an 'all right' girl in your eyes. I'm asking you to try, one day, and I know I shouldn't ask anything of you.

Please, then, if you can't, know that I cannot, will not, don't want to forget you. This period of disfavour must lessen one day. Don't you ever want it to? I should have written this in just one line, 'My true love for you is forever.' I want you to know if you need to be with or want to talk to me, I will be here, and my private life cannot touch my devotion to you, it's not the same thing. Can we not be exceptional people who can talk without bitterness, remembering all that was good, is it too much to ask for?

There, sweet Serge, is my letter that I have wanted to write to you and didn't know how.

Jane X

Summer

Dearest Serge,

Just a little word via Charlotte to give you a kiss and to wish you *bon voyage*. I also gave you the letter I wrote Monday which is of no importance apart from the fact that I'd written it to you, therefore it's yours. Luckily I had you on the phone, and I could tell by your voice that what Madame Hazan had told me wasn't altogether what you wanted.

I kiss you, dear Serge, and don't forget my monkey's trousers.

* * *

I had great fortune in that he was willing to become my friend, even though it was terribly difficult for him at the beginning. When I had Lou, he agreed to become her godfather, calling himself 'Papa 2', and if he had worries, it was to my joy that he called me. He turned up at my house at Rue de la Tour around midnight, driven by policemen or a G7 taxi. There were two dinners, me and Jacques and the children, and then, at any old hour, Serge turned up, sometimes with Charlotte, sometimes with Bambou, and we'd start again. For me, Bambou was just the most generous of people. She stopped Serge from hurting himself, from going downhill; she gave him a child, a new family; she was young, beautiful and she accepted his behaviour towards her. She let me have a professional and private rapport with Serge, without putting anyone in any danger. She had understood how necessary it was for me to still be a part of his life and maybe to have become his confidante. And then there was Charlotte. It seems to me that they were practically the same age. They could be naughty together. And for Charlotte another life started on the weekends at Rue de Verneuil. Serge created an identical house for Bambou and Lulu that was an exact replica of Rue de Verneuil but in Chinatown. Serge met Bambou not long after I left, and from then on I knew he was safe.

1982

Rome, Babington's Tea Room

My dear Lou has been moving about all night, so the repose has been particularly brief! Lou, are you a girl or boy? My little vice, have you got black hair like him, little queen? I do hope so. And his eyebrows, and his cheekbones. That's what I want. The rest can look like me. What an idea. Just silly ideas that must come from the heat at Babington's or the iced tea or thinking back on my lunch with Ferrara. The visions of quite so many producers at the Bolognaise quite made my head spin. So here I am, feeling rather soppy near the Spanish Steps, drinking cold tea instead of climbing the steps towards that English chapel, Keats's house, oof! Too hot for culture. Here, amongst the American tourists, it's more restful for body and soul. Jacques is doing his ad for babies' nappies, poor thing! He didn't want me to come onto the set because he was so ashamed, he said. Oh là là, nappies in this heat! And three-month-old bambinos with their mamas coming from Paris, it really is a test of love – and money for Lou – we must, we must. Loulou, what are you up to? Come on, I'll give you a walk.

INDEX